George Ballentine

The Mexican War, by an English Soldier.

Comprising Incidents and Adventures in the United States and Mexico with the

American Army

George Ballentine

The Mexican War, by an English Soldier.
Comprising Incidents and Adventures in the United States and Mexico with the American Army

ISBN/EAN: 9783744748636

Printed in Europe, USA, Canada, Australia, Japan

Cover: Foto ©ninafisch / pixelio.de

More available books at **www.hansebooks.com**

ADVENTURES
OF AN
ENGLISH SOLDIER
IN THE

UNITED STATES ARMY.

New York:
W. A. TOWNSEND & COMPANY.
1860.

THE

MEXICAN WAR,

BY

AN ENGLISH SOLDIER.

COMPRISING

INCIDENTS AND ADVENTURES

IN THE

UNITED STATES AND MEXICO

WITH THE

AMERICAN ARMY.

NEW YORK:
W. A. TOWNSEND & COMPANY.
1860.

American Publishers' Preface.

DURING the discussion in the Senate of the United States, upon the bill to confer additional military rank upon General Winfield Scott, in acknowledgment of his great services to his country, General Shields remarked that no worthy history of the Mexican war had yet been written. The truth of the observation was everywhere felt. What has hitherto appeared on the subject, beyond the official despatches, has more resembled romance than history, being in the main confined to dashing narratives of the personal adventures of roving or belligerent Hotspurs, who knew little and cared less about the discipline and routine of the every-day life of the regular soldier; or on the other hand to eulogistic compilations, prepared for sale, rather than as contributions to history. The writers of both classes have "cast discreetly into shade" whatever would "offend the eye" of the readers they sought to appreciate.

As a partial remedy for the evil complained of by the gallant officer above referred to, the publishers put forth the present volume. If it does not rise to the dignity of history, it at least partakes of that faithfulness of record and clearness of detail which give history its value. The author is manifestly superior to that class of his countrymen ordinarily found in the rank and file of an army, in intelligence, in education, in observation, in descriptive and narrative power, and in candor and liberality of sentiment. Something of foreign misapprehension, possibly some degree of foreign preference or prejudice, may be found in his pages; and it is by no means improbable that some of his criticisms upon men and events may be unjust; but there is throughout the volume an evident desire to be just as well as independent, both in criticism and in narration.

The publishers confidently express the opinion, in which they are confirmed by the verdict of the literary gentlemen to whom the work has been submitted for supervision, not only that nothing has yet issued from the American press that gives so intelligent and lively a description of the *actualities* of the war in Mexico, but that no work is extant in the English language which presents so interesting a picture of a soldier's life—his round of conversation, his employments, his toils, dangers, and escapes—what he sees and does, and how he does it—as this autobiography. The reader will find it difficult to part company with the author. There is no "fine writing" to pall upon the taste. Everything is told naturally, and everything is described earnestly. The style is nervous yet chaste, and free from the coarseness which too often disfigures a soldier's narrative. Yet there is no sentimentality. The manliness of the true soldier is apparent on every page. The charm of the work is in the impressive distinctness of every picture of place or incident. The reader will feel as though he accompanied the hardy soldier from the moment of his enlistment to that of his discharge; messing with him on Governor's Island, marching with him to join the forces under General Scott, sleeping with him on the mountain side, where the bed is made *softer* by putting aside some of the larger stones, circuitously approaching the scene of action, exchanging a repartee or a word of encouragement with a comrade, mingling in the mêlée, and finally entering the city of Mexico in triumph, and realizing all the peculiarities of its buildings and its people. So vividly is every scene painted that a stranger, with the volume as his guide, might trace the entire route of the American army through Mexico, locate every bivouac, and comprehend every manœuvre or military movement. The publishers feel assured that this commendation of the volume will be verified by every intelligent reader of its pages.

Contents.

CHAPTER I.

I arrive in New York, and make several strange acquaintances, — — — — — — — — — — 9

CHAPTER II.

My first experience as an American soldier, and attendance at military punishment, — — — — — — — 17

CHAPTER III.

Embarkation at the Battery—Yankee opinion of Soldiers—Fort Adams—New comrades—Defects of organization—Routine of duties—Life in quarters — — — — — 30

CHAPTER IV.

Departure from Fort Adams—Providence—Robbing the Orchard—Boston—Life in a Transport—The Captain and the Nigger, — — — — — — — — — — — 42

CHAPTER V.

The Soldier at Sea, — — — — — — — — — 51

CONTENTS.

CHAPTER VI.
A Modern Soldier of Fortune, - - - - - - 66

CHAPTER VII.
Land in Sight—Pensacola Bay—Fort Pickens—Rough Lodgings—Smuggling Whiskey—A Carouse, - - - - 86

CHAPTER VIII.
The Surprise—Doctor Brown—Fishing at Pensacola—Bathers and Sharks, - - - - - - - - - - 92

CHAPTER IX.
Tampa Bay—Indian Paradise—Beautiful Squaws—Forest Life —The Hummocks—Snakes—Rumours of War—Lost in the Wood, - - - - - - - - - - - 100

CHAPTER X.
General Scott—The Coast of Mexico—A jolly Captain—A Gale of Wind—The River—Tampico, - - - - 121

CHAPTER XI.
The Town and its Population—Reinforcements—General Shields—Bill Nutt as Orderly—Expedition to Vera Cruz, - 137

CHAPTER XII.
Sacrificios—The debarkation—A bivouac—A night alarm, - 145

CHAPTER XIII.
General Scott—The Shell—Naval sporting—Investment of Vera Cruz—Vergara—Spoiling the knapsacks, - - - 152

CHAPTER XIV.
A prophecy fulfilled—The bombardment—Visit to Vera Cruz, 162

Page

CHAPTER XV.

Sickness—March on Jalapa—Position of the enemy—Order to attack—The counter-order and its effect, - - - 167

CHAPTER XVI.

Arrival of General Scott—Ascent of the ravine—The charge—The loan of a pipe—Colonel Harney—General Pillow—Bill Crawford—Victory, - - - - - - - 177

CHAPTER XVII.

After the battle—The wounded—Mexican surgeons—The litter of dead—An unexpected regale, - - - - 190

CHAPTER XVIII.

Santa Anna's leg—Distribution of spirits—Colonel Childs—Interring the dead—March to Jalapa, - - - - 197

CHAPTER XIX.

Santa Anna's house—Aspect of the country—The ladies of Jalapa—A Mexican funeral—Description of the city—The priesthood—Procession of the Host—Paying the troops, - 203

CHAPTER XX.

Departure from Jalapa—Deserters—On the march—Captain Walker—Perote—Tepe Agualco—Puebla, - - - 215

CHAPTER XXI.

Puebla—Convents and Public Buildings—Newspaper Generals—An Indian City—San Martin—Valley of Mexico, - 231

CHAPTER XXII.

San Augustine—Reconnoissance—Guard-house luxuries—A convivial party—An unexpected interruption, - - - 239

CONTENTS.

CHAPTER XXIII.
The Field of Battle—King's Mill—The Execution—The Pursuit, - - - - - - - - - - - 249

CHAPTER XXIV.
Ravages of War—Entry into San Cosmo—Character of the Population—Markets—The cemetery, - - - - 265

CHAPTER XXV.
Conclusion, - - - - - - - - - - - 281

AUTOBIOGRAPHY

OF AN

ENGLISH SOLDIER IN THE U. S. ARMY

CHAPTER I.

I arrive in New York, and make several strange acquaintances.

I LEFT home for the United States in the summer of 1845, for the same reason that yearly sends so many thousands there, want of employment. I had both read and heard a good deal about America, and knew that money could not be picked up in the streets there, any more than at home ; but I was scarcely prepared to find the scramble for the means of living so fierce and incessant, as I found it in New York.

Being a handloom weaver, I called on several persons belonging to that business, and from the same town as myself, Paisley, in the west of Scotland. They told me they had to work very hard to earn three dollars and a half, or at most, four dollars a week ; while loom rent and other expenses, with loss of time, changing and putting in new sorts of work, reduced their wages to an average of less than three dollars, or about twelve shillings a week. There were some weavers in carpet factories in Philadelphia they told me, and also a few in New York, who earned five or six dollars a week ; but only a few could find employment at these places, which were also subject to periods of stagnation of business, when the cost of living soon exhausted the savings of those who were provident enough to save a little for a rainy day. They generally, while informing me of plenty of places where I might find employment at weaving, such as it was, advised me to try and find employment as a labourer in preference; which some of them declared their intention of doing as soon as they had finished their engagements.

While walking along the wharfs at the East River one morning, my attention was arrested by a placard above one of the shops which front Brooklyn, stating, in the usual Brobdignagian typography of these announcements, that one hundred able-bodied men were wanted for whaling. Applicants were directed to walk up stairs. With a vague idea that possibly a South Sea voyage might answer my peculiar situation, I walked up and presented myself to a man whom I found sitting at a desk in a large room, barely furnished, and very dirty. I asked him if he could inform me as to the terms of engagement. "I can't do anything else," he replied, as he got up from his desk, and coming close up to me, asked if I meant to join the money-making business of whaling. He was a small cadaverous looking being, with sandy hair, sallow complexion, and red eyes that glittered like a ferret's, as you caught an occasional glimpse of them from behind a pair of green spectacles. I told him in reply, that I was out of employment, and not particularly nice as to what I tried, if I were able for it, and it promised tolerable pay. "Ah!" said he, "Stranger, I guess you are in a particular all fir'd streak of good luck; we are nearly filled up, that is a fact, but if you are in good health—let me just look at your arm," he continued, as he seized hold of one, feeling it up to the shoulder for the purpose of testing its muscular condition. Being satisfied with his examination, apparently, he asked me if I was an American citizen. I told him I was not, having only arrived in the country a few weeks before. "That is no matter," said he, winking one of the ferret eyes, "I can fix that right away." He then congratulated me upon being in a fair way to make my fortune, and informed me that the men employed in whaling were paid by shares, which they called lays, and that their wages were proportionate to their luck. He had known a young man have eight hundred, or a thousand dollars for his share, or lay, in a voyage that did not last over eighteen months. A whale ship would have very bad luck if the men aboard of her did not clear three or four hundred dollars a year. Bad health alone, he said, had prevented him from going a voyage or two; and so he went on with a great deal more to the same effect, most of which I thought too good to be true. Thanking him, however, for his information, and promising to call again after thinking the matter over, I left the office. I can't deny that his statements made a considerable impression on me at the time, though of course I believed that he greatly exaggerated. Still it is probable that I would have doubled Cape Horn in one of these whalers, perhaps touching at Nukuheva, and a few of the islands in that vicinity, and realizing some of those scenes of enchantment of which the inimitable Herman Melville has given such charming and graphical descriptions in his Typee and Omoo, but for the following incident.

Going down the steps from the office, I met in the street one of the sailors of the ship in which I had arrived, a fine old fellow with whom I had often had a chat during the passage. After the usual salutations, he asked me if I would help him to " splice the main brace," the nautical phrase for taking a glass of grog. I assented, and while taking a glass and a cigar together, he confidentially informed me that he had considered me a Christian ever since the fourth of July. My claim to this high character, which the old fellow I suppose considered perfectly valid, rested on the following rather slender foundation :—The night preceding the fourth of July had been wet and stormy, the wind blowing a pretty stiff gale. In the morning, the crew having been on deck all night, were tired, cold, and wet; and the vessel being on the temperance principle, they had no grog, at which they grumbled sadly. The sailors were mostly Americans, and the fourth of July, the anniversary of the Declaration of Independence, being held as a day of jubilee and general festivity in the States, the contrast suggested to their minds by their present condition, made them feel the deprivation more acutely. I had brought a small stock of whiskey with me, and not requiring it for my own use, I served out an allowance to each man; thus cheaply earning the reputation of a Christian. He proceeded to acquaint me with his having "shipped" in a vessel which was to sail in a few days for the East Indies. He had drawn a month's pay in advance, for the purpose of having a spree, as he was going on a long voyage. "Look here, matey," said he, "I have a few of the shiners left yet," and pulling a handful of silver from his pocket, he insisted that I should take part of it. I thanked him for his offer, which I said I would cheerfully accept if I required it. "Avast there, mate," said he, "did I not see you coming out of a land-shark's office there on the wharf?" I acknowledged having gone into an office there, telling the object of my visit, and repeated part of the statements made by the shipping agent. "I thought so," said Jack, with a sneer, "but listen to me, lad." He then gave me a history of his own experience on board a whaler, with a number of anecdotes gathered from different messmates, all tending to show that it was a life of great hardship, with very poor wages. He strongly advised me to look for some other sort of employment, and as to sharing his money, if I didn't it was all the same, he could pitch it into the river; he never carried any money on board with him when going on a long voyage. As I was not greatly above the want of a little pecuniary assistance, though not quite destitute of resources, having a good suit of clothes, and other articles easily convertible into money at my lodgings, I accepted a dollar from him as a loan. I did this the more readily, as I saw he would be grievously offended should I persist in refusing his kind offer. " Ay, ay," said the honest and warm-hearted old fellow, as we shook hands at parting, "you and I may happen to meet some other time, when your luck's better than mine. If we don't, and you should ever see a messmate on his beam ends, give him a lift, God bless you, and it will do all the same."

My interview with this honest fellow having dissipated any idea I had previously entertained of going to sea in a whaler, I strolled about for the remainder of the day, meditating on my future prospects, which presented a rather cheerless aspect at this juncture. Having served for a considerable time in the English army, from which I had purchased my discharge about five years previously, I finally resolved, as a sort of last resource, to try five years in the American service. The bills advertising for recruits, stated, that a few enterprising young men, of good character, were wanted for the service of the United States; and promised good treatment, as far as physical comfort was concerned, being somewhat to the following effect:—That soldiers of the United States' service were provided with good quarters, an ample sufficiency of good and wholesome diet, an abundant supply of clothing, and in case of sickness, the most careful attendance, and the most skilful medical aid. The statement concluded with the amount of money which could be saved by sergeant, corporal, or private, during their period of five years' service, varying from four to seven hundred dollars.

It was about the middle of August, 1845, that I called at the recruiting office in Cedar street, for the purpose of enlisting. The sergeant in charge of the establishment, having asked me if I had been in the British service, to which I replied in the affirmative, said in that case he was afraid they could not enlist me, as they had lately received an order from Washington to that effect; deserters from the British service having generally turned out bad soldiers. As I saw he was under the impression that I was a deserter, I explained that I had purchased my discharge, which I could produce if required. This, he said, altered the case; he was going to the recruiting officer's quarters, and if I had no objection he would take me along with him. I went with him, and was soon ushered into the presence of Lieutenant Burke, a tall handsome man, with fine expressive dark eyes, and large black whiskers, but a rather melancholy cast of countenance. He became Captain Burke soon after, in consequence of the war in Mexico, which caused considerable promotion among the officers for some time; but he did not live to enjoy it, being killed at the battle of Churubusco, outside of the city of Mexico, in August, 1847, about two years after my enlistment. After asking me a few questions, he said he would be glad to have me if I passed the surgeon's examination, and could procure a document to show that I had been discharged from the British service. I accordingly went to my lodgings, and returned with my certificate of discharge, which he slightly glanced over, and remarking that it was quite satisfactory, directed the sergeant to go with me to the inspecting surgeon. I then underwent an examination similar to that which recruits undergo when enlisted in the British service, and immediately after, went with the sergeant to the office of a magistrate, and took the usual oath of allegiance.

Being a soldier once more, and desirous of ascertaining the actual condition of one in the American service as soon as possible, I asked the sergeant when it would be requisite for me to be ready to go over to Governor's Island. This is a small island in the Manhattan Bay, where recruits are stationed until sent to join their respective regiments. It is rather more than a mile in circumference, and about a mile from the battery. The sergeant, who seemed a civil fellow, said that I might either go over in the garrison boat at sunset that evening, or if I had anything to arrange in New York, I might defer going over until next evening. He advised me to sell my clothes, and purchase old ones in New York, as I would get almost nothing for good clothes in the island, and would have no opportunity of coming over to sell them, as recruits after landing never obtained permission to leave the island until sent to join their regiments. I followed his advice with regard to the clothes, for which a purchaser was easily found, replacing them with a light linen jacket, and chip hat, which cost a mere trifle, but were good enough to throw away in a day or two, when I should put on soldier's uniform. I also sold my trunk, and a few other articles which, as a soldier, I had neither much use for, nor convenient means of carrying; and being desirous of going over the same evening, I then returned to the recruiting office.

At sunset the sergeant accompanied me and two other recruits down to the boat, which lay in front of Castle Garden. The garrison boat was a large, handsome, and neatly painted cutter, rowed by six soldiers, with a corporal acting as coxswain. Seated in the stern of the boat were a couple of young officers smoking cigars. They were probably chagrined at having been detained a minute or two while we were coming down, for one of them called out in a petulant tone to us, to jump in and be damned. I looked with a little surprise at the would-be aristocrat specimen of equal rights who had spoken, and could perceive that he had the apology of youth and inexperience, being little more than a boy. One of the recruits muttered loud enough to be heard by the gentleman, who stared and coloured, but perhaps thought it prudent to decline a reply, "Faith and there's many a strong word comes off a weak stomach."

The evening was delightful, and in a few minutes we were landed on the wharf at Governor's Island. The other two recruits and myself were shown to a tent, where we were to sleep for the night. We found that it contained only two straw mattresses, and two blankets, but as the weather was very warm, we slept that night very comfortably.

CHAPTER II.

My first experience as an American soldier, and attendance at military punishment.

WE were roused next morning by the reveille, which is always beat a little before sunrise. Having got up with the assistance of a good-natured recruit who happened to look into our tent, we rolled up our mattresses, and folded the blankets according to regulation, and then, falling into the ranks formed in front of the tents, we answered to our names as they were called by the sergeant who had charge of us. All hands were then distributed in separate parties, each party in charge of a corporal, to "police" or clean round the garrison. A portion of this duty, at which the recruits grumbled loudly, and which I soon learned was one of several standing grievances of which they complained, was being sent to the barrack-square, where a company, called the permanent company, were stationed. As the recruits lay in tents outside, and at a considerable distance from the barracks, they naturally felt indignant at the unjust degradation to which they were subjected, in being compelled every morning to act as a scavenging commission for the permanent company. The refusal to obey orders, caused by this foolish regulation, was the means of many of the recruits being confined in the guard-house while I was on the island. At six o'clock we were assembled and formed into squads for drill; we were then drilled until seven, when we were dismissed.

At half-past seven o'clock, at beat of drum, we again fell into the ranks, having our leathern stocks on, and jackets buttoned up to the collar. The roll was again called, after which we were marched to the cook-house to breakfast. It is a rule in the American service that soldiers shall breakfast, dine, and sup in the cook-house, a very absurd and inconvenient regulation, for which I never heard any satisfactory reason assigned. Our breakfast consisted of six ounces of bread, a slice of salt pork, and a pint of weak unpalatable coffee, totally innocent of the useless extravagance of milk, instead of which we were permitted to season our sumptuous fare with vinegar at discretion, a large black bottle full of that condiment being placed at each end of the table.

Before commencing, and as I was about to sit down to my first breakfast on Governor's Island, a recruit, Sawney, belonging to New York, one of the "bhoys," as they delight in being called, and a recognised and privileged wit among the recruits, volunteered to ask a blessing. It was evidently a preconcerted arrangement with several of his influential friends, who used all their address, and a considerable degree of exertion to obtain silence. Having finally succeeded, Sawney rose with a face of the utmost gravity, and commenced a profane and irreverent parody. He concluded by d——g all those infernal scoundrels who rob poor soldiers of their rations; amen. "Sawney, get up, and go to the guard-house," said a sergeant who entered as he sat down, after finishing this singular grace. "Ay, ay," grumbled Sawney, "I expected as much; I said how it would be. If a poor devil wants to be ever so religious, it's no use a trying of it here. I suppose that's what you call liberty of conscience in this blessed free republic of ours. Hang me if it is not enough to make a man curse Washington, or his old grandmother even." So saying, and swallowing his indignation

CLOTHING, INSPECTION, AND DRILL. 19

along with a gulp of the wretched coffee, and taking his bread in his hand, amidst the sympathy of his admiring friends, he walked off to the Guard House, muttering curses, not loud but deep.

After breakfast, the sergeant in charge of the recruits took me and the two others who came over on the previous evening to the clothing store, where each received the following articles of clothing. A forage cap, leather stock, jacket, and trousers of coarse blue cloth, two cotton shirts, two pairs of socks, one pair of half boots, a blanket, a great-coat, a knapsack, and a havresack. Having brushed our clothes, cleaned the metal buttons of our jackets, and polished our boots, at 10 o'clock, we again fell into the ranks for inspection and drill. After a minute inspection by the officer who had us in charge, to see that we were smart and clean in our appearance, we were formed into a number of separate squads for drill; those who had joined earliest, and consequently were the most forward with their drill, being placed in the first squad, and so on in succession. The other two recruits, Murphy and Finnegan, and myself, were turned over to a corporal named Bright, to be taught the preliminary steps of a soldier's drill, as "the position of a soldier," or the manner in which a soldier should stand in the ranks; "the facings," or mode of turning on the heels to the right or left, with slow marching, and a few of those things which usually commence the course of instruction with recruits.

Corporal Bright, who was an Irishman by birth, was a United States soldier by profession, and long custom. He had served three enlistments, and entered on the fourth. He was a stout, punchy, little fellow, rather round-shouldered, slightly bowlegged, nose carbuncled, and portending an addiction to strong potations. In addition, he had a very decided squint from a pair of dull, grey, and glassy-looking orbs, which, as Finnegan when criticising his personal appearance remarked, " stuck out of the crathur's head like the eyes of a boiled cod fish." Notwithstanding these slight drawbacks, Corporal Bright had an idea that he was a very handsome and well-made man, and on this account became the unconscious butt of all the recruits he got to drill. " Murphy, arrah bad luck to you for an awkward-looking omadhaun," he would call out, " can't you hold up your big head, and look me straight in the eyes ?" (Murphy aside)—" Be the hokey, my bright-looking customer, and that's what I defy mortial man to do." Corporal Bright (marching in front), " Look at me now Murphy, and yourself too Finnegan ; there now, do yez iver see me duck my head like a gandher going under a gate or bent two double like some old Judy going to a wake ?" Finnegan (aside)—" Faith, an it's a Judy you make of yourself, sure enough, you consated crathur." Corporal Bright (addressing his squad), " Be my sowl, I'm ashamed of yez for counthrymen ; *stand at ease ;* I'll just march a few paces in front now to show yez how yez ought to march ; now if yez plase will yez take a patthern." So saying, he would step off, and march twenty or thirty paces to the front, with such a ludicrous imitation of the *beau ideal* graceful ease, and dignified carriage of body which he recommended, as to sometimes prove rather too much for the gravity of his pupils. These performances he would intersperse with a few instructions, and self-laudatory remarks, such as, " There now, do yez persaive the difference, can't yez carry yer shoulders back, yer heads ereck, and march as you persaive I do, as bould as a lion, and as straight as a ramrod." Finnegan (aside)—" Arrah, look at the gommagh, with the airs and consate of him, marching in front there as bould as Julius Cæsar ; sure it's a holy show the unfortunate crather makes ov himself with his ' straight as a ramrod ;' faith, the ramrod that's no straighter than you, would do to load the gun that shoots round the corner. Murphy (aside in reply), "Faix, but it's the beautiful cook they spoiled, when they made the same fellow a corporal; he could have one eye up the chimney, and the other in the pot at the same time." Such is a faint sketch of Corporal Bright and his squad of recruits, on the drill ground at Governor's Island.

Having been well drilled while serving in the British army, I found no difficulty in acquiring my drill on the island, the systems of English and American drill being essentially the same. I therefore escaped a good deal of that annoyance to which recruits are often subject, upon first joining the army, and which frequently proceeds from the ignorance or bad temper of the non-commissioned officer appointed to drill them. The proper combination of intelligence, firmness, and mildness of manner, requisite to form a good drill instructor, is of rare occurrence, and owing to this cause, many a young and high spirited recruit, discouraged and fretted by the bullying and blustering tone of those who ought to be his patient instructors, is tempted to desert the service, when, with proper treatment, he might have been made a good and efficient soldier.

At half-past eleven o'clock the squads were dismissed, and the greater part of the recruits who possessed money, or had credit at the sutler's store, went over to it to buy crackers and cheese, pies and other eatables, and to drink cider, ginger, and root beer, all of which articles, with tobacco, and several other necessaries, were sold there at the slight advance of 100 per cent. upon the price at which similar commodities could be purchased in New York.

The sutler's store is a shop kept in every garrison, and is somewhat similar to a canteen in the British service, only the sutler's stores are prohibited from selling spirits. Recruits, on arriving at the island, were allowed credit in the sutler's store to the amount of two dollars, which sum, or the amount taken by the recruit, was remitted by the captain of his company on the first pay-day after he joined his regiment. Those recruits who had exhausted their credit at the store, either went to their tents, or lay stretched on the grass, under the fine shady trees that ornamented the parade ground, reading, dozing, or smoking, and chatting, according to their various inclinations.

At twelve o'clock the dinner call beat, a fifer and drummer playing the regulation tune, "O the Roast Beef of Old England." We again fell into the ranks, buttoned up as at breakfast roll-call, and having answered our names were marched to the cook-house to dinner. This meal consisted of six ounces of bread, a slice of salt pork, and a basin of bean soup. This compound was very salt, and very fat, and contained a quantity of half-boiled beans. I have seen some strange and rather uninviting dishes, both before and since, but never anything so utterly unpalatable as the bean-soup of Governor's Island. A few of the more verdant of the recruits occasionally swallowed a portion of it, under the false impression that it was a species of military soup, which might possess some hidden nutritious virtues, though so singularly uninviting in taste and appearance. For this venial error, however, they were pretty sure to suffer a moderate degree of penance, until led by experience to see their mistake. The old and more experienced hands, usually preferred to wash down their dry victuals with a drink of water, so that the quantity of Spartan broth, and salt pork, daily left on the dinner table of the recruits, was quite enormous, a fact easily cited to refute any complaint of an insufficient dietary.

At three o'clock we again fell in for drill, and were

dismissed at half-past four; and at five o'clock we were marched as before to the cook-house for supper, which consisted of six ounces of bread and a pint of coffee. I need not insist upon the inadequacy of the diet furnished to the recruit, both as regards quantity and quality, at Governor's Island, where a complete organization seems to exist, for the purpose of robbing the recruit, and disgusting him with the service at the very outset. The diet and general treatment are much better when the soldier joins his company; although I am free to confess that, throughout the service generally, a very wide field still remains for improvement. I am aware that it will seem to many a thing quite incredible, that in a country abounding as America does with cheap food, a standard grievance with the soldiers should be the manner in which they are fed; it is a fact, nevertheless, quite notorious to every soldier who has ever served in the American army.

After supper, we usually had an interval of rest until nine o'clock. " Now came in the sweet of the night," while the old and sedate portion of the recruits strolled along the foot-walks that intersect, and surround the island, or sat in small parties conversing in front of their tents, the younger and more volatile among them engaged in a variety of pastimes and amusements. Foot-ball, leaping, wrestling, foot racing, leap-frog, throwing the stone, or dancing when music could be procured, were a few of the more prominent of the diversions commonly resorted to. Later in the evening, after having answered our names at retreat, which was beat precisely at sunset, groups assembled round the tent doors, to smoke, chat, tell tales, or sing songs. Nigger songs or the broadly humorous, formed the staple of these social entertainments, except with the German portion of the recruits, who, having been taught to sing in their national schools had acquired a more refined ear, and a taste for music of a rather superior quality. They generally arranged, therefore, a separate party, forming a very pleasing concert among themselves, by singing their national songs; these, when heard a little distance off, on a still evening, had a very beautiful and harmonious effect. At nine o'clock we fell in, to answer our names at tattoo roll-call, when the drums and fifes played a few merry tunes, after which the roll was called and we were then dismissed to bed. About fifteen minutes were then suffered to elapse, when the drummer beat three distinct taps on the drum, at which signal every light in tents or quarters had to be extinguished, and the most strict silence preserved, on pain of the offender being sent to the guard-house—the immediate punishment for all wilful infractions of the rules of the service. Such is a summary of one day, and, with but slight variations, of every day of the three weeks I spent on Governor's Island.

I had been upon the island about a week, when a large draft of recruits was ordered to Texas, where they were to join different regiments, preparing for that expedition to the frontier, which resulted in involving the United States in the war with Mexico. The popular feeling in the United States, at that period, seemed to be strongly in favor of a war. Texas had just been annexed, and the papers teemed with paragraphs calculated to rouse the war spirit, dwelling on the indignities offered to the States by the Mexican Government; especially in refusing to pay certain indemnities claimed by American citizens, for injuries received by them from Mexican civil functionaries, in their trading relations with that nation. In the meantime the refusal of Mexico to recognize the independence of Texas, or to listen to any statement of American grievances, with the circumstance of her having an army on the Rio Grande, showed that she was careless how she provoked the coming struggle, which she probably now began to consider inevitable; and tended to show that hostilities would soon break out between the sister republics.

I cannot say how far the near prospect of a war may have operated upon the minds of recruits to cause desertion, but certainly the number of desertions at the period I speak of was very great. This crime I had imagined would be almost unknown, or of very rare occurrence in this army, where the period of service was limited to five years, and which professed to treat its soldiers so liberally on all other points. But the practice of putting all recruits who join at Governor's Island during the summer months, into tents, where they are roasted as if in an oven during the day, and frequently drenched with wet, and starved with cold during the night, must produce a degree of disgust to the service in the mind of the recruit at the very outset. For a tent, though excellent accommodation to the soldier on a campaign (especially if one has been compelled to rough it for a week or two occasionally with the blue vault or the black sky for a canopy), is a miserable substitute for a substantial barracks. And it certainly must produce a rather unpleasant impression on the recruit, to reflect, that probably the most miserable loafer in New York is in a more comfortable lodging than himself. It is to this practice, together with the confinement to the island, and the wretched system that prevails in regard to their food, that much of the desertion among the recruits is to be attributed. In fact, throughout the American service generally, desertion, though the only offence for which the disgraceful punishment of flogging is permitted by the military code, is not looked upon in the light of a crime by the soldier. This is principally owing to the conviction that they are not treated justly. No great amount of logic is required to perceive that a contract, to be binding must bind both parties; but it would take a good deal to convince the soldier, that he is bound to observe an oath which he has taken under certain implied conditions, which he finds are not observed.

The common method adopted by the recruits who wished to desert from Governor's Island, was to engage a boat to come over in the night time to take them off, while others trusted themselves and their fortunes to a single plank in the following manner. Watching when the tide was setting into the harbour, they fastened their clothes to a plank, and by swimming and holding on to it while they directed its course, with the assistance of it and the tide, they easily reached New York, or Brooklyn. One morning we missed two large tubs which we had made by sawing a hogshead in two, and which always stood at the pump, being used as washtubs by the recruits, who were under the necessity of scouring their own linen on the island. Many and various were the conjectures as to the missing utensils, until some one suggested the probability of their having been used to ferry over the two recruits who were reported absent that morning. This surmise was soon after confirmed by one of the permanent company who had been in New York on the previous night, and who stated, that he had seen two small strange-looking craft, answering to our description of the missing tubs, paddling, in the gray twilight of the morning, alongside one of the wharfs in New York, where there is little doubt that their adventurous navigators effected a safe landing.

A rather ludicrous circumstance happened to a captain of a schooner who picked up one of these deserters in the bay. The deserter had left Governor's Island on a plank, and having miscalculated the run of the tide, he was rapidly drifting out to sea, when he was seen and picked up by the schooner. It would seem, however, that the poor fellow had only escaped one danger to run into another, for the captain, on questioning him, and finding that he was a deserter, not being of those who think that a good action is its own reward, resolved upon obtaining the more tangible one of thirty dollars, the sum paid for the apprehension of a deserter, by delivering him up to the authorities as soon as they should arrive at New York. However, he concealed his design from his intended victim, to whom he appeared exceedingly kind and attentive, giving him a good stiff glass of grog, and some dry clothes, to wear until his own were dried. On arriving at the wharf he told him he had business ashore, and recommended him to stay where he was until evening, as there was danger of his being apprehended should he go on shore in daylight. At all events he was not to think of going till he should return. So saying, and locking the cabin door upon the deserter, he went off to Governor's Island to procure a party of soldiers for his apprehension.

Meanwhile the deserter was not idle or asleep, and having "smelt a rat" from the captain's manner, especially from the circumstance of his having locked the cabin door, he resolved upon turning the tables upon him. The result of this resolution was, that on the return of the captain with a party of soldiers, he found that not only had he lost his trouble, but that during his absence his chest had been broken open, and a considerable sum of money, together with a valuable silver lever watch, had been abstracted by the miserable-looking wretch on whom he had calculated for turning in thirty dollars. The captain, who looked extremely foolish, had evidently caught a Tartar instead of a deserter, being minus sixty, instead of plus thirty dollars, and in place of receiving sympathy was laughed at by all who heard the story. What added flavour to the jest among the recruits, was the curious, half-witted, and simple looks of the deserter, who was generally considered deficient in intellect, but who clearly proved himself more rogue than fool upon this occasion.

In order to check the frequency of desertion, great efforts were made to apprehend some of the soldiers in the act of escaping from the island, for the purpose of inflicting a punishment that might deter others from following their example. At length, having succeeded in apprehending two who were trying to cross in a small boat to Brooklyn, the commanding officer immediately caused a court-martial to be summoned for their trial; and after the lapse of a few days, during which the proceedings of the court were sent to the commander-in-chief for his approval, the prisoners were brought out on parade to receive sentence and punishment. Both of them having been proved guilty of the crime of desertion, were sentenced to "undergo the infliction of a corporal punishment of fifty lashes on the bare back with a raw cowhide, and further to have their heads shaved, and be drummed out of the service with ignominy."

They were young and good-looking men, one of them a native of the States, the other a German, and both received their punishment, which was inhumanly severe, with admirable fortitude. A number of the recruits were compelled to fall out of the ranks and go to the rear, owing to a sensation of faintness caused by witnessing this exhibition of modern torture. This is a common occurrence with young men, both officers and soldiers, many of whom seem to suffer nearly as much as the recipient, at witnessing these barbarous punishments for the first time. Fifty lashes is the full extent of corporal punishment that can be inflicted in the

American army, and that only for the crime of desertion; but as far as physical suffering is concerned, or the damage done to the constitution by that inhuman mode of punishment, fifty lashes with a cowhide are fully equivalent to three hundred with a cat, such as is used in the British army.

After being flogged, the prisoners were marched back to the guardhouse, where they had their heads shaved bare, in pursuance of their sentence. Next morning they were brought out to the parade-ground under the charge of a file of the guard, and marched from thence round the garrison, a fifer and drummer playing a tune specially used on these occasions called the "Rogues' March," being the same tune used in the British service on a like occasion. They were then marched down to the wharf, and sent over in the garrison boat to New York. A subscription was secretly got up, and several dollars collected for them among the recruits, by whom their condition was generally commiserated, though some of them did not hesitate to say that they considered them lucky fellows, and had better be flogged and drummed out, than shot up in Texas or Mexico.

CHAPTER III.

Embarkation at the Battery—Yankee opinion of Soldiers—Fort Adams—New Comrades—Defects of Organization—Routine of Duties—Life in Quarters.

ABOUT the latter end of the month of August a draft of forty recruits were ordered to Fort Adams, Rhode Island, to complete two companies of artillery stationed there. I had the good fortune to be included in the number selected for this draft, and was happy at any prospect which promised a relief from the disagreeable confinement of Governor's Island. About five o'clock on the evening of the thirty-first August we got on board a sloop belonging to the garrison, which landed us at the Custom-house wharf near the battery. There we were met by a crowd of idlers, who gathered round us, curious to have a look at the soldiers who they imagined were ordered to Texas to fight the Mexicans; the most trivial movement of troops being magnified into an event by the rumour of the approaching war with Mexico. We marched round the Battery to the wharf on the North River, where we went on board a steamboat, and shortly after started amidst the cheers of a crowd of urchins, several of these precocious juveniles, apparently not more than ten years of age, shouting with intensity of glee at the idea of the fun, "O won't they give the Mexicans hell?" But, "as the old cock crows, the young one learns," as the old proverb has it.

For some time after starting, we amused ourselves by admiring the delightful villas and beautiful scenery of both the

Manhattan and Long Island side of the channel, which glowed in the rich mellow colouring of the autumnal sunset like the realms of a fairy land. But evening soon closed over us, and as we were at our destination early next morning, we had little opportunity of seeing much of the scenery on our voyage, however much we might have been disposed to admire it. Our men were directed by the officer in command of our party to keep together in the fore part of the boat during the night, and to sleep on the deck in the best manner we could. As the night air at that season of the year was beginning to feel rather cold, we grumbled a little at this arrangement, but there was no help for it. The boat was full of passengers, a few of whom occasionally entered familiarly into conversation with the soldiers, and showed their good breeding by various acts of civility and kindness. But we could scarcely help remarking that the majority of them seemed to look upon us in the light of a degraded caste, and seemed to think that there was contamination in the touch of a soldier; for it is a singular fact that though Jonathan is so vain of his military prowess, and a little too apt to boast of the wonderful exploits of those armies of his that can whip all creation so easily, it is only in the collective term, or as an abstract idea; he is exceedingly shy of the individuals who compose it. In reply to some casual observation made by a fellow passenger upon our appearance on board, I chanced to overhear an old fellow of most vinegar-looking aspect drily remark, " Ay, ay ! they are a fine set of candidates for the States prison." I was standing partly concealed by some boxes that stood upon deck, and to do the old fellow justice, I believe he did not intend that his remark should reach a soldier's ears: however, I could not resist the impulse of the moment which prompted me to repeat for his edification Sir John's reply to Prince Hal, when criticising his soldiers rather too curiously, " Tut, tut, good enough to toss, food for powder, food for powder ; they'll fill a pit as well as better : tush, man, mortal men, mortal men." My quotation, while it rather took the old fellow by surprise, and raised a smile among a few of the surrounding passengers, had the more substantial effect of being the means of procuring me a good bed that night ; a luxury which I believe I was the only one of the party who enjoyed. A young gentleman overhearing the conversation, in whom I afterwards discovered an enthusiastic admirer of the " Mighty Poet," invited me to take a glass of brandy. We afterwards engaged in a conversation, which being enlivened and promoted by an occasional tribute to Bacchus and a fresh supply of cigars, lasted until pretty late in the night. Upon getting up to go to bed, and learning that I was to sleep on deck, he said, that must be a mistake, but he would rectify it : and going to the steward, he immediately returned with a ticket for a berth, which he gave me, nor would he hear of thanks for his kindness ; insisting that it cost him nothing, and that the circumstance of the soldiers sleeping on deck must have originated in a mistake. I hardly knew what to think of it at the time, but afterwards upon reflection I felt convinced that he had paid the steward for the accommodation, which he wished to offer me in this delicate manner. Bidding him a friendly good night, I availed myself of my ticket by going down below, where I found a good bed, and slept comfortably until roused by beat of drum next morning. On getting upon deck I found we were near our destination, being opposite Fort Adams, which is about a mile from the town of Newport, where we landed, but as the road from Newport to the Fort skirts a deep bay, we found the distance by land about three miles.

We had now reached the head-quarters of our regiment,

and having taken off our knapsacks, rested a little, cleaned ourselves, and taken breakfast, we were marched to the hospital to undergo a final medical inspection. Stripping off all our clothes at the door of a large apartment, each of us entered in succession, one going in as the other came out. I could scarcely help smiling when in marching into the room *in puris naturalibus*, the surgeon thus addressed me, " So, an old British soldier, I suppose?" which taking for granted, without waiting for any answer, he continued, " Have you been much in hospital while in the British service ?" I told him I had enjoyed very good health while serving there. He then asked me how long I had served, where stationed, and in what regiment, and, after making me walk about a little and extend my arms, dismissed me. I admired his acuteness in thus telling at a glance that I had served in the British army, for as our names were not called as we entered, he could not have ascertained the fact except from observation. The result of the examination was, that we were all without exception declared fit for service; indeed it rarely happens that recruits are rejected on joining their regiments, as they are minutely examined by the surgeon at the recruiting station where they enlist.

We were now to be told off to our respective companies, an important event to the soldier, as each company forms a separate and distinct family, from which during his five years' period of service he is seldom transferred. It is true these companies are all subject to the same general regulations, but their whole internal economy, discipline, and the general comfort of the men are altogether dependent on the methods adopted, and the interest manifested in its arrangements by the officer intrusted with its command. Company K, commanded by Captain Taylor, and company I, commanded by Lieutenant Capron, were the two companies

2*

stationed at Fort Adams at that time. We were to be distributed between these two, and the simple method of taking a man alternately from the top to the bottom of the roll having been decided on as the most fair and impartial, I found myself at the end of the proceedings, along with nineteen more of my comrades, told off to company I.

We were now shown to our quarters, large, arched, bomb-proof rooms. They were tolerably comfortable, with the exception of the wooden bedsteads, and the exceedingly disagreeable custom, still universal in the United States service, of sleeping two in a bed—a custom which has been abolished in every barrack in Great Britain, and the Colonies, to the infinite comfort of the soldier, for the last twenty years. The orderly, or chief sergeant of the company, a rank which corresponds with that of colour sergeant in the British service, told us off in twos, and appointed the beds we were to occupy; affixing a label with the names of the occupants upon each. I happened luckily to get a very good comrade, the usual term for a bed-fellow in the army. He was an Englishman, named Bill Nutt, a regular cockney; who had been brought up in London to the trade of a carver and gilder, by his father, once a respectable master-tradesman in that business there. He had run away from home when a boy, and served a three years' cruise in a British man-of-war, where he had "seen a little service," having been, to use his own language, "in a bit of a shindy with the Dutch boors at the Cape of Good Hope." He was a witty, pleasant young fellow, and a general favourite with the men for his cheerful temper, and good nature. Still, a real specimen of the John Bull family, he was keenly sensitive to any ill-natured reflections thrown upon his country, or her institutions. He also felt grievously annoyed at the insolent and impertinent tone assumed by native Americans to all foreigners; indeed I learnt that he had left several workshops in New York from quarrels arising out of this circumstance.

Company I to which I now belonged, though nominally artillery, had precisely the same duties to perform as infantry; being armed with muskets, and in every respect equipped and drilled in the same manner, with the exception of an occasional drill at the battery guns of the Fort. The company, after having received our draft of twenty recruits, consisted of sixty men, including non-commissioned officers and privates; of these, two were English, four Scotch, seven Germans, sixteen Americans, and the remainder Irish. Such was its composition at the time I entered, but in the American service a company soon undergoes a change in its component parts. During the five years which I served, from the combined causes of deaths, desertions, and discharges, more than two-hundred-and-fifty had joined it; although its strength never exceeded one-hundred-and-twelve, to which it was augmented while in the city of Mexico, being then a light battery. The infantry companies were also augmented to about eighty privates each, during the war with Mexico.

The short period of service in the American army has obvious disadvantages. The men, from being so frequently changed, never seem to acquire that feeling of brotherly regard for one another, or any of that kindly forbearance, and good will, which a long acquaintance naturally produces; and which helps so materially to form and promote the *esprit du corps*, which is found to animate more or less, according to the good or bad qualities of the officer commanding, every regiment, troop, or company in the British service, as regards the mutual relation in which officers and soldiers ought to stand to each other. It has also the following prejudicial effect—the American officer, from want of a habit of strict attention to the management of his company, partly caused by the transitory interest he must feel in a perpetual current of strangers, becomes careless of either learning the characters, or caring for the interests of his men. Thus, frequently the seeds of distrust and ill-will are sown between the two classes; a serious evil in the service, which sometimes produces a bitter result. A signal instance of this occurred at Churubusco in our Mexican campaign, of which I shall have to speak hereafter.

We were now in better circumstances than we had been while on Governor's Island; we had comfortable quarters in place of tents, and our diet was considerably improved by the produce of a garden, which belonged to the garrison; it being on ground belonging to the government, and planted and cultivated by the soldiers. The potatoes, cabbages, and onions, raised by their labour, formed a welcome addition to the rather indifferent fare furnished to the soldier by government. The cheapness of dairy produce, too, at Rhode Island, where butter was sold at ten cents, or five pence a pound, and cheese at one half of that price, enabled us to improve our diet at a trifling expense. In addition to this abundance, fish of excellent quality were plentiful in the bay close at hand, where we could easily at any time catch a few trout, rock fish, flounders, lobsters, eels, crabs, and a variety of others, of a richness and flavour which might tempt the palate of an epicure, and whose names I have forgotten at present, but a grateful recollection of whose merits remains in the catalogue of the good things of that period. In the intervals between the hours of drill we amused ourselves by fishing in the bay, by sea bathing, or by rambling about the country in the vicinity of the garrison. Sometimes we went over to the town of Newport, a distance of about three miles by the highway, but which a short cut through the fields reduced to two. To go more than a mile from the garrison without a written permission signed by an officer, is forbidden by a regulation of the service, a soldier being liable to severe punishment for its infringement; but this rule is not often rigorously enforced, and officers seldom restrict their men to any particular distance from the garrison, unless circumstances require it, as long as they are regular in their attendance on their duties, roll-calls, and parades.

Recruits are treated with a certain degree of indulgence for some time after joining the regiment, or company, to which they belong. They are usually excused from the performance of all duty while learning their drill, a period of about two or three months. When the adjutant of the regiment, who is responsible for its discipline, considers the recruit sufficiently drilled, he dismisses him from drill, and sends him to duty, as it is termed; he has then to take every duty in rotation. As soon as he mounts his first guard, he drops his title of recruit, which is thenceforth merged in that of soldier; and proud of his newly acquired distinction, he speedily adopts the manners, customs, vices, and virtues of his model, to be like whom has been for some time the highest object of his ambition. But if the recruit has gained in his own estimation by advancing to a level with the old soldier, he soon finds that the duties imposed upon him by his new position are a considerable drawback upon his newly attained dignity. In the first place he has to mount guard once every fourth day on an average; this duty commences at nine or ten o'clock in the morning, and terminates at the same hour next morning. A soldier remains on guard for twenty-four hours in all ordinary cases, during which he is not permitted to put off his clothes or accoutrements, or to quit his guard, even for an instant, without permission from the officers in charge of it. There are three sentries to each post, who are relieved every two hours in succession; thus each man is two hours on post and four hours off, giving each eight hours sentry during his twenty-four hours on guard. When off post, he is permitted to stretch himself upon a sloped wooden bench, with a wooden pillow, called the guard-bed, where he may sleep if he chooses, being at liberty to select the softest boards he can find for that purpose, but strictly prohibited from taking off any of his accoutrements. When relieved from guard he cleans his musket and appointments, which, with an hour or two of drill, occupies his time until evening.

The next duty to be performed is that of "general police," all who came off guard on the day previous being appointed for that work. The principal duties of the general police are to clean the parade ground and the purlieus of the garrison, and to cut wood and carry water for the use of the officers and soldiers. They are under the superintendence of the orderly officer, a duty which is taken in rotation by all, except the commanding officer of the post. The orderly officer has also the supervision of the barrack guard, and the duties of the garrison generally; all reports are made to him, and, in the event of any extraordinary occurrence, through him to the commanding officer; in short, the duty corresponds to that of officer of the day in the English army. A very objectionable part of the duties required from the general police, and the source of a good deal of discontent, is a practice which exists of causing them to do a considerable portion of work for officers, which ought to be done by their own domestic servants. The men consider it quite reasonable that they should clean the garrison, and perform the necessary duties of cutting their own wood, and bringing water for their own use; but they very naturally grumble at doing the same for their officers, who they know are furnished by government, in addition to their pay, with a liberal allowance of money and rations, for the express purpose of providing themselves with servants from civil life. This custom of making the soldiers do the domestic drudgery of the officers' household, thus converting the soldier into a degraded menial, a Gibeonite hewer of wood and drawer of water, is universal throughout the American army, although at direct variance with the rules of the service. It has a most deteriorating effect upon the character of the soldier, whom it renders disaffected to his officers and the service, careless in his habits, and slovenly in his appearance. It is chiefly owing to this bad practice, I have no doubt, that the American soldier is so much inferior in smartness of appearance, and in the neatness of his uniform and appointments, to the English soldier, who is accustomed to see the rules of the service as stringently binding upon the officers as they are upon the men. What serves to render this breach of discipline more glaringly inexcusable, on the part of the American officers, is that the Commander-in-Chief, General Scott, aware of the existence of the practice, and the bad effects which it produces, has, time after time, issued circulars, calling the attention of officers to the existing regulations on this subject. These circulars, as directed, are frequently read on parade; and the perfect indifference with which the system is carried on, in open defiance of the prohibition, shows the complete degree of impunity with which an officer of the United States army may disregard the orders of a superior, however high his rank, when they happen to be disagreeable to himself.

These duties of mounting guard, and general police, are the principal part of the American soldier's duty when in quarters; in addition to these he is occasionally on company police, which consists in keeping the barrack rooms and passages clean, and doing any work that the Captain or Orderly Sergeant may require in connection with company affairs. There is also the daily cleaning of his arms and appointments, a thing which a good soldier seldom neglects, and which generally occupies an hour or two; and the usual drills and parades, which generally occupy two or three hours each day; the remainder of his time is pretty much at his own disposal.

While we remained at Fort Adams, we had a great number of visitors from the town of Newport, which is a fashionable resort in summer for sea bathing, and parties of ladies and gentlemen came over from it daily to look at the fort. Some of the old hands made a dollar now and then by acting as cicerone to one of these parties; but the practice, upon what principle I must say I could not clearly perceive, was generally considered low and disreputable. The fortifications at Fort Adams are on a scale of great magnitude, and must have cost a great deal of money. They had been a number of years in progress of erection, and were not quite finished when we left. The fort commands the entrance to the Sound, and is a very strong and complete defence, having a series of subterranean passages connected with its interior defence, parts of which can be suddenly filled with water in a manner highly ingenious. There are also bombproof vaults, capable of accommodating a sufficient force for the garrison of the place, which has an immense number of very heavy guns on its various batteries.

While we lay at Fort Adams, we had church service performed in one of the barrack rooms every Thursday evening, by a Methodist preacher from town. This was in consequence of the distance being too great to march the men to church in town upon Sunday. The attendance not being compulsory, very few of the men went, but our officers, with their wives and children, attended regularly, with as many of the men as they could persuade, a thing which they sometimes tried with but indifferent success. I recollect hearing a Lieutenant ask one of the men, whom he met in the square as he was going over to church service, if he would not come over and hear a sermon. "Heaven forbid, sir," was the reply of honest Dennis O'Tool, a Munster man, and a staunch Catholic. " Eh ! what's that you say, Dennis ?" said the Lieutenant, in a bantering tone. " Sure, Lieutenant, the Blessed Virgin knows I'm bad enough already, without sinning my soul any more by going to hear a swaddling preacher mocking the holy religion," was the reply of Dennis ; at which the Lieutenant's wife lifted up her eyes in pious horror, while the Lieutenant himself went away laughing heartily.

The regiment I had joined had been expecting a change of station for some time, and about a fortnight after the arrival of our draft, the order came for us to be in readiness to proceed to Florida. Most of the old hands were sorry to leave good quarters and a healthy situation like Fort Adams ; many of them had formed acquaintances and connections in the town of Newport also, which made them still more sorry at leaving. The recruits, however, seemed rather pleased at the idea of change, and the bustling interest and excitement of a sea voyage and change of scene had its charms for some. For my own part I believe I felt rather indifferent on the subject. We were to go to Boston, where we would take shipping for Pensacola.

CHAPTER IV.

Departure from Fort Adams—Providence—Robbing the Orchard—Boston—Life in a Transport—the Captain and the Nigger.

ON the morning of the 13th of September, having put our baggage on board, our head-quarters, consisting of the band and the two companies K and I, embarked in the steamer at the Garrison Wharf. As we sailed past the wharf at Newport, to which we came very close, the captain of the steamer directed the speed to be lessened, to enable us to bid farewell to our friends, who were assembled on the wharf to see us pass, and wave us their adieus. On leaving, they gave us three hearty cheers, which we as heartily returned. Our band struck up Yankee Doodle, and the flutter of scarfs and handkerchiefs was soon lost in the far distance.

It was a fine sunny morning, and enlivened by the strains of a good band of music, and the view of some fine river scenery, we soon had more the appearance of a pleasure party than a detachment of Uncle Sam's troops, ordered to a distant and disagreeable post. The green undulating banks of the clear, smooth, and wide stream, which lined the sandy or pebbled beach of a succession of sylvan coves, were dotted here and there with neat cottages. Farm-houses peeped occasionally through a clump of trees on some gentle rising eminence, round which one might see the plough had been at work, from the lively alternations of colour which distinguished these portions of the landscape. But the land seemed principally occupied with the pasturage of cattle, large herds of which were grazing close to the water's edge, and adding to the picturesque effect of the scene. On sailing up to the wharf at Providence, I observed several whale vessels lying close up; their appearance was not very inviting, and from what I have since learned of these craft, I think I should almost prefer another campaign in Mexico to a three years' cruize in one of them.

Providence is a neat and thriving place, like most of the New England towns, very clean, quiet, and orderly. Yet there is a considerable appearance of bustle about it: it contains several cotton mills, and is finely situated in a pleasant and healthy locality. But we had no time to go through it, as we had to take our baggage from the steam-boat and put it into the railway cars; this being done, we got into the cars ourselves, and started immediately for Boston. We passed through a rather sterile country from Providence to Boston, relieved and diversified occasionally by a farm-house, a neat village, or a few smiling orchards. A nicely whitewashed cotton factory also now and then enlivened the landscape, but the grey rocks, dwarf timber, and stunted fir trees, gave ample proof of the general poverty of the soil, which is principally occupied in raising stock and grazing cattle.

Our progress by the railway was rather slow, for a wheel belonging to one of the cars having broken, we had to wait until it was repaired or replaced. In the meantime, we got out of the cars, and having found our way, in an evil hour for their owners, into some of the orchards near the road, we helped ourselves plentifully to the apples and peaches with which the trees were loaded. Soldiers, especially on the march, seem to have exceedingly imperfect and confused ideas on the subject of *meum* and *tuum*. On the present occasion, I believe the most conscientious among us considered ourselves completely exculpated by the fact, that being hot and thirsty, we could find no good water to drink. Besides, I dare say there was a sort of vindictive pleasure in this sort of spoiling of the Egyptians: were we not going on a long voyage to a distant and unhealthy post, while the owners of these apples and peaches were living at home at ease! "Faith, it may be a long time before we see an apple orchard again," remarked one, as he industriously filled his havresack with the fruit. A long time certainly! Many of the poor fellows never entered another orchard, and never will! Two years afterwards, when rambling with some of my comrades through a beautiful orchard near St. Augustine, a small town on one of the most deliciously fertile and richly cultivated skirts of the valley of Mexico, I recalled to their mind the conversation we had held while plundering the orchard by the wayside, as the cars were being repaired. In the short space of two years we had got almost an entirely new company. There were only about a third of the original number remaining, who had left Fort Adams two years previously—deaths, discharges, and desertions had made awful inroads on our community.

We arrived at Boston about four o'clock in the afternoon, and after transferring our baggage from the railway cars to waggons, we marched through the city with our regimental colors displayed, and our band playing in front, which attracted a great crowd around us. On our way through the common, we got a glimpse of the famous Bunker's Hill monument.

"A very common-place looking affair, but a remarkable monument for all that," observed Bill Nutt, "it being the only monument known to exist that has been erected to commemorate a defeat."

"Arrah, whisht with your blather, man, don't you per

ceive the illegant allegory of the thing; it's only a standing real genuine American bull, set up in opposition to the old English one," said Paddy Bynne.

We had no opportunity of seeing much of the city of Boston, as we were marched on board the ship in which we were going, as soon as we arrived at the wharf where she lay. It was a fine large new vessel, called the Albatross, of about one thousand tons burden. She had been built for the cotton trade, and was to take in cotton at Mobile, after landing us at Pensacola. There were two other companies of our regiment on board, making four companies in all; but each company was only about sixty strong, and we had not a great number of women and children, as several of the married men had left their wives and families behind, being near the expiration of their service. We had a fine large vessel, well fitted up, and had, therefore, more room and better accommodation than commonly falls to the lot of soldiers aboard ship.

We had not been long on board when a guard was mounted, and a number of sentries placed all around the deck, and at the gangway. These sentries had orders to prevent the men from going ashore without permission, the smuggling of spirits into the vessel for the use of the soldiers, and several things of that nature. These measures, I could plainly perceive, had only the effect of making the men resort to a little more strategy in effecting their objects, which it was soon tolerably apparent had a diametrically opposite tendency to the tee-total principle. A number of the men, having applied for leave to go on shore for the purpose of procuring necessaries for the voyage, were not only refused, but told that all such applications would be useless, as the commanding officer was resolved to grant no leave for either non-commissioned officers or soldiers to go on shore while in harbor. This extreme caution of the commanding officer was bad policy, as it enlisted the sympathies of the sentries in favour of those who wished to go on shore; the non-commissioned officers also, finding that they were prevented from going as well as the men, made common cause with them in endeavouring to nullify the arbitrary prohibition. As a consequence of this state of things, I could soon see that the sentry winked at all sorts of irregularities; rather assisting to mystify his officers, by helping his comrades to elude their vigilance in going in and out of the vessel, than trying to detect or prevent them. The method commonly adopted to get out of the vessel was, to substitute a straw or tarpaulin hat, and a Guernsey frock, or red woollen shirt, for the soldier's cap and jacket. This disguise, so effective as to deceive the most acute of the officers, was easily procured from some of the sailors on board, and by means of it a constant communication was kept up with the grog stores while we lay there, fortunately not a long period, being only during the next day and night. Thus, while our commanding officer, I have no doubt, flattered himself with the idea of his own sagacity, in refusing his men these indulgences, which it should have been his pleasure, as it certainly would have been his best policy, as well as his duty, to have granted, he was weakening his authority by stretching it too far—a more common mistake in the service than officers are at all apt to imagine.

A rather ludicrous circumstance, which occurred while we lay here, helped to enliven a little the usual monotony of a ship's deck while in harbor. A comical sort of fellow, of the name of Morris, belonging to one of the companies on board, who used to sing Nigger songs, and who, being a very good mimic, could act the Nigger admirably, resolved to turn his talents to account by assuming the character while in harbor, and passing himself off among his comrades, except a few who were in his confidence, as a black cook belonging to the ship—his twofold motive for thus "working the dodge," as he styled it, being partly the fun he expected from the mystification of the men and officers, and partly that he might be allowed to bring whiskey into the ship, there being no hindrance to the ship's crew bringing goods on board, as our sentries could not interfere with them. Borrowing, therefore, an old pair of canvas trousers, a Guernsey shirt, and tarpaulin hat from a sailor, and thoroughly engraining his face and hands with the sooty composition requisite to give him the true Ethiopian complexion, he became quite invulnerable to detection by his coat of darkness. In this disguise he rolled about the deck during the whole of the forenoon in a partial state of intoxication, and came and went between the vessel and shore, carrying baskets and parcels of suspicious import with the most perfect impunity. Towards evening, he began to sing snatches of Nigger songs, varying the exhibition with a "flare-up" jawing match with some of the soldiers, in the sort of gibberish and broken English so peculiar to the woolly-headed sons of Ham. This comedy afforded considerable amusement, especially to those of his comrades in the secret of his disguise. As he was dexterous in the tongue fence of those encounters of rude wit, and knowing the chinks in the armor of his opponents, he was sometimes able, by a seemingly careless though cunning thrust, to administer a sickener to their vanity, which was the more galling as seeming to come from a dirty and half-drunken Nigger. "Ah, soger," he would say to some poor fellow whom he saw casting a longing eye towards the busy thoroughfares of the city, "captain not let you go shore, eh? Too bad, eh? much sooner be black ship's cook than soger." "What's that you say, you Nigger?" would most probably be the reply of the soldier, not being in the best temper, and rather indignant at the idea of being an object of commiseration to a Nigger. "Who you call Nigger, eh? Nigger yourself, sar; more Nigger, a good sight, than ship's cook, sar; ship's cook go ashore when he please, and get drunk like gentleman, sar; you a white soger Nigger, me black ship's cook Nigger—dat all de difference." Then, as if in soliloquy, in a deprecatory tone, "Eh! by Jorze, boff poor Niggers; soger moss as spectable as colored Nigger when he keep heself sober and behave screetly, like color gemman." Stung and irritated by the mock sympathy of the Nigger, the soldier would now be for taking a summary revenge out of his ignoble carcase, when some of the darkey's friends would interpose, declaring that he was a good fellow, and they would not see him illused. In the meantime, Morris was supposed by the orderly sergeant of his company to be absent in town, and as such reported to the captain. Thus far, all had gone on swimmingly; but there was a bit of a rather unpleasant surprise preparing for him as the denouement to this farce, which he had acted with so much success, which had probably not entered into his conception of the character, but mightily increased the dramatic effect of the representation as a whole.

The captain of his company, who was a bit of a humourist, either having detected the masquerader himself, or having been informed by some busy person of the strange metamorphosis which one of his men had undergone, it occurred to him that he had an opportunity of giving him a taste of Nigger discipline, that might make him feel more vividly the character he had been representing with so much applause. Sauntering, accordingly, along the deck, with his hands behind him, until he arrived opposite the circle where Morris was exhibiting his antics, he deliberately stepped forward and seized him by the collar, and pulling out a raw cowhide, from behind his back, he began to vigorously belabour poor darkey's shoulders. " O Lor, massa! O Golly! What you trike poor debil for ? What hell dis ?" shouted Morris, who had no idea that he was discovered, and was willing to submit to a moderate degree of chastisement rather than drop his disguise at that particular juncture. " You infernal grinning scoundrel," cries the captain, still vigorously applying the cowhide, "I have been watching you quarrelling with and aggravating my men all this afternoon ; what do you mean, you black rascal, eh ? Curse your ugly black countenance, I'll beat you to a jelly, you scoundrel." As he still continued his discipline with the cowhide, showing no symptoms of speedily leaving off, Morris, who was smarting with pain, at last began to think more of preserving his skin than his incognito, and called out lustily, " Captain, I say— stop! I am no Nigger—I am a soldier!" At this there was a general burst of laughter from the soldiers, who crowded round, and seemed to enjoy the scene amazingly; those who did not know that Morris was actually a soldier, laughing still more obstreperously at the seeming absurdity of the Nigger's assertion. The captain, though evidently tickled, seemed in no hurry to let him go : " Do you hear the impudence of the black rascal ? he says he is a soldier !" said the captain, addressing the men who were standing round. " There, does he look like a soldier ?" he continued, as he turned him round for inspection. " Go along, you black rascal, and don't let me catch you among my men again, or I will certainly serve you out with a few more of the same sort." So saying, and administering a few parting salutations of the cowhide as he released him, the captain walked off, chuckling to himself at the joke, which I saw him relating afterwards to some of his brother officers, to their infinite mirth, if one might judge from the peals of laughter which his story elicited. In the meantime, Morris was fain to get rid of his Nigger character as quickly as possible; and having, with the aid of warm water and soap, effected this, he made his appearance on deck, and reported himself as having been asleep in the hold when the roll was called. This the sergeant reported to the captain, who, satisfied, it is probable, with the punishment he had administered with the cowhide, affected to believe his statement, and sent him word by the sergeant to take better care in future.

While we lay at the wharf, we had a crowd of inquisitive idlers in constant attendance round the vessel, all of whom seemed particularly anxious to learn our destination. To the often-repeated question on this all-absorbing topic, the invariable answer was that we were going to Mexico. This being in the most perfect accordance with the preconception, as well as the ideas of propriety of the inquirer, was of course perfectly satisfactory, and therefore implicitly believed. The fact is, that had they been told the simple truth that we were going to Florida, they would either have suspected their informant of telling a lie, or considered him ignorant of the true destination. They had made up their minds that we were going to Mexico, and our men thought it just as well to agree with them for the short time we were to be in their company.

CHAPTER V.

The Soldier at Sea.

ABOUT nine o'clock, on the morning of the 17th, the tide being full, we unmoored ship, and with a fair wind, stood out of harbour. With a fine, steady, though light breeze, we sailed pleasantly past forts and light-houses, gliding along by a miserably barren-looking coast, consisting for the most part of strangely rugged and fantastic looking piles of grey and weather-beaten rocks, and low sandy islets, covered with rushes or stunted grass, the only sign of vegetation visible. In the evening we caught a glimpse of Cape Cod in the distance, but passed it during the night, and on the morning of the 18th we found ourselves on the open sea.

A soldier at sea generally finds himself very disagreeably situated. Accustomed to strict personal cleanliness, and in the habit of keeping his arms and appointments in a high state of order when in quarters, he feels completely out of his element in a transport, where, even under the most favourable circumstances, he is utterly unable to attend to a number of those things so essential to his feelings of comfort. On the present occasion, however, we were more comfortably situated than is usually the case with soldiers in a government transport, the vessel we were in being double the size of that we were entitled to by the rules of the service. Yet we were by no means too comfortable, or in possession of a great deal of superfluous space; the fact is, that in ordinary cases soldiers are usually stowed away when at sea, more like cattle, or hogs, on a Dublin and Liverpool steamer, than human beings; and the exemption from this in the present instance was hailed as a blessing. But this circumstance, so much in our favour, was not caused by any extraordinary or particular extension of courtesy or kindness shown to us by those in authority. It arose simply from the *Albatross* being in want of a cargo for Mobile, a port within a short distance of the one we were destined to, and where she was to ship a cargo of cotton for Liverpool. A vessel of half the size, if specially chartered for the purpose, would have cost government as much, or probably more; while adding most incalculably to our discomfort, and giving rise to innumerable heinous infractions of the third commandment, had the present chance not turned up in our favour.

The arrangements for accommodation between decks, were much the same as those usually made in emigrant vessels; a row of two berths, one above the other, ran along each side of the vessel, and a third similar one in the centre; leaving a tolerably wide passage on each side of the centre row as a gangway. A portion of the hold was separated by a boarded partition, for the use of the married people. In time of peace, three married men of each company are allowed (their wives being laundresses, and washing for the soldiers,) to bring their families along with them when moving. Each of these married men is allowed separate quarters for himself and family when in garrison, also rations for his wife, who is paid a stated sum by each soldier for whom they wash. When one of these married men is discharged, if more applicants than one should apply for the vacant situation, the Captain gives it to the one he considers the best deserving. When going on active service, neither officers nor soldiers are permitted to take their wives or families along with them.

On the evening of the 18th, the breeze having freshened, a number of the men began to experience the usual effects produced on the stomach of a land-lubber by the motion of a vessel at sea. Of course we had a repetition of a few of those mouldy old practical jests which have been in use on board ship on these occasions from time immemorial; those in the enjoyment of their usual health and spirits seeming to consider the unfortunate individuals suffering from this annoying sickness fair game, and a legitimate object of mirth, in place of sympathy. One of the oldest jokes perpetrated on these occasions, must be familiar to every soldier who has ever made a sea voyage, and is played-off somewhat after the following manner. The hoaxer pretending great sympathy with the sufferings of the afflicted, states that he has heard of a most excellent remedy, of simple and easy application, and certain in its results. Should he succeed in engaging the interest and attention of his audience, the insidious design of the hoaxer is accomplished; he immediately proceeds to describe the simple and never-known-to-fail remedy, which consists of the following recipe, "Take a good large slice of fat pork tied to a string." The bare mention of fat pork, without the rank atrocity and diabolical intent implied in the attached string, is quite sufficient to raise the gorge of his intended victims, who seldom wait to hear the conclusion of the recipe; while the hoaxer shows the cloven hoof by an obstreperous and demoniacal fit of laughter as the pale faces flit past him to lean over the bulwarks, and wonder, while paying their tribute to Neptune, what pleasure one rational being can derive from the sufferings of another.

This practice of turning the sufferings of the sea-sick into ridicule, and which seems so strange and unfeeling, arises, I am inclined to think, from a good rather than a bad motive; owing its origin, probably, to the circumstance that the exertion requisite to overcome sea-sickness and its consequent torpor, is most effectually promoted by the fear of this ridicule. I have often seen strong men, from a want of the requisite energy to throw off this torpor and counteract its effects by moderate exercise and the fresh air of the deck, sink into a critically dangerous state of illness, nearly ending in death from exhaustion, the stomach ceasing to perform its functions, and the whole frame being reduced to a mere skeleton.

The sailors on board ship are always told off into two watches, one of which is constantly kept upon deck for the performance of the necessary work of the vessel. These watches relieve each other every four hours, but in a gale, or when a sudden squall is apprehended, all hands remain constantly on deck until the danger is supposed to be over. Soldiers being reckoned worse than useless in a gale of wind, are bundled below with very small ceremony when the weather looks dangerous, with the occasional exception of a few of the more active, retained to assist the seamen. Owing to the dislike of the soldiers to remain below, it sometimes happens that the Captain or mate of the vessel finds it necessary to complain to the officer of the day, that the soldiers are in the way of their men in working the ship. In this case the officer gives instruction to the sergeant of the guard, who soon sees all the soldiers down below; after which the gratings are put on the hatchways, and a sentry placed over each, with orders to allow none of the men to come upon deck. In the meantime the scene below is one of "most admired disorder," women ejaculating, children screaming, soldiers cursing, swearing, singing, dancing, and making every sort of uncouth and dissonant noise imaginable, a few of the more energetic radicals, locofocos, or physical force chartists, haranguing their comrades meanwhile upon the propriety of breaking the hatches open, and forcing their way upon deck in spite of the sentry, and the arbitrary and tyrannical prohibition of the officer of the day, a proposition usually hailed with acclamation and adopted *nem. con.* But, ere " screwing their courage to the sticking point," " The native hue of resolution is sicklied o'er with the pale cast of thought," and the suggestion thrown out by some milk-and-water moral force advocate, relative to the pains and penalties attached to mutiny, and deforcement of sentries, in the " *Articles of War*," cautions the rash and fiery spirits of incipient rebellion, that " tis better to bear those ills they have, than fly to others which they know not of." And thus this enterprise of such pith and moment, like most of those of the physical force chartists, ends in "mere sound and fury, signifying nothing." This confinement, however, being only for the purpose of preventing the sailors from being impeded in their work while taking in sail, seldom lasts more than half an hour, or an hour. As soon as everything is snug upon deck, the gratings are removed from the hatchways; and glimpses of light, and hope, and currents of fresh air, circulate through the hold once more; while our moral force advocate emerging from the pestiferous atmosphere, triumphs in the progress of a rational sanitary reform.

Soldiers on board ship are usually told off into three watches; this is done to prevent the over-crowding the hold, by keeping one third of their number constantly on deck; each watch remaining four hours on deck in succession. On the present occasion the custom of telling off into watches was dispensed with, very much to our satisfaction; the *Albatross* being large and roomy enough, in the opinion of the officer commanding, to render the observance of the regulation unnecessary. Still, throughout the whole of the voyage the rules for cleaning and ventilating the ship were strictly maintained; these being of the most essential importance to the health and comfort of troops on board ship, too much rigour can scarcely be used by officers in enforcing their observance. A sergeant, corporal, and twelve men mounted guard every morning at nine o'clock; two sentries were posted between decks, one at each end of the vessel, for the purpose of preserving order, and taking charge of the lights which hung in large glass globe lamps, one at each hatchway, during the whole night. Other two sentries were placed on deck, one having charge of the water cask, where our daily supply of fresh water was kept, to prevent any waste, or undue use of it; while the other had orders to check quarrelling, or gross improprieties, and preserve order generally on deck. Every morning immediately after guard mounting, all hands, men, women, and children, were turned upon deck; unless in rough, or very wet weather, when the rule was not enforced. The police, consisting of the non-commissioned officers and men who came off guard on the previous morning, then went below, and scraped, and afterwards washed the floor of the lower deck. Afterwards they fumigated between decks with tar, and sprinkled the floor with chloride of lime; they also brought up a day's supply of fuel and fresh water from the lower hold for the use of the soldiers. The soldiers always brought up their own wood and water, and had a cook and cooking place of their own; as well as being lodged in a distinct portion of the ship called the forecastle. After the hold had been cleaned, it was inspected by the officer of the day, to see that the duty had been properly performed, and that the bedding and clothes belonging to the men were neatly folded and arranged in their respective berths. In fine weather the whole of the bedding was brought upon deck and well aired, and none of the men were permitted to go below without special permission, until the whole were allowed down in the evening. When I speak here of bedding, I mean the soldier's blanket, which in the United States service he always carries along with him; there are no mattresses for a soldier to lie upon on board ship in the American service.

As these were all the duties we had to perform while on board, it will be seen that we had very little to do, or to occupy our attention during the greater portion of our time, which, as usual under like circumstances, hung heavy on our hands. The fortunate few who could obtain books, were assiduous in their endeavours to convert the tedium of a sea voyage into a source of enjoyment, but unfortunately the supply of literature fell far short of the demand; the natural result followed; holders grew firm, and books were at an immense premium. I could scarce help fancying how exceedingly gratifying it would have been to the literary vanity of the authors of "The Bloody Bandit of the Lion's Glen," "The Mysterious Hand," and others of that genus, could they have witnessed the surprising request in which their productions were held, and the apparent gusto with which their intensely melo-dramatic scenes were devoured on board our vessel. It was truly wonderful, the sudden change wrought in the value of scraps of printed paper; everything of which sort seemed to "suffer a sea change into something rich and strange." An old newspaper became suddenly invested with a remarkable degree of literary interest, and a dozen would have bespoken, and be waiting in rotation for the perusal of the fragment of some old third-rate novel, or antediluvian magazine, as eagerly as the most impatient reader watches for his favourite monthly. Under these circumstances, unless one had something to offer by way of *quid pro quo*, reading was totally out of the question. In this emergency it occurred to Bill Nutt, the young man whom I mentioned as having been told off as my comrade in a former chapter, to offer a sort of *succedaneum* a written journal of the transactions on board. Accordingly on the morning of Sept. 20th a placard containing the following announcement might have been seen pasted up on a conspicuous part of the hatchway of the good ship *Albatross*.

'*Albatross*, 20*th Sept*. 1845.

"THE JOURNAL OF THE ALBATROSS.

" To-morrow morning will appear the first number of a journal bearing the above title, to be published daily (weather permitting), at our office near the cook's galley, on board of the *Albatross*. This journal will consist of at least eight quarto pages in legible handwriting : it will contain, besides 'The News of the Day,' 'Critical Notices,' 'Letters of Correspondents,' and 'Advertisements,' a general summary of all the stirring and striking events, daily, hourly, and minutely acted and transacted, before the eyes, and as it were under the noses, of this strange conglomeration of unfortunate humanity now on board. Amalgamated, mixed up, and bound up, as it were in our fortunes, by the inextricable and inexplicable decrees of the three sisters, and the immutable and inscrutable workings of destiny, who in forging the chain of circumstances that at present surround us, has obviously decided that, sink or swim, we should sail down the stream of time in this wooden prison for a certain period in company ; it becomes us to make the term of confinement seem as short as possible. With a view to this result, several of the motley individuals forming part of the worshipful society here assembled, have come to the resolution of publishing this daily record of remarkable events and occur rences; for which contributions are respectfully solicited from all lovers of light literature. In the confident expectation of receiving the cordial support of the community, we have only to announce that contributions will be received at our office near the cook's galley, where terms of subscription and full particulars may be learned."

Next morning accordingly, and with one or two exceptions in squally weather, every successive morning that we remained on board, there regularly appeared a sheet of miscellaneous matter, written in a plain legible hand; it was attached by a string to the cook's galley, and extensively read by sailors and soldiers, exciting considerable merriment and good-humoured criticism. Several of these fugitive pieces, written by Nutt, I preserved until lately, and as a specimen of his humour, and a sample of the Journal, I insert one or two of them.

"SOMETHING IN THE WIND.

" Last evening before going to press, we could see with half a glance of our weather eye that there was something serious in the wind, something exceedingly ominous looking, in short, something more than merely dirty weather. The term dirty weather, by the bye, we may as well remark for the information of several and upwards of our readers not perhaps aware of the fact, being a vague definite term, generally used by spoony individuals in the vain efforts they make to stimulate indifference, and conceal their apprehension of a severe blow. Instantaneously stopping the press, we immediately hurried upon deck, and found that, as usual, we were tolerably correct in our surmise. In fact, there were several palpable and distinct indications of a stiffener to wind'ard, sufficiently alarming to the owners of weak or delicate nerves; who, if they cannot resolve upon leaving such articles ashore, are most decidedly in the wrong box with them aboard. On going for'ard to where the second mate—one of those hardy weather-beaten sons of Neptune with whom we are on tolerably familiar terms—was standing gazing at the rigging, we asked his private opinion of things in general, and the present rather critical aspect of affairs in particular. He replied in his gruff 'deep-toned voice,' that we are sure 'did not falter,' that we were 'a going to catch particular d—n—n, and no mistake.' In the meantime, the gallant crew of the *Albatross* behaved with the cool decision one naturally expects to characterise a crew, composed principally of freeborn and full-blooded Yankee sailors. We distinctly observed one gallant fellow while holding on by a bowline waiting for orders, deliberately put his hand into his breeches pocket. This reminds us that we have heard sneering sceptics deny the existence of pockets in sailors' smallclothes, a malignant slander, which we here refute in the most emphatic manner, as the egregiously contemptible fabrication of ignorant and presumptuous blockheads. This gallant son of Neptune, we reiterate, putting his hand into his breeches pocket, drew from thence a plug of Virginia tobacco, and eyeing it with a look of affection, as if calculating the probability of its being the last time it should ever express its fragrant juice, he heaved a sigh, took a vigorous bite, returned the plug to his pocket, and stood calmly awaiting the order of his superior. In the meantime, the 'blustering railer, rude Boreas,' seeing our state of preparation, and that we were not to be easily hove aback, or finished with a blow, sneaked off to le'ward; where, should he catch an unfortunate skimmer of the seas napping while in his present humour, with out walking into several of his sails and spars, you may have our hat. In the meantime, we may look out for squalls, the usual phenomena of these latitudes, but in the words of the song—

"'With a stout vessel and crew,
We'll say let the storm come down.'"

"LOST.

"A good sound apitite as bin lost sum wares on board of the Halbert Ross by a wery nice sort of yung man, who remanes in a most diskonselat stat ever sense the misfortun okurd, not bein abel to konsum mor nor a trifel of fore or five pounds of bisket and pork in a day sense the axident. Who ever as found the same on deliverin it at the office of the jurnal, will be ansumly rewarded. N.B. The yung man as lost his'n, as found an osses, wich will be glad to part with reznabel."

"FREE CONCERTS.

"On our way home last evening, we called at the free concert held in the forecastle, which, we were glad to perceive, was very well attended. We were highly amused with the singing of several of the distinguished vocalists who favoured the company with their sweet voices, and which, as the 'Bard of Avon' somewhere remarks on a similar occasion, 'To hear by the noise, it sounds like dulcet in contagion.' In fact, the singing, while it might have been worse, one could scarcely, under the circumstances, expect it to be much better. As a slight qualification, however, to what may appear our too partial encomiums, we would beg, with all due deference to the superior judgment of the gentlemen having the direction of the proceedings at these social entertainments, to offer a suggestion. It is simply this, that every gent. on rising to sing, ought to state to the company whether the song with which he intends to favour them is of the comic or sentimental class. At a first glance, we have no doubt our honest suggestion will appear to the fastidiously critical, or the critically fastidious, to be invidious or uncalled for; we are prepared for this; but it is with a just pride that we announce to our readers, that we have never yet swerved to the right or to the left, or shrunk from the performance of a stern or necessary duty by the fear of criticism or consequence. With this animating reflection actuating us, we candidly put the following question:—If sentimental gents will sing sentimental songs, out of all tune, and with a comic voice, accent, and manner, and if comic songs are treated *vice versâ*, how is an unsophisticated person able to comprehend this inverted system of 'untwisting all the links that tie the hidden soul of harmony?' I assure my readers I went last night to hear the singing, with a desire to be pleased, if ever mortal critic had that desire (which may be questioned). What was the result? Disgust, disgust of the most unqualified, unmitigated, and contemptuous character. One of the gents in the sentimental line tried 'Alice Grey' and 'Oft in the Stilly Night,' and the audience were convulsed with laughter, while a comic gent tipped them 'Nix my Dolly' in such a doleful and lugubrious style as to cause the company to wear the air of a funeral-party. I need say no more. I trust, in future, that each gent. who rises to sing at these free concerts will signify in a plain, straightforward, off-hand, and up and down manner, whether his song

is sentimental or comic, in which case they may safely calculate on the favour and slightly qualified applause of
"DANIEL DAMPER."

Among the methods adopted to pass time on board, card-playing was the most popular and engrossing. Non-commissioned officers and privates, seated in groups on the forecastle in fine weather, and between decks when it rained, played at the game of poker from morning till night. Poker is the national game of cards in America. It is played by gamblers of all classes, to the exclusion of almost all other modes of gambling, and being a peculiarly exciting game, it exerts an inconceivably fascinating influence over its votaries. During our present voyage, I have frequently seen a private soldier rise from a single sitting the winner of forty or fifty dollars; and in a few hours, having again sat down to play, he would probably have lost it all, and as much more as he could borrow, without seeming either much elevated or depressed by the smiles or frowns of the fickle goddess. It may surprise some how soldiers could be in possession of such large sums of money. It happened simply thus :—Two of the companies had been paid a short time previous to their embarkation, the men had thus no opportunity of getting rid of their superabundant capital; an operation which, when ashore, they usually perform with astonishing facility. A private's pay in the Infantry is seven dollars a month, and he is paid every two months; one dollar a month is retained until the expiration of his service. Thus at pay-day the private receives twelve dollars; the sergeant twenty-six; the corporal eighteen; the musicians sixteen; no pay being retained from any of these ranks except the private. Most of the soldiers are more or less addicted to gambling, and thus large sums of money are frequently in the hands of the practised gamblers about pay-time, sometimes amounting to hundreds of dollars in possession of five or six of the most skilful. Gambling is strictly prohibited by the rules of the service, but the difficulty of enforcing the rule, owing partly to laxity of discipline, and partly to the exceedingly badly-arranged system of paying the soldiers two months' pay at a time, in place of daily or weekly, renders the prohibition a dead letter.

We had an excellent regimental band on board, and in fine weather our officers had it up on deck to play for an hour or two in the evening. This practice had a markedly enlivening effect upon the spirits, and must have helped materially to promote health, as it evidently exerted a beneficial influence in promoting a cheerful hilarity and good-humour among the men. It was interesting to observe the sudden change from blank and listless apathy to brisk and animated cheerfulness which some well-known and favourite air produced in the countenances of all; the strains of "Auld lang syne" calling forth the latent smile on cheeks and lips, and kindling the languid eye of the most melancholy and morose. My friend Nutt, when remarking on this effect one morning, said he could almost believe in the authenticity of the miracles ascribed to the music of Amphion and Orpheus, as he had himself witnessed a most astounding transformation effected in the person of the boatswain of the ship, whose "savage breast" had been so thoroughly soothed by music's magic spell, that he had observed him once, while under its powerful influence, talking in the tones, manner, and accent of a civilized being.

I mentioned that Nutt had been on board a British man-of-war during a three years' cruise. One day, when seated in a quiet corner of the deck, I reminded him of a promise he had formerly made to give me a sketch of the events of his earlier years, which had resulted in a young man of good abilities, and brought up to a good trade, being seduced into such rambling and unsatisfactory modes of life as that of a sailor or a soldier. After a preliminary " well here goes for a yarn," he commenced the following narrative. As it professes to be a true chapter in the early life of my comrade, I will give it as nearly as I can recollect in his own manner, devoting a chapter specially to the purpose.

CHAPTER VI.

A Modern Soldier of Fortune.

I suppose you know that I am a Cockney. I was born and brought up within the sound of those famous bells of Bow, whose voice, speaking through the legends of childhood, has warned many an incipient mayor and alderman to turn again, when half inclined to "cut" the paternal mansion, and the precincts of their guardians' influence; and who, following the admonition of the affectionate monitors, have risen to emulate the wealth at least, if not the fame or the virtues, of the renowned Whittington, of " thrice Lord Mayor of London " celebrity. I really can't recollect whether these bells warned me or not on the morning when I resolved upon leaving "the old house at home," and looking out a little into the world. Certainly, if they did, I paid very little attention to them, being wholly taken up with my object of getting off unnoticed by any of my acquaintances, who might, when they heard I was gone, be likely to indicate the route I had taken, in which case I was afraid my father would follow and bring me back.

My father, who was a carver and gilder in extensive business, had brought me up to the same trade, which I had learned with facility and aptitude, and for a year or two previous to my leaving him, though then only seventeen years of age, I had been of great use to him, as I did as much work, and of as good quality, as many of the journeymen to whom he was giving employment. My mother died when I was a child in the arms of a nurse, and before I was old enough to recollect the event, my father had married again. My stepmother was a very good sort of woman as stepmothers go, and I had no fault to find with her treatment of me ; perhaps she liked her own children, of whom she had three by my father, better than my sister and myself, and it is probable that home might have been happier if my own mother had lived. Still our stepmother never showed any marked preference for her own children, nor ever treated my sister or me harshly or unjustly ; and could not be blamed if she did not possess all that warmth of affection which a mother can have only for her own. My father unfortunately had a quick and violent temper, which was a good deal aggravated by a habit of tippling into which he had fallen ; and frequently for trifling causes of offence, when he happened to be in one of his ill-tempered moods, he beat me so severely that at last I became apprehensive he would one day do me a serious injury. It was after receiving one of these drubbings that I resolved upon leaving home. I was then about seventeen years of age, and wanted four years of being out of my apprenticeship ; my father having bound me by indenture to serve him for seven years ; but, as I said before, I could work at the business as well as a good many of the journeymen. Here, in America (and this is one thing in which I must give Jonathan the credit of having gone rather ahead of the old countries), it matters not whether a man serves an apprenticeship, or how he acquires the skill or proficiency to work at his trade or calling. " Is he able to do his work ?" is the only question asked, and ability is the only test required. But in England the case is widely different, as I had soon reason to deplore. I was leaving home with the intention of working at my trade in some country town out of the knowledge, and beyond the reach, of my father.

I had only about fifty shillings when I left home, twenty of which I got from my sister, whom I made my confidant, and who did all she could to alter my determination, but seeing that I was firmly resolved upon going, she gave me a sovereign, making me promise to write to her, a promise which I never fulfilled.

I had no fixed intention of going to any place in particular when I left our house; but in passing a coach-office where a coachful of passengers was on the point of starting for Portsmouth, and on inquiry, learning there was room for one on the outside, I took a seat, and was soon rapidly whirling along the road. We soon left the dome of St. Paul's an indistinct, dim, and visionary outline, and away we burst with a glorious canter into the fresh air of the open country, where even the cloud of the foggy Babylon itself was soon left far behind. There was a young sailor on the top of the coach, going to Portsmouth to join his vessel, having been up in London on a visit to his friends. He and I were soon engaged in conversation, when he gave me a long account of his cruise in the Mediterranean, and the adventures of his last three years on board a man-of-war. He described the life of a sailor in glowing terms, and wondered how any person could prefer a dull life on shore, who had the choice of the merry and easy life led on board one of Her Majesty's ships. Though I was much amused with his conversation, I did not feel in the least inclined to wish myself one of the jolly crews he talked of. More especially as he spoke of some of the officers he had served under as regular Tartars, one of whose eccentricities consisted in making a few of the men kiss the gunner's daughter of a morning before breakfast. This kissing the gunner's daughter, which rather puzzled me at first, I found on inquiry was an amusing practice they had of tying a sailor up to the breech of a gun, and inflicting two dozen lashes on his bare back with a cat o'nine tails, by the hands of the boatswain.

We arrived in Portsmouth early in the evening, and I accompanied the young sailor to a tavern, where we had supper together, and engaged lodgings for the night. We afterwards went to the theatre, and passed the night away pleasantly together. I told him I had left home, and was strongly persuaded by him to enter the vessel in which he was going; it would take me, he said, on the ratings as a boy for a three years' cruise, during which I might learn to be a good sailor; the vessel was for the West India station and would sail in a few days. But I steadily resisted all his arguments, thinking I had only to look for employment to find plenty of it, and not having the slightest desire for a sea life, which I had always pictured to myself as one of great hardship and ill-usage. Next morning after breakfast, I went down to the Point with him, and saw him take a boat to go on board of his vessel, which lay at Spithead.

I wandered about Portsmouth for the remainder of that and several succeeding days, looking for employment at my trade; but though I found several shops where the masters would have been willing to employ me if I had been able to show that I had served an apprenticeship, I soon found that without that, I had no chance. It was in vain that I offered to work for half wages, it was quite against the rules of the trade, and though tall and stout of my age, any person might see I was too young to have served an apprenticeship; in fact I believe most of them guessed the true state of the case, that I was only a runaway boy. This was a serious disappointment to my hopes; however, partly through pride, and partly through a dread of the punishment I would receive in all probability from my father if I returned, I determined to stay away until reduced to the last extremity. In the meantime I resolved to try the country towns, thinking it possible that by jobbing, and showing my ability to work, together with offering to work for low wages, I might eventually, perhaps, succeed in finding permanent employment. Flattering myself with this idea, I started for the country. I travelled through several counties on foot, sometimes getting a few days' work in one town, and then compelled to set off to another to look for fresh employment. During this period I often dined off beans, or turnips, in the fields, and very glad I was to get them too; and I have several times been glad to find a bed in some convenient hayrick. At length one evening I was standing at a toll bridge, fairly beaten up; starved with hunger, tired, and footsore. To make matters worse, the churlish tollman, cursing my impudence in attempting to set up a plea of poverty to induce him to let me pass free, threatened to set his dog on me if I did not take myself off the same way I came. "Friend, thou art sparing in good deeds, and liberal in thy use of bad words, I fear," said a mild voice a short distance behind me, and turning round I saw a good-natured looking gentleman, in the broad brimmed hat and plain coat of the Quaker. The tollman became very suddenly red in the face at this address, not having observed the approach of the old gentleman, who probably had some control over him in his situation, as I saw him talking to him for some time in a tone of rebuke. On going away he motioned me to follow, which I was not slow to do, you may be sure, especially as upon glancing at the tollman I saw he did not consider himself much obliged to me for the lecture he had just received from the Quaker.

The old gentleman, who though stout and healthy looking, and of a cheerful and ruddy complexion, was, I should think, close upon sixty years of age, waited until I came up to him, when he began to ask a few questions relating to my present condition, and how I came to be travelling in that destitute manner. I told him I had been travelling and looking for employment as a carver and gilder, mentioning some of the towns at which I had found a job, but that not being able to find permanent employment in the country, I was making my way back to Portsmouth. But he was not satisfied with this statement apparently, which I imagined he suspected left the main point untold, and continued to question me, until I became fairly puzzled, and involved in several contradictions. You will think it strange that a big lad of seventeen should begin to cry at an old fellow asking him a few simple questions, but such was the case though. It is now six years ago, and I recollect it as if it were yesterday; it is strange how easily the head pumps are set a-going sometimes. The kind and benevolent tones of the old gentleman as he questioned me, mingled with a feeling of shame at the incoherence of my replies, fairly overcame me; at the same time I was weak, and probably hysterical, from a long abstinence from food, and so sitting down by the roadside I hid my face in my hands, and blubbered like a big schoolboy after a whipping.

On recovering, I found the old gentleman was still alongside, evidently resolved to keep me in tow. "Come, my lad," said he, when I had got up on my feet, "thou art tired and footsore, my house is not far off, come along with me and thou mayest have thy feet washed, a supper, and a bed, and if thee doesn't like to tell thy story I shall not ask thee." Rousing myself up, and feeling ashamed at the false statements in which I had been detected, and which had led to the singular childish symptoms I had exhibited, while travelling along the road, I gave him a true and succinct relation of my circumstances, and my reason for quitting home. When I had concluded, he said he thought he could give me some employment that would occupy me a few days, and during that time my feet would recover, and he would think of some advice that might be useful to me.

We soon arrived at the old gentleman's house, a genteel cottage a little off the highway, with a fine ornamented lawn in front, and a spacious garden in rear. His wife, a fine, cheerful, quiet looking old lady, came to the gate to meet him. He told her in a few words the circumstance under which he had found me, and it was speedily evident by her actions, that she rejoiced at the opportunity of exercising her benevolence. An abundant supply of warm water, with soap and towel, were speedily at my disposal, and having washed my feet, I was furnished with clean stockings and slippers. I then partook of an excellent supper, to which I did ample justice, and soon afterwards was shown to a good bed. I was treated with unvarying kindness while I remained with these excellent people, a period of eight days, during which I cleaned, and freshly gilded, the frames of a number of pictures belonging to them. I received much excellent advice from them both, and the old gentleman, to whom I had faithfully promised to proceed home, gave me a letter addressed to my father, and two sovereigns, on the morning I left. I had not earned more than half the sum, but I knew he calculated on paying my coach fare to London in this manner, and I would have pained him by refusing it. Having bid my kind and benevolent friends a sincere farewell, I travelled to the next town, which was only a few miles off, and there took the stage coach to Portsmouth. But though I had promised to go home, when staying with the worthy Quakers, and intended it also I believe, now when away from their influence, the old motives of pride and fear were in full operation again; and before I arrived at Portsmouth, I had resolved to enter a man-of-war.

Accordingly, to make a long story short, I entered as a boy on board the frigate *Blazer*, at that time fitting out for a three years' cruise on the coast of Africa. I cannot say that I expected to lead a very easy or pleasant life when I entered Her Majesty's service; it need not surprise you therefore to learn, that for some time after I joined, having suffered a good deal from sea-sickness, as we encountered several stiff gales before leaving Spithead, I felt my bitterest anticipations of the discomfort of a sea life fully realized.

We lay for a fortnight at Spithead, during which time we were occupied chiefly in getting in stores and provisions. A few days before sailing, our captain came on board, and having mustered the men, he read the commission appointing him to the command of the frigate. When he had done reading, a few of the men were commencing to cheer. " Hold your d——d jaw," he shouted in the voice of a Stentor. " Now men, mind what I say to you, I will have no cheering in this ship without my orders. If you should have the luck to board an enemy's vessel, you may cheer like devils the moment you set foot on her decks, but not a moment before. When you are paid off and ashore, too, after our cruise is over, I have no objection to your cheering as much as you think proper; but while on board this ship, mind I wish you to recollect it—no cheering if you please, except at an order from me. As you are all here I will take the liberty of making a few remarks which may save some misunderstanding in future. We sail in a few days for the coast of Africa, I have taken the command, and as all reports will henceforth be forwarded to me, I hope that all irregularities of conduct will immediately cease. I am exceedingly averse to corporal punishment, but, however painful to my feelings, there are some crimes for which I feel that I shall be compelled to award it if distinctly proved; these are drunkenness, disrespect to officers, and disobedience of orders. I will be happy to render you every indulgence in my power while you are under my command, and shall use every means to make you as comfortable as possible; which I trust you on your part will do your endeavour to merit. Now, my lads, you may go."

Such was the address of our captain, who did not seem to be known to many of the crew except by hearsay, which gave him the name of a "bit of a sharper," or, in other words, a strict disciplinarian. The short speech he had just delivered, which was freely commented upon, I could plainly see had lowered him a few pegs in the estimation of the men, and especially among the old tars. "O, d—— all such canting humbug about painful to his feelings, and 'compelled to award it.' Why the deuce didn't he tell the brats of middies, when they wanted a man flogged, just to report him sulky, or worse for liquor, and he would order him two dozen," grumbled an old veteran, as a few of them sat discussing the subject on the evening watch. "For my part," he continued, "I never knew one of your very feeling gentlemen but what was devilish good at making a poor fellow's back feel." "The very blessed same remark I made to Sammy here as we came aft," responded another old tar. "What's the use of trying to come to windward of an old sailor in that way; why don't he out with it in plain English, somewheres in this fashion :—My lads, I have always been in the habit of seeing plenty of flogging, which I think a good custom, and means to keep it up."

I must confess that I thought these old tars a complete set of croakers, not being able to perceive anything in the speech to call for such illiberal construction, and severe animadversion. In fact, for my own part, I had considered the speech most admirable, both in matter and manner. But a few months on board fully verified the correctness of their prognostication, which I found had been the sound deduction of observation and experience. The fact of the case is, that if a captain is an enemy to flogging he strikes it altogether from his catalogue of punishments; and therefore never makes allusion to it when addressing his men, any more than if he was not aware of its existence. There are a number of captains in the British service, who have abolished flogging within their own jurisdiction, as effectually to all intents and purposes, as if it had been done by act of parliament. And this also, very much to the improvement of the discipline of their respective crews; and thus practically giving the lie to those who insist upon the necessity for the continuation of this degrading punishment. But our captain was none of these, and the cat was by far too often in the boatswain's hands. A person who has never been at sea in a man-of-war, with a captain who has got the idea that flogging is necessary for the maintenance of discipline, would not believe the extent to which this punishment is administered in some vessels. I believe that during the first six months that I was aboard, nearly one half of our ship's crew had received a flogging. The merest trifle, a pair of trousers not perfectly clean, or having a grease spot on them at a Sunday's muster, or an article accidentally left out of the clothes bag, when the vessel was inspected by the officers of the watch, was quite sufficient to qualify a man of even good character to receive this disgraceful punishment. The boys were not stripped and flogged with the cats, except in extraordinary cases, but when found fault with by an officer, the boatswain was instructed to give them a taste of discipline. This consisted in a piece of three quarter inch rope with a knot at the end, called a colt, which the boatswain carries in his pocket, being smartly applied to the back and shoulders in a series of successive jerks; an exhibition highly amusing to the spectator, but producing the most startling effect upon the recipients, whom it causes to throw themselves into the strangest contortions and grotesque antics imaginable. I sometimes had a taste of this discipline, and must say that I did not find it much calculated to increase my liking for the sea service.

There was a bag kept by the boatswain on board the Blazer, which was called " the boatswain's save all," by the sailors. In it were carefully stowed by the boatswain, all the clothes found between decks which were left out of their owners' clothes-bags, when the decks were inspected by the officers of the watch. Once a week, at a stated hour, the clothes were turned out of the bag, the officer of the watch standing by to see who claimed them, as the party so claiming was marked down for a dozen lashes for each article; which he received at the regular punishment hour next morning. Very few of these articles were claimed of course, most of the men preferring to lose the article, even though compelled to go to the purser and draw a new one, being in this case a virtual fine equivalent to the value of the article, which was charged against their wages in the purser's books. But we had several old salts aboard who never paid the purser for an article of clothing while on the cruise. One of these, when he saw an article of clothing produced from the bag, which he considered worth taking a dozen for, deliberately walked up, and picking up the article —shirt, trousers, or whatever it might be, he would begin to apostrophise it as that d——d unlucky shirt, or jacket, that was always getting him into a scrape. The officer of the watch who would know the old fellow to be a regular customer on these occasions, smiling at the ruse, would mark him down for his dozen; and careless of the jests of his comrades, the old tar marched off with his trophy. The unclaimed goods were thrown overboard.

There was a young boy of the name of Billings, who died on board the Blazer when we had been about eight months out, and who all hands agreed in thinking fell a victim to a flogging which he received on board. He was no great favourite in the ship, yet on account of his youth everybody seemed to pity him ; for strange to say, old fellows who are careless of a flogging in their own persons, often show sympathy for others whose spirits they see broken down under the agony of shame caused by the degradation of the punishment. Billings was a remarkably clever and handsome boy, about sixteen or seventeen years of age, rather delicate in his appearance, and exceedingly proud-spirited and fiery in his temper. It was supposed that he had run away from home, and that his people were in better circumstances than common ; but he was very reserved in his communications, and never made a confidant of any person until near his death ; when he told the doctor, who had been very kind to him, something which he wished him to write to his mother who lived at Bristol. The doctor tried to persuade him that he would live to go home and see her himself, but nothing would content him, until the doctor had taken down what he wished him to write, together with his mother's address, in a memorandum book. Shortly after, the captain came down with the doctor to see the boy. The captain spoke very kindly to him and asked him if he would like some wine. A tear rolled over the wasted cheek of poor Billings, as he whispered something into the ear of the captain, who seeing his lips move, stooped to hear him. I was attending on him that morning, as we took it in turns, but although standing pretty near, I could not hear a word of what he said to the captain. Whatever it was, it seemed to affect him a good deal. He told Billings to keep up his spirits, that he would send him some wine, and if there was anything on board that he would like to eat, if the doctor permitted, he would order the steward to bring it to him. After that, wine, and everything that was supposed to be good for him, was sent from the captain's table; but it was all of no use, the poor fellow died a few days afterwards. He had been flogged about a month previously, for calling a midshipman who was beating him with a rope's end, a bastard; since which time he had done no duty, and constantly complained of a pain in his chest. Some of the old sailors said they had seen cases of the same sort before, that it frequently happened to boys through flogging, and that the boy Billings died heart-broken. A few days' confinement on bread and water would have been a far better punishment for this boy's offence, while the midshipman who had caused this breach of discipline, by striking him, (contrary to all good discipline, and the regulations of the service,) might have been put under arrest for some time to show the captain's displeasure at his conduct. Whether the death of this boy caused the alteration or not I cannot say, but certainly the punishment of flogging was not of such frequent occurrence for some time subsequently.

It is a strange fact that a considerable portion of the sailors, and more especially that portion who oftenest suffer the infliction, believe that the service would be ruined if the custom of flogging were abolished in the navy. But even among the most bigoted tars of the old school, this opinion is fast wearing out, and the time must soon come when the cat will be consigned to the locker of Davy Jones, in place of that of the boatswain; and only be recollected as one of the instruments of torture used in the barbarous ages.

After cruising two weary years on the most monotonous and unhealthy station that ever a man-of-war had the ill-luck to be sent to, during which we lost a number of our best hands from fever, and made prize of two slave vessels, we received orders to proceed to the Pacific. This was good news to all, especially to those poor fellows who were sick when the order arrived, and who soon felt the benefit of a change of scene and climate. For my own part I was delighted with the appearance of those enchanting islands of which I had often read when a young boy with so much relish, and Tahiti and a number of others, seemed like scenes which I recollected having visited in dreams. We sometimes spent eight or ten days in the harbour of one of them while we refitted, and took in fresh water, fruits, vegetables, and other supplies, and during these periods, parties of us were permitted to go ashore. I had now learned my duty as a sailor pretty well, and consequently felt a little more reconciled to my situation than when I first entered the Blazer. Indeed, were it not for the perpetual dread of the petty tyranny, which his officer may exert over him at any time, for faults real or imaginary, and of which no sailor serving in a vessel where flogging is customary, can ever wholly divest himself, a sailor on board a man-of-war would not have a bad time. For my own part I had begun to form such a liking for the service, while cruising in these delicious latitudes, that, but for the slight drawback just mentioned, I believe I would have entered at the expiration of my time, for another three years' cruise in one of Her Majesty's ships, in which case you would have been spared this long yarn.

During our cruise here, we sometimes overhauled a whaler, and on several of these occasions, a sailor or two, on the plea of ill-usage, volunteered to enter our vessel. These we always accepted when sufficient cause of complaint could be shown, the captains of many of those whalers being most tyrannical scoundrels, and using their men in a most brutal and cruel manner in many instances. When such is the case, the means of redress in the hands of the sailor are as follows : Whenever a man-of-war approaches near enough to render the signal distinct, a red or blue shirt is fastened to some conspicuous part of the rigging of the whaler, where it cannot remain a dozen seconds until it is observed by some one on board of the man-of-war, and is reported to the officer of the watch. The result of the manœuvre is, that in a very short space of time, an officer from the man-of-war, having been on board of the whaler making inquiry into the state of affairs there, returns with captain, complainants, and witnesses, who are speedily standing on the quarter-deck of Her Majesty's ship. The captain of the man-of-war, having listened to the complaint, the defence, and the witnesses *pro* and *con*, gives a prompt decision on the case, from which there is no appeal. The complaints usually consist of having been brutally beaten by the captain or mate, of insufficiency of food, or food of bad quality. They are seldom made without good foundation, and are mostly easily substantiated, as witnesses against the captain may volunteer into the man-of-war, as well as the complainant. The proof of ill-usage by striking is frequently easy, by the men showing the marks of wounds and recent bruises on their bodies. When bad food is complained of, the provisions they have on board are examined, and when insufficiency is the cause of complaint, the physical condition of the crew often affords confirmation or disproval of it. Summary, and promptly carried into execution, are the decisions of these floating courts of justice, being generally somewhat to the following effect: " Captain, pay these men up to the present time, and send them aboard with their chests in less than half an hour." It is no use for the captain to say that he has not got money to pay them; if money cannot be found, goods will be seized to the amount required; a few barrels of oil, for instance, have frequently been taken, and sold, when convenient, to pay the seamen's wages.

I recollect seeing one of these cases decided in a manner that gave great satisfaction to the beholders. A poor, half-starved looking object, reminding one of Smallbones, in Marryatt's novel of *Snarleyow*, brought a complaint against his captain for beating him, and, as the boy said, making him afraid of his life, besides keeping him on short allowance of bad food. His statement was fully borne out by the evidence of several of the crew, besides the marks of bruises and ulcers on various parts of his body. The captain, a big, ill-looking scoundrel, " whose looks would have been enough to hang him with any honest jury," as an old tar remarked, seemed quite careless of refuting the evidence, which exhibited a case of monstrous injustice and cruelty. Our captain, having heard the case, ordered the captain of the whaler to go aboard with Smallbones, and see that he found all his property, and afterwards bring him on board of the Blazer and pay him his wages in his presence. The captain and Smallbones having come aboard, and the latter having received the wages due to him, the captain of the whaler, thinking the case over, was for proceeding immediately to his own vessel, when he was told by our captain to stop a few minutes, as he was not quite done with him yet. In the meantime our boatswain had been dispatched for the cats, and having returned in a few minutes with a bagful of these implements, amidst the grins and ill-concealed glee of the crew of the Blazer, who thought it a capital joke to see a skipper get his back pickled, the captain of the whaler was ordered to strip. He appeared to hesitate at first for a minute or so, probably thinking it might be a mistake or a joke, but on our captain calling out to him, to strip and be d——d, or it would be worse for him, he saw resistance or delay would be useless, and began very deliberately to take off his coat and shirt. He was then tied up to a gun, and received three dozen on the bare back, which the boatswain seemed to give *con amore*, having selected the thieves' cat for the purpose, a heavier sort than those in common use. On his going over the ship's side to go to his own vessel, " a sadder and wiser man" than when he came aboard, our captain hoped he would not let him catch him in a similar scrape again, or he would give him a double dose of the same physic. This was the only case in which I saw the captain of one of these vessels flogged, and I thought our captain must have greatly exceeded his powers by the proceeding; but I was told by some of the old hands that it was not at all uncommon, and that they had often witnessed similar occurrences. For my own part I must say that I highly admired this simple and primitive mode of administering justice, and could scarce help thinking that the good old plan of the commander of the Faithful, Haroun Alraschid of glorious memory, sometimes possessed its advantages.

Notwithstanding the delights of this enchanting region, few of our men were sorry, when, our three years having nearly expired, we were ordered home; at least if one might judge from the appearance of the crew, who, when the news was communicated, seemed all as happy as if they were going ashore on a day's leave, or had just been ordered a double allowance of grog. We soon reached the Cape of Good Hope, but on arriving there, we found that a rebellion had broken out among the Dutch boors; and that this would occasion our being sent up the coast a day or two's sail, to the relief of a small body of soldiers who were hemmed in by a large force of the rebels. These soldiers had been sent to quell the insurrection, but the force they had taken was too small: they had been surrounded by overwhelming numbers, and compelled to construct a temporary breastwork, which they had gallantly resolved to defend until the last extremity. On sailing to the bay where we were to land, we saw that the rebels had made an attempt to fortify the harbour, having mounted a few guns on a height near its entrance. Our captain, either from a desire to spare an effusion of blood, or because he had received instructions to that effect, sent a lieutenant ashore in the barge with a white flag, to try and persuade them to listen to reason. But clemency was thrown away upon the stupid boors, who would not allow the boat to land, and fired several shots at it from the guns of the fort; on seeing which the lieutenant returned to the vessel.

We now ran in until within a mile or so of the fort and dropped anchor, receiving meanwhile a brisk fire from their batteries, but which from their ignorance of gunnery did us no damage. Before opening our fire, however, a chance shot of theirs killed two of our men, and wounded three more, putting all ideas of lenity to the scoundrels out of the captain's head, and he immediately gave the command to commence firing. A tremendous fire was now opened from our vessel upon the fort, which never fired another shot in return, in a few minutes its only occupants being the wounded, the dying, and the dead. The temporary fortification they had been occupying was situated on a promontory, between which and the wooded country behind, there was a sandy neck or isthmus, which was completely exposed to our fire, and over which the enemy had to pass in retreating to the country. In a few minutes after our firing commenced, seeing it was not returned, our captain ordered us to cease firing; when we could see a crowd of several thousands running in a state of the utmost confusion across the isthmus. Two or three guns were directed and fired among them, doing dreadful execution, when the captain ordered the firing to cease, remarking that the poor devils would have had enough of it. Our marines and sailors armed with muskets and cutlasses were now landed, when we found some hundreds of killed and wounded, in and around the fort, presenting the most shocking spectacle I ever beheld. Our surgeon and his mates set to work on the wounded, and spent a few hours in zealously trying to repair those injuries, which we had as zealously tried to inflict a short time previous.

Having ascertained that the party of soldiers who were about eight miles in the interior, still held out, one of the most slightly wounded having had his wound dressed, was placed on a mule led by one of our men, to conduct us to the place. On arriving, we found that the siege had been raised that morning, the insurgents having left in great panic on seeing the flight of the routed party, who had scattered in all directions. The soldiers were in a pitiable condition, having been in a state of starvation for the last two or three days. They had been closely besieged eight days, and their position frequently assaulted, but they had always repulsed the enemy with great loss. In fact they had killed so many of the assailants, that they had resolved rather to die of starvation than surrender, as they felt certain of being killed by the enemy in revenge for the loss caused by their obstinate resistance. Many of them were so weak that we had to take spell about of carrying them in litters, which we made of the branches of trees; and it ook us all that day and part of the next to bring them aboard. After having destroyed and dismounted the guns at the fort, we sailed for Cape Town, and having put the soldiers ashore there, we proceeded on our homeward voyage. In less than two months after this we were paid off at Portsmouth, when I received fifty sovereigns as my three years' pay and share of prize money. I bought a decent suit of clothes and proceeded to London. On arriving there, I learned that my father was dead, my sister had married and gone with her husband to America, and my step-mother and her family had gone into the country to live with some of her friends. I came out to New York, where I found employment easily enough at my trade, and where, if I had not been a bit of a fool, I should still be, I believe. Such are a few of the events in the experience of my comrade, Bill Nutt.

CHAPTER VII.

Land in sight—Pensacola Bay—Fort Pickens—Rough lodgings—
Smuggling Whiskey—A Carouse.

THE captain of the Albatross had brought his wife along with him; he was an excellent sailor, all the men said, but had the prevalent fault of sea captains, he was a little fiery in his temper; which the presence of his wife it is likely would help to moderate. Be that, however, as it may, it is certain that her excellent and remarkable sailor-like qualifications made her the admiration of all on board, as, so far from being afraid, she seemed rather to enjoy the excitement caused by the appearance of a squall, which at that season of the year in these latitudes, are often anything the reverse of safe or pleasant. On a stormy and disagreeable night when the captain considered it to be his duty to be upon deck, there was she to be seen along with him; either sitting alongside of her husband in front of the cabin beside the wheel, or pacing backwards and forwards on the quarter-deck, now and again taking a knowing squint at the rigging or the horizon, and anon as abstracted seemingly, as if ruminating on some deep problem in navigation. The sailors declared that she could navigate a vessel as well as any captain that ever stept in shoe leather. There might be some exaggeration in that statement, however; and perhaps they magnified her powers of managing the ship, from sometimes witnessing the apparent ease with which she occasionally succeeded in managing the captain when carried away by those hurricanes of passion which now and then seized him. Still if she had studied navigation I see nothing to hinder her from being an expert navigator, as she certainly would have shown no lack of intrepidity.

After a prosperous voyage of sixteen days, the low sandy coast of Florida became distinctly visible. The first appearance of land on approaching Pensacola is very singular. Long bright lines of silvery white, crowned with a mass of dark green vegetation, stretched far athwart the blue horizon, suggesting the idea of a strong surf everywhere rolling in upon the shore. On a near approach we discover that which we thought surf is the beach, the sand of which here is as pure and white as drifted snow, which it exactly resembles at a distance. The bright and varied hues of the water, from dark blue or green to the lighter shades of these colours, which the sea presents as we close on the land, the dazzling white of the sandy shore, and the heavy masses of the dark green pines, strongly relieved against the clear blue sky, impart a unique, and at the same time a highly picturesque appearance to the bay of Pensacola.

Fort Pickens, where we were to land two companies, to one of which I belonged, is built on the point of a low sandy tongue of land, and together with Barrancas and Munroe, the two forts opposite, where our other two companies were to be stationed, completely commands the entrance of the bay. As the water was deep enough to admit of vessels coming close to the wharf at Fort Pickens, the Albatross was hauled close up and firmly moored. It was near sunset when we arrived at the fort, and only a few of the old soldiers who expected to meet friends and comrades in the company stationed there, went ashore, and also the whole of the officers, who of course preferred (the lucky dogs) a good dinner, and a jovial night ashore, to being cooped up in a ship. Early next morning we disembarked, and after placing our arms, equipments, and personal effects in our quarters, which were only distant a few hundred yards from the wharf, we were employed for the remainder of the day in bringing the regimental property ashore.

The numerous uncomfortable circumstances from which soldiers usually suffer during a removal, and more especially in the United States service, where the idea of having quarters comfortably arranged for the soldier's reception, on his arrival at a new station, is seldom thought of, is the cause of a great deal of the drunkenness that commonly prevails upon these occasions. The first object of most soldiers upon entering a new garrison is to discover where liquor can be procured; neither is this, in spite of all penalties enforced and precautions taken, ever a matter of difficult accomplishment; for according to the amount of the prohibition and restriction, so is the amount of bounty on the smuggling of the article. At Fort Pickens, for instance, when we landed, whiskey was sold at a dollar a bottle, an advance of nine hundred per cent. upon what it cost at Barrancas on the other side of the bay. Having once discovered a sly grog shop, the intelligence soon spreads, and in a very short period intoxication in every progressive stage, and producing every variety of effect, is the order of the day, and sobriety only the remarkable exception. In these saturnalia of course a few fights occasionally take place, and individuals of pugnacious propensities usually find "ample room and verge enough" for their exercise, an excellent field here offering for the display of what is fancifully termed *the science.*

On the present occasion, the appearance of our quarters at Fort Pickens was just the sort of thing to justify or encourage this predisposition to drown care, and the idea of the disagreeable and uncomfortable, in a bumper. They consisted of a large bomb-proof casemate, exceedingly dirty, having been occupied up to the day of our arrival by a party of negroes, who were employed in making repairs on the fort and garrison. There was not a particle of furniture of any description in this room; the floor, which was composed of bricks, was covered with mud and wood ashes, as the negroes had kept a fire burning on the floor to keep the mosquitoes away; notwithstanding this, they were still plentiful here, though the cold weather was setting in. The ashes had been allowed to accumulate on the floor, which was also additionally garnished and ornamented with skins of yams, fish bones, dried peppers, and other tropical litter of a lazy negro's hut, giving it much the appearance of a tolerably dry dunghill. Nutt and I swept a corner of this miserable den, and having, on a search round the garrison, procured a few boards, on these we spread our blankets, and thus prepared our bed for the night; the absence of a mattress was not of great importance, as we had been accustomed to dispense with that needless luxury while on board ship. In the American, service by the bye, soldiers always lie on the boards when on board ship; in the British service, where the health and comfort of a soldier are objects of study and solicitude, a different custom prevails; a clean blanket and mattress being issued to the soldier on his going on board, and taken into store when he leaves the vessel. However, my comrade Bill Nutt and I congratulated ourselves on our good fortune in having procured the boards to lie upon, as the majority seemed to have no alternative but to sit, stand, or lie down on the brick floor, cold, damp, and dirty as it was, and at the imminent risk of catching a cold, or a touch of rheumatism.

Under these circumstances, it need excite no extravagant surprise, that whiskey, when it could be procured, was speedily had recourse to, as a cure for all those discomforts and annoyances from which there seemed no other mode of escape. Such, at all events, was the practice of most of our men on this evening; and such seemed to be the course decided on by a party of honest fellows belonging to the company, who, on their way out, stopped to ask Nutt and me to go along with them. As neither of us were teetotallers, and as we felt rather fatigued with our day's work, carrying boxes up from the wharf, we could offer no reasonable objection to the proposal: so accepting the invitation, we were soon on our way to the place where the whiskey was sold. This illicit traffic was carried on by the blacks, at the time employed in the repairs of the fort. These blacks were slaves, and hired out by their owners to government; some of them had been taught the trade of bricklaying, and their owners received upwards of twenty dollars a month for their labor, after deducting the cost of the slave's living. One of these slaves could not have been purchased under a thousand dollars; they were young, healthy, and intelligent-looking negroes, speaking remarkably good English with great fluency, better than most of the soldiers in the fort. They had an abundant supply of the corn whiskey used in the States, a coarse liquor, unpleasant in taste, and intoxicating in the proportion of about two bottles to one of the low priced Irish or Scotch whiskey. This whiskey is sold in New York, New Orleans, and most large cities of the Union at twenty cents a gallon, and could be obtained on the opposite side of the bay, at Barrancas, where these negroes bought it, at fifty cents a gallon. They retailed it at a dollar a bottle, or five dollars a gallon, clearing the very moderate profit of nine hundred per cent. on their business, but they incurred the risk of a severe flogging if detected selling liquor to soldiers. One of our party having gone up to the window of one of the huts in which these black fellows lived, speedily returned with four bottles of whiskey. With these, having adjourned to a convenient distance to permit our indulging in free discourse, without any risk of being disturbed, we sat down on the sand, and passing the bottle round, we drank in succession without the useless accompaniment of glasses.

CHAPTER VIII.

The Surprise—Doctor Brown—Fishing at Pensacola—Bathers and Sharks.

It was a beautiful calm evening, and the stars were shining with the lustrous brilliancy peculiar to tropical skies, the atmosphere was deliciously warm, without feeling in the least oppressive, the breeze being just enough to moderate the heat, and keep the mosquitoes at their proper distance. Our party was comfortably reclining on a sandbank facing the bay, whose murmuring waves rippled within twenty or thirty yards of our resting-place; all seemed to enjoy the scene, and all agreed in declaring the whiskey, which circulated with astonishing rapidity, to be a very good article. We were soon, thanks to the whiskey, in a philosophic and good-humoured disposition, and quite ready to laugh at all the petty miseries and annoyances of human life, as a very good sort of joke, and one not in the slightest degree interfering with our present delightful entertainment. One of the party, named Davis, being of a speculative turn, favoured us with a short dissertation on the excessive absurdity of the common opinion, that there ever could be such a quality in existence as positive good or evil, these terms being convertible or comparative. This position he proceeded to illustrate in a manner which I have no doubt would have been highly satisfactory and ingenious, when he was requested to "cut it short," by Bob Madden, a man of a practical turn, who wished to favour the company by singing the "Cruiskeen Lawn."

This having been sung accordingly, and duly chorussed, drinking, smoking, singing, joking, and laughing, passed the time until near tattoo, by which time we had got pretty deep into the third bottle, and began to think of retiring. Unfortunately, however, for the harmonious ending of what had been so well begun, the whiskey now began to show some of its usual effects, by producing a strong inclination for exhibiting, and

"Each, for madness ruled the hour,
Would prove his own expressive power."

Davis lectured with much apparent earnestness of manner and animation, on what I believe he called " The *Political Policy* of the *Peruvians*," to several of the party, who were straining their energies in a vain attempt to follow the tropes and figures of his rhetoric. Bob Madden, who hated long speeches, as he hated an unfilled can, bawled at the highest pitch of his voice, " Cease, rude Boreas, blustering railer," which Davis, construing into a designed intention of insult and interruption, became perfectly savage, and declared his intention of taking it out of Bob, by pitching into him. At this stage of the proceedings, the officer of the day, who had heard the noise our party had been making for some time previous, dispatched a corporal and a file of the guard to convey us prisoners to the guard-house. Nutt, who was generally upon the alert, and who had been looking for some such interruption, gave us the hint just in time, and we started to our feet and ran, with the guard in chase. But on these occasions the guard is seldom anxious to make prisoners, and only that one of the party, named Dymond, happened to fall and get stunned, so that he could not run, there would have been no prisoners made. As it was, he was taken to the guard-house.

Unluckily for the prisoner, the officer of the day had followed the party of the guard himself, and observing the bottles, which, in our hurried retreat, we had left on the sand-hill, he picked them up, and found one of them full and another containing a portion of whiskey. The empty bottles, by "the scent of the whiskey that hung round them still," gave sufficient indication that they had been recently emptied of similar contents, and were the cause of the present fracas. The officer ordered the corporal of the guard to secure these bacchanalian trophies, and give them in charge to the sergeant, and next morning he had them sent for and produced before the commanding officer, as a proof of the extent to which this illicit traffic in whiskey was carried on in the garrison. Dymond was then sent for, and questioned as to where he got the liquor, and the parties who were along with him. But neither threats nor promises could prevail on him to betray either the one or the other, and he was kept in confinement for nearly a month, during which time he was not forgotten by his comrades, but being considered a martyr to an honourable principle, was furnished with everything that was supposed likely to soften the rigour of confinement. As for the remainder of our convivial party, we answered our names at tattoo on going home that evening, after which we went to sleep, and were never questioned about the matter.

Such is a specimen of our proceedings on the first night after landing at Fort Pickens, and such is the mode in which drinking is commonly practised in that service. A degrading custom, producing habits of beastly intoxication, and having its origin in the erroneous manner in which soldiers are treated in that service, where a systematic course of procedure, calculated to degrade a soldier, and annihilate his self-respect, seems to be in constant operation. If in place of prohibiting the soldier from ever going into a tavern, or tasting spirits, under a regard, forsooth, for his morals, and a pretence of keeping him sober, they were to make him a little more comfortable in his quarters, they would probably succeed a little better in regulating the soldier's conduct. And if, in addition, they were to establish, as in the British service, a tavern in every garrison, where riotous conduct or drunkenness would not be permitted, but where the soldier could sit down and enjoy himself in a moderate and rational manner, I could safely venture to predict, that the practice, now prevalent, of drinking out of bottles until beastly intoxication ensues, would cease to exist.

On the second morning after our arrival we had our quarters thoroughly cleaned, and were supplied with bedsteads, but we soon discovered that no cleaning would render the quarters comfortable. They were dark, damp, and badly ventilated, the walls in rainy weather dripping with wet, and in the still, close evenings, they swarmed with mosquitoes. A good deal of sickness was complained of by the men, though the winter had set in, which in the south is the healthy period of the year, and the approach of which is welcomed as cordially by the whites, as the summer is by the inhabitants of cold or temperate climates. This was commonly attributed to the badness of our quarters, and I have no doubt that was a principal cause; still the change of climate and water, and the careless and intemperate habits of a large proportion of the men, with the hardships and privations of the voyage, might sufficiently account for much of the disease prevalent, which consisted of fever and ague, colds, rheumatism, and diarrhœa. Our surgeon, who came over from Barrancas every morning to visit the sick, was rather an original and eccentric individual in his manner. When a patient described his malady and its symptoms, he invariably assured him that he need be under no apprehension or alarm about it, as it was a mere trifle, and easily subdued by refusing to yield to it. He had the same complaint himself, he said, but luckily his duty compelled him to move about, so that he could not give way to disease, for want of time. As he told every description of patient the identical same story, he became at last quite an object of curiosity; for though of thin and spare habit, this victim, according to his own account, of the most complicated variety of diseases that ever afflicted one poor individual at a time, was yet cheerful, active, and vigorous. While giving his patients medicine, it was his custom to inculcate strongly the advantages of abstinence and exercise, in the prevention and cure of disease; he generally quoted his own case as an example in point, sometimes remarking that he would have been dead long ago, if he had not made a resolution not to die as long as he could help it. Our men gave him the sobriquet of Doctor Brown, from the resemblance which his advices bore to those given by Doctor Brown to his apprentice, in the song, the following distich of which was often sung in his hearing as he passed through the barrack square, though if he perceived, he never took any notice of the allusion :—

> "He often says, with much elocution,
> Hard work, low diet, and a good resolution,
> Are the only things for the constitution.
>   Oh! Doctor Brown."

Davis, who was fond of propounding theories on the perplexing and inexplicable, said he considered that the great variety of diseases to which the doctor was subject was probably rather in his favour, as their antagonistic properties, by neutralising and counteracting each other's bad effects, might preserve a beneficial balance in the system. To which lucid explanation Bob Madden responded, by asking Davis if he saw anything particularly green about him, a remark which Davis of course considered beneath reply.

Shortly after our arrival at Fort Pickens, at the suggestion of our officers, we subscribed a dollar apiece for the purchase of a seine, by means of which we procured an abundant supply of fish, as the bay literally swarmed with them. We usually hauled the seine twice or thrice a week, procuring with ease a barrel or two of excellent fish, weighing from half a pound to three or four pounds each; any of smaller size we threw into the sea again. The fish we principally caught were mullet, which are very delicious fish; for four or five months during the winter, when they are in season, immense shoals of them frequent the coast of Florida; they feed on mollusca and are never caught with bait, neither are they ever found on the northern coast of America. Sheepshead, another very excellent fish which we commonly caught, has its name from the appearance of its mouth and teeth, which have a striking resemblance to those of a sheep. These last, with perch, cat-fish, trout, and various others, might easily be caught by fishing at the wharf with a line, but as the seine furnished a superabundant supply for the use of the garrison, fishing with the line was not much practised. There was one species of fish in the bay of Pensacola, however, which we could have very gladly dispensed with; these were sharks, which were both numerous, and of most incredible size and voracity. A short time before the arrival of our regiment a sailor, who had fallen overboard from the rigging of a man-of-war lying at the Navy Yard, was almost instantly devoured by these ravenous monsters, in the sight of his horror-stricken shipmates, who could render him no assistance, so sudden was the catastrophe. The crew of the man-of-war, while they remained there, had waged an incessant war with the sharks, in revenge for the loss of their comrade; and had killed a great many, but without having produced any apparent decrease in their numbers. The offal which is thrown overboard by the men-of-war, one or two of whom are constantly lying off the Navy Yard, is probably the cause of the presence of so many of these unwelcome visitors. One of our officers, desiring to have a specimen of these sharks, employed the ordnance sergeant to catch one. Accordingly a stout shark's line was furnished for the occasion, consisting of fifty or sixty fathoms of what would be considered tolerably thick rope for a horse halter. A shark's hook, consisting of three or four branching out of a single stalk, and about the size of butchers' hooks, attached to a stout iron chain, and baited with a four pound piece of pork, the whole being well fastened to the line, which was made fast to a mooring post on the wharf, was thrown into the sea opposite the wharf. The line was left in charge of the sentry on the wharf, who had orders to send up word to the garrison as soon as he perceived that a shark had taken the bait. But the sentry had neglected the order, and seeing the line tight he began to haul in upon it with all his might. The shark, taken by surprise at the novelty of his situation, yielded a little at first, and then suddenly making a desperate rush, he dragged the sentry into the water, and he very narrowly escaped drowning, but was luckily saved by holding on to the line till some of the men who were near came to his assistance. A sufficient number of men having speedily arrived, the shark was hauled on the beach alongside the wharf, and dispatched with bayonets and cutlasses; when measured it was found to be eleven feet long. Its frightfully capacious jaws, full of jagged, saw-like teeth, were taken out of the head and preserved by the ordnance sergeant; when fully extended the jaws would easily admit a stout man's shoulders to pass through them. I had frequently seen them caught when at sea, five or six feet in length, but never anything to compare with this monster of the deep.

One would imagine that with a knowledge of the existence of such creatures in the bay, swimming in deep water would have been totally out of the question at Pensacola, but there are strange reckless beings everywhere fond of excitement, and of the credit of doing something of which everybody else would be afraid. One morning two or three of the men being on the wharf, and the conversation happening to turn on the shark which had been caught a few days previously, and the danger any person would incur by swimming there; one of them offered for a trifling wager to jump in from the wharf, and swim in deep water for a period of five minutes. The wager was accepted, and the fool-hardy hero was stripping to jump in, when the sentry stationed on the wharf interfered, and ordered him to put on his clothes. This he refused to do, and the sentry very properly made him a prisoner, and sending for the corporal of the guard, he was taken to the guard-house. The commanding officer, on learning the circumstance, complimented the sentry on his conduct; and issued an order prohibiting soldiers from bathing in deep water.

CHAPTER IX.

Tampa Bay—Indian Paradise—Beautiful Squaws—Forest Life—The Hummocks—Snakes—Rumours of War—Lost in the Wood.

THE surface of the ground, both within the garrison, and everywhere in the vicinity of Fort Pickens, is entirely composed of fine sand, which is so white and dazzling, especially when the sun is shining, as to have a most unpleasant and injurious effect upon the eyes. The situation is also very unhealthy during the summer, the fatally destructive yellow fever being frequently prevalent during the hot season. It was therefore with a great deal of satisfaction that the company to which I belonged, after having been about a month at Fort Pickens, received the order to proceed to Tampa Bay. We embarked in a brig called the Isabella on the 2nd of November, and bidding adieu to those of our comrades whom we were leaving behind at Fort Pickens, after a pleasant voyage of two days we anchored about seven or eight miles from the village and garrison in Tampa Bay, that being as near as vessels above the size of a light schooner can approach, on account of the extreme shoalness of the bay.

It was evening when we arrived, and early next morning a small government sloop called the "Star," arrived from the garrison for the purpose of taking us ashore. About one-half of us contrived to stow ourselves into it, along with our muskets and knapsacks, though rather crowded. She was to go back for the remainder after we were landed.

After tacking about in the bay until near evening, the wind being nearly ahead, we finally succeeded in reaching the wharf. The appearance of the land, when viewed from the deck of a vessel in the bay, is like most of the views along the coast of Florida, of a rather tame and circumscribed character; as, owing to the perfectly dead level of the country, a green belt of vegetation covering a sandy beach is all that the eye can discover. On a nearer approach, however, as its distinctive features become more easily defined, they arrange themselves into something more nearly akin to the beautiful and the picturesque.

Tampa Bay is a neat little village of wooden houses, situated at the mouth of the river Hillsboro, and close to the garrison. There is a small traffic carried on between it and the few scattered settlers of the neighbourhood, who bring in their surplus produce and exchange it here for goods or money. Its situation is reckoned to be one of the most healthy and salubrious in Florida; but as the land in the vicinity is mostly of a poor quality, and as the bay is difficult of approach for shipping, it does not seem destined to rise very rapidly in importance. The barracks, which may almost be said to be part of the village, are a long range of log buildings erected by the troops during the Florida Indian war in 1837. They have a covered gallery all round, and are well adapted to the climate of Florida, being raised about three feet from the ground, high in the roof and well ventilated. They are also built on the highest part of the garrison, about fifteen feet above the level of the sea, an unusually great elevation on the coast of Florida.

We were all delighted, on landing, with the appearance of the garrison, its neat white-washed buildings, and its grassy parade; while round the neat cottages in which the officers and their families lived, grew rows of orange and lime trees thickly covered with their golden fruit, then nearly ripe. In front of the barracks there stood a noble grove of live oak trees, which afforded a delicious shade from the scorching heat of the sun, and gave an air of quiet, and an expression of sylvan beauty to the scene. The long greybeard and wierdlike Spanish moss, that droops in huge masses from the rough brawny arms of these giants of the primeval forest, gives them a venerable and druidical appearance which is exceedingly picturesque. This moss, which takes root in the bark, grows on many of the trees in Florida, though I never saw any on the pine. But above all it seems to love the live oak, to whose strong arm it clings with devoted affection; depending in long flexile drapes that swing most gracefully in the breeze. The proper name of this plant is *tillandsea;* it is of a grey colour, and not unlike long rough beards of a gigantic size in appearance. It has a very small yellow blossom, and pod containing seed, and is very valuable when properly cured, being commonly applied to all those purposes for which curled hair is used, such as stuffing mattresses, sofas, and chairs. To prepare it for this purpose it is gathered from the trees with long hooks, and afterwards put into water for a few days to rot the outer part, and then dried. The substance obtained by this process is a fine black fibre resembling horse hair. A mattress stuffed with this substance may serve for a year if not wetted; it then becomes dirty, and requires that the moss should be taken out and well beaten; by which means it becomes more elastic than ever. I had a mattress filled with it thus prepared, when I was at Tampa Bay, and I thought it one of the most comfortable beds I ever slept on.

On arriving at Tampa Bay we found another company of our regiment stationed there, two companies being considered requisite for the protection of the inhabitants against any sudden outbreak of the Indians. These, to the amount of several hundred warriors, besides squaws and children, still occupy a large tract of Florida called the Everglades; where they live in the same state of rude savage life to which they were accustomed ere the first of the pale faces left a footprint on their sandy shores. They have game in abundance, herds of deer roam through the plains and glades, and crop their luxuriant herbage; numerous flocks of wild turkeys roost in the hummocks at night, and feed in the openings and pine barrens by day; and in the creeks and bays of the sea coast, or in the large fresh water lakes of the interior, incredible quantities of delicious fish are easily caught. Round their villages, in the selection of a site for which they display excellent taste and judgment, they usually cultivate a small portion of the soil in raising maize, or edible roots; and the little labour which this requires is performed by the women and children. In this delicious climate, where there is perpetual verdure, and where the existence of cold or winter is scarcely known or felt, the mode of living of these savages seems not so very disagreeable, and with their ideas of comfort they must find Florida a complete Indian paradise. It is not much to be wondered at, therefore, to find them so reluctant to leave for a new home among the tribes of the Indian Territory. Sooner than submit to this, about fifteen years ago they waged an unequal war with the United States; which lasted several years, and cost America nearly as much, it is said, as the late war in Mexico. At the present time there are not in Florida more than a fourth, it is supposed, of the number who were there at the commencement of the war; as a great many of them at various times accepted the terms offered by the government of the United States, and were transported to a tract of land called the Indian Territory, lying between Arkansas and the Rocky Mountains. Those who refused to leave, and who were finally permitted to remain in a portion of Florida defined by certain boundaries, have been variously estimated at from three to five hundred warriors. But as they have almost no intercourse with the inhabitants, white men not being suffered to approach their villages, it is very difficult to form anything like a correct estimate of their numbers. The government agent, stationed at Fort Charlotte, a small settlement near their boundary line, for the purpose of trading with them, and who has been desired by the government to endeavour without exciting their suspicions to ascertain their numbers, reckons them at five hundred, exclusive of women and children. Those who remain are part of the tribe or nation of Seminoles; they were as tall on an average as the men of our regiment, and though not near so athletic or muscular, generally more graceful in personal appearance. They have more yellow than copper in their complexion, and have the high prominent cheek bones, and that quick, furtive, and suspicious glance of the Indian race, which seems watching every moment to make a sudden spring in the event of any appearance of treachery. Some of their young squaws have a very pleasing expression of countenance, and I have seen one or two of these who I believe would be pronounced beautiful if compared with the prouder belles of European cities. The men, or warriors, walk with a most dignified and majestic carriage, and an air of stoic composure highly imposing. They wear moccasins made of deer-skin, and of their own manufacture; and go bare-legged in a short-sleeved sort of tunic, confined at the waist and falling down nearly to the knees in the manner of a Highlander's kilt, to whose ancient costume that of the Florida Indians of the present day bears a considerable resemblance, especially when seen at a short distance. Some of them ornament their dress with beads and shells, which they sometimes wear in their hair also, and both men and women are fond of wearing large silver rings in their ears and through their nostrils.

Parties of twenty or thirty of these strange-looking visitors frequently came into the village of Tampa Bay while we lay there. They were always accompanied by a sub-chief, a sort of lieutenant, who had charge of the party, and their object was to exchange deer-skins for powder and other necessary articles. They frequently brought a few turkeys or a few pieces of venison, part of the game they had shot as they came along; these they sold cheap enough, a turkey fetching a quarter, and a piece of venison of fifteen or twenty pounds weight, half a dollar. They always visited the barracks when they came to the village, walking through the rooms and shaking hands with the soldiers in a perfectly friendly manner. None of them, however, understood English, and we were all equally ignorant of the Seminole, so that our discourse was necessarily limited to the language of pantomime, at which they seemed a vast deal more apt than our men. They showed us marks of gunshot wounds they had received in the Florida war on various parts of their bodies, pointing to our muskets at the same time and shaking their heads; and they seemed highly delighted when one or two of our soldiers, who had been in the Florida war, showed them similar marks, making signs that they had received them from the Indians. They laughed and talked to one another with great animation and glee at this circumstance. But the great attraction for them was two six-pounder pieces, which stood in front of the quarters; they always approached these with looks of the greatest curiosity, and apparent awe, cautiously patting them as if to propitiate

5*

them. They have the most exaggerated ideas of the destructive effects of artillery, of which they stand in horrible dread; and some of our men who were in the Florida war asserted that a chief cause of so many Indians having surrendered towards the close of the war, was owing to the Americans having procured two or three light field-pieces, though, owing to the swampy nature of the country, they could not have used them. As they always behaved quietly in the garrison, they were never hindered from strolling round any part of it, strict orders being given to the soldiers not to molest them. They used no more ceremony with the officers than with the men, frequently walking up to them on the parade, or into their quarters, and offering to shake hands with them with the most perfect *nonchalance*.

On paying one of these visits to the village it was customary for them to have a bout of drinking and dancing; a sort of Indian ball, which they held in a yard behind a house in the village appropriated exclusively to their use. The entertainments of the evening, on these occasions, usually consisted in smoking and drinking whiskey until pretty late, a few of them dancing at intervals in the most ungraceful and even ludicrous attitudes imaginable. They wound up the evening generally with a war dance, in which all who were not too drunk joined. This dance commences slow at first to a low monotonous chaunt, and increases in rapidity of time and movement until, like the witches' dance in Tam o' Shanter, "the mirth and fun grow fast and furious," and they yell and whoop like a set of demons or incarnate fiends. On these occasions, they sometimes quarrelled among themselves, and ended the night with a general squabble; yet as care was always taken, on their arrival, to have their arm taken from them and locked up, until they were ready to return home, there was no danger of any serious accident occurring.

GENERAL DESCRIPTION OF FLORIDA.

Florida received its name from Juan Ponce de Leon, from his having discovered it on Palm Sunday (in Spanish Pasqua Florida), in 1512; and not, as many of its inhabitants believe, on account of the beauty of the wild flowers and the shrubs which it produces, and of which it certainly exhibits a splendid profusion. It is natural, however, to suppose, that the charm of the scenery, and especially the singular beauty and luxuriance of many of the strange shrubs and trees, which would seem so wonderful to the Spaniards on their first landing, may have confirmed the adoption of the idea originally suggested by its striking appropriateness. A great portion of the peninsula of Florida is sandy, and not much adapted to cultivation; but there are rich tracts here and there composed of hummock and swamp, which may yet, when cleared and drained, yield a rich reward to the cultivator. There are some pretty extensive cotton plantations on some parts of it, and sugar-cane, tobacco, rice, Indian corn, and every other variety of tropical produce or fruits, may be successfully cultivated where the soil is good. Still, as long as the Indians remain in its borders, its resources will never have a fair chance of development, as the distant settler can have no security for life or property while they are in the vicinity. During the winter the weather in Florida is delightful, the ground being quite dry and the atmosphere clear, and of that exquisite medium with regard to heat, neither too hot nor too cold, which one feels to give a bracing and invigorating tone to the constitution, and a pleasant buoyancy to the spirits. In summer the ground is wet and swampy, a large part of the surface resembling a complete marsh, owing to the frequent and heavy rains which fall during that season, the level nature of the surface, and bad natural drainage. It was purchased from Spain by the United States in 1821, and was constituted a state in 1845.

Our duties were very light while we lay at Tampa Bay; we mounted guard about once every fourth day on an average, and when off guard we had two parades each day, succeeded by an hour's drill. On the morning after that on which we came off guard we had to work a few hours in policing the garrison, and in cutting the usual allowance of wood for general consumption; the rest of our time, except that required for cleaning our clothes, arms, and accoutrements, was at our own disposal. Our commanding officer, while we lay at this post. adopted an excellent method for teaching young soldiers how to use their muskets with effect. As we always loaded with ball cartridge when we mounted guard, in place of drawing the cartridge when we were relieved on the succeeding morning, we were marched down in front of a target, which stood with its back to the sea; and being placed at a distance of about a hundred and twenty yards from it, each of the guard discharged his musket at it in succession. The sergeant of the guard accurately marked each shot, and he whose ball went nearest the centre of the target was excused from mounting guard the next time it came to his turn. This produced a great deal of emulation amongst all hands, and the result was, that most of them soon became excellent shots.

Having so much spare time on hand, our men frequently took long rambles into the woods, especially during the fine dry weather; and on these occasions, for some time after our arrival in Tampa Bay, there was a danger of getting so utterly lost in the woods, as not to be able to find the way home; thus incurring a serious risk of dying of starvation. An occurrence of this description happened shortly after our arrival, showing the necessity of caution in making these excursions, at least until we were a little better acquainted with the surrounding country. A young man belonging to our company had gone out shooting one day, by himself, and in his eagerness for the sport he had gone a considerable distance away from the path, without having paid sufficient attention to the direction in which it lay, to be able to find it again. When he began to think of returning, he found himself completely bewildered by the resemblance which one part of the flat, monotonous pine forest bore to another, and wandered about until evening, trying to find the footpath, but without success. As he had not returned next morning, his absence caused much speculation, and our lieutenant, thinking it probable that he might be starved in the woods if not soon discovered and assisted, sent a party of twelve men out to search for him. They were to go in parties of two or three, and to fire their muskets occasionally, at some distance from the road, taking care not to lose their way back to it themselves. After a few hours' search, he was discovered about six miles from the garrison, and within a mile from the footpath. He was very nearly exhausted when found by the party, and but for the measures taken by the lieutenant, it is probable that he would soon have died of sheer hunger and fatigue, as he had not the slightest idea of being able to find his way home, and was so nearly worn out, that he could not have walked much further. He had been without food for about thirty hours, during which time he supposed he had walked between thirty and forty miles, in the hope of arriving at some habitation or road that would lead to one, but without success; and he was beginning to lose all hope, when he heard the firing of the party. In this portion of Florida, it is impossible to travel above a few miles without having to make a circuit to avoid an impassable swamp, or impenetrable thicket called a hummock; and being diverted from pursuing a straight course by these obstacles, he had probably been describing a series of circles within a short distance of where he was discovered. All his ammunition had been expended before he knew that he had lost his way, so that he had not the means of killing game or kindling a fire ; but at night he had pulled a quantity of long grass which grew there, and covering himself up with it, he managed to sleep a few hours. One of the party, at the suggestion of the lieutenant, who furnished it himself for the purpose, had brought a flask of brandy along with him, and having given him a portion of it mixed with water, and a sandwich, he was soon so far recovered, as to be able to walk home to the Fort along with the party.

The hummocks of Florida are a peculiar feature of the country. The uncleared lands, consisting of what is called pine barrens, are wholly composed of large pine trees open to air and light, and between which there thrives a luxuriant undergrowth of palmettoes, and a great variety of richly scented and gorgeously-coloured flowering shrubs. A savannah of tall strong grass, five or six feet in length, which occurs here and there, and an occasional swamp, are the only relieving features, besides the hummocks, which diversify the dreary monotony of these interminable pine barrens, covering nearly the whole surface of the state, of which there is, comparatively speaking, but a small portion under cultivation. At intervals of a few miles, dense forest thickets, containing magnificent trees of every description common in Florida, except the pine, occur in travelling through these pine barrens. Oak, liquid amber, hickory, chestnut, cotton-wood, and magnolia, are among the varieties found in the hummocks, which vary in size from about one mile to two or three in circumference. The bottoms of many parts of them are usually swampy, and there is a thick undergrowth of thorny shrubs and vines, which makes it exceedingly difficult to penetrate into their dark recesses. During the Florida war, the constant places of refuge for the Indians were the hummocks, and woe to the soldiers who followed them too rashly: Uncle Sam's troops being no match for the red men in those natural and almost impregnable fortresses. Wounded deer frequently fly to them for shelter, and when one of them succeeds in reaching the skirts of a hummock, after having been wounded at some distance, without the assistance of a good dog, there is small chance of discovering its dying place. I have sometimes been seduced into their dark and sombre shades, in following a flock of turkeys which had taken shelter in the branches of some of the gigantic trees; on such occasions I have generally been compelled to emerge from their treacherous recesses with torn clothes, face and hands scratched, and bemired up to the middle with the mud of the swamp. In going through these hummocks, one sees the fallen trunks of large decayed trees lying scattered on the ground in all directions; these are very inviting to step on, when one imagines he is in danger of sinking up to the armpits in a swamp hole. Beware, however, I would say to the inexperienced and incautious stranger, how you tread on these fallen trunks; try them with your foot gently, and see if they are sound; many of them are rotten and hollow, and some of them contain dry lodging for a numerous and thriving colony of moccasins or rattlesnakes, a single puncture from the venomous tooth of one of which would make you grievously rue your reckless intrusion on their domestic privacy.

Snakes of a great many different varieties are very numerous in Florida. During the winter they remain in their holes in a torpid state, seldom making their appearance for two or three months during that season; but in spring and summer I never went out to take a walk without seeing a number of them. The rattlesnake, adder, and moccasin, are three different species found there, whose bite is exceedingly dangerous, and, in many cases, fatal; but they all luckily possess a very quick sense of hearing, and generally contrive to get out of the way before they are trod upon. I never heard of a single person being bitten while we lay there, though in summer we seldom went into the woods without wearing a pair of very strong boots, as a protection against a chance bite. These boots came up to the knees, and were worn over the pantaloons.

Alligators are numerous in the ponds and rivers of Florida, and may often be seen floating with the stream like the trunk of a tree, while watching for their prey, on the surface of the Hillsbro' river, close to the garrison at Tampa Bay. One of the soldiers who caught a young one, brought it to the garrison, designing to rear it as a pet, but as it gave no signs of profiting by the opportunities of improvement afforded it, utterly despising the soothing system, and exhibiting in the most undisguised manner the natural depravity and apparently incorrigibly vicious propensities of the alligator family, by snapping at dogs, children, and all who came near it, he was forced to destroy it as a nuisance.

Opossums, racoons, squirrels, and rabbits, were found in the woods round the garrison, and a great variety of the feathered tribes frequented its vicinity, among which were pelicans, cranes, ducks, didappers, partridges, pigeons, parroquets, vultures, and a host of others. Among the small birds I observed several species of the humming-bird, the blue-jay, the scarlet oriole, the redbreast, the woodpecker, the whip-poor-will, with that glorious bird of inimitable song, the mocking-bird. It commences to sing about the beginning of the month of March, and continues to the month of June. The celebrated ornithologist, Wilson, has given a description of this bird, which I had read, and could scarcely help thinking must have been rather too highly coloured and laudatory, until I had heard a few of its extraordinary performances, when I freely admitted its truth. Its song, to which I have often listened on a still and clear moonlight night, for that is the time in which it warbles its most melodious strains, is indescribably sweet. It is the only real good singing bird in America; but I would prefer it to all the linnets, larks, thrushes, and blackbirds of the old world.

The lagoon-like bays and creeks on the coast of Florida abound with many excellent varieties of fish, and turtle are very numerous and easily caught. We often had turtle soup at Tampa Bay, as turtle could be bought at two or three cents a pound. A species of land tortoise called a gopher, which burrows in the sand, is obtained in the woods by digging them out of their burrows with a spade; this made a very delicious soup, which some preferred to turtle. There is an excellent oyster-bed on a sand bank in the bay, about six miles from the garrison; and occasionally a few of the men, having obtained the permission of the Quarter-Master, would take the barge and go down for a supply of oysters. Going down at low water, it was no hard task to collect as many oysters as the whole of the two companies could consume; nearly all parts of the coast of Florida furnish these excellent shell-fish in inexhaustible quantities.

I had been about six months in Tampa Bay, when a vacancy happening to occur, through the discharge of a corporal, I was appointed in his place. I could easily perceive, before I had been long in the service, that a corporal or serjeant held no very enviable position; that his duties were ill-defined, and the system of discipline loose and unsatisfactory. On this account I felt no satisfaction at my promotion; besides I had no adequate motive for submitting to the increased trouble and responsibility, as I had no intention of remaining long in the service. There were many things transacted of which I strongly disapproved, and I did not like the idea of sacrificing my individuality and conscientious opposition to these, by accepting this office. Owing to these rather peculiar views of mine, I would most decidedly have declined the distinction, had the opportunity occurred; but I was not aware of the circumstance of my having been recommended for the office until after I had been appointed, so that I had not even the chance of refusal. Not considering myself, therefore, bound to a subservient silence, seeing that I had not been a voluntary acceptant of the office, I continued to disburden myself occasionally by strictures and remarks, which I have no doubt must have appeared excessively ungrateful to several of my superiors. I have always been rather partial to opposition.

The expected war with Mexico became a very engrossing topic while we lay at Tampa Bay, in the summer of 1846, especially after the news arrived of General Taylor's first battle on the Rio Grande. The mail, which was carried through by a man on horseback from Augustine, a town on the seacoast, about a hundred miles distant, arrived only once a fortnight. Sometimes, on account of the flooded state of the rivers, which had all to be forded, as there are no bridges in Florida, it did not arrive until several days after its time; on such occasions its arrival, an event at any time, caused the most intense excitement and eager expectation, our officers on those occasions frequently walking down to the post-office, and waiting for their own letters and papers. On the day on which the news of General Taylor's victory at Palo Alto and Resaca de la Palma arrived, one of our officers having torn the envelope of a newspaper and read a paragraph or two, suddenly took off his cap, threw it up in the air, and began to huzza and caper, in the height of his exultation, much to the astonishment of the spectators, until he explained that General Taylor had gained a victory. As for the soldiers, I believe they were all very glad that, as there had been a battle fought, General Taylor had won it; but there was very little enthusiasm, I must say, at the reception of the news. All seemed to feel a presentiment of those "coming events" that "cast their shadows before;" the Rubicon was passed, and the present victory we felt to be the precursor of a campaign that would leave the bones of many a gallant fellow rotting in the soil of Mexico. As for the officer here alluded to, he was shot dead in the vicinity of the city of Mexico; had he seen the fate that awaited him, it would probably have moderated his transports at the news of the first battle.

As a means of passing the time which hung rather heavily on our hands at Tampa Bay, a debating society was formed in the company to which I belonged. The orderly sergeant of the company, a young man named Beebe, belonging to the State of New York, gave his aid in its formation by becoming an active member himself, and procuring the use of a large room for the purpose of holding the meetings. The rules adopted for the government of the society were few and simple, and any soldier, by paying a small stated sum as a subscription for the current expenses, &c., and reading and subscribing to the regulations of the society, kept by the secretary, might become a member. Out of one hundred and twenty men in the two companies stationed here, only about a dozen joined the society. The meetings were held once a week, the hours being from seven until nine o'clock on Friday evening: they were open to all who chose to attend, the room being always well filled; and if they added no great amount to the valuable, though rather unwieldy and unclassified, stock of materials called useful knowledge, they at all events contributed considerably to the stock of amusement. These meetings were conducted with the customary decorum of similar societies in civil life; a president, a treasurer, and a secretary, were elected for a month at a time; these formed a committee, and regulated the affairs of the society. The president gave out the subject for the ensuing week's discussion, and appointed the member whose turn it was to open the discussion by a short essay on the question to be discussed, at the close of each night's proceedings. The essay was either read or spoken, at the option of the party delivering it.

When it was first proposed, believing that it could do no harm if it did no good, at the solicitations of several of its projectors, I agreed to join it. Among them were several rather clever young men, possessing a good deal of general information, mingled a little too much, perhaps, with that sort of consequential air of self-conceit, too often engendered by the debating society system. They had all belonged to debating societies in various parts of the Union. Amongst these, Benthall, an American, had belonged to one in his native city, Philadelphia; Williams and Vanduzer, Americans, to one in Boston; and Beebe, to one in some town in the State of New York. These four were Americans, possessed of a good deal of natural acuteness, along with a good education, and considerable information. Davis and Nutt were Englishmen; Donahoe, Lonergan, Madden, and one or two more, were from the green isle; while I was the sole representative of the land o'cakes.

The question proposed, as the subject of the first night's discussion, was as follows: "Whether is love or anger the more powerful passion?" I had been appointed by the pre-ident to open the discussion by the introductory essay, which I had been at considerable pains in arranging, as I wished to deliver it without the assistance of notes, calculating of course on producing an effect by this studied carelessness of manner. The vanity of wishing to be considered wise, is not wholly confined to young men of learning; and the ambition of being thought a distinguished orator, or a clever chopper of logic, may sometimes be found lurking beneath the worsted epaulette of the soldier, as well as under the dignified and patrician toga of the bar or the pulpit.

In the meantime, a trifling misadventure came very near turning my anticipated triumph into a complete disgrace. That no lack of exertion on my part should be the cause of failure, if the fates had decreed adversely to my success, I resolved on practising a recitation of my essay in the woods. Accordingly, on the afternoon of the day appointed for the debate, sallying out with a rifle on my shoulder, I soon reached a convenient spot, and thoroughly repeated my exercise, having done which I pursued my way still farther into the woods, until warned by the lengthening shades of the tall pines that evening was rapidly approaching. It only wanted about an hour of sunset when I began to plod my way homeward to the Fort. While walking leisurely along, I observed a small blue bird, about the size of a sparrow, sitting on a twig that overhung the path. In a moment of thoughtlessness I stopped and took aim at it with my rifle; I was about seventy or eighty yards from it, the point blank range of my piece, which carried one hundred and twenty to the pound. As I had not practised much with the rifle then, I could not have expected to hit at that distance; I drew the trigger, however, and the bird dropped from the branch. I looked with remorse on its mangled and torn corpse, and felt that I had committed an unhallowed violation of the quiet sanctity of the wilderness, that seemed to call out for vengeance. Angry at myself for doing that which I had frequently reprobated in others, and desirous of leaving those frowning pines, which one might also fancy were accusing, though silent, witnesses of this needless slaughter, I turned into another path, which I thought led by a shorter way into the Fort. After walking about two miles, I found that I had overrated my knowledge of that part of the country, and that I was completely at fault. To go back to where I had left the main road would have been the most certain way to correct my error; but it would have delayed me considerably, and I should have nearly seven miles to walk if I retraced my steps. Besides, by so doing, I might be too late for the meeting, and I felt that if I failed to make my appearance, my absence might be construed into a want of confidence in my own ability. I therefore resolved upon taking a straight line for the highway through the bushes, by which I hoped to reduce the distance to about two miles. I started on this resolution, and for the first mile or so I got on very well, the ground being firm, and the bushes not too thick. But at last difficulties began to multiply, in the shape of thorny vines, that sometimes tripped my feet, and at others, enveloped my whole body in their meshes, tearing my clothes and skin. At other times I got up to the middle in a swamp, when I was forced to go back and make a circuit to avoid it. At last I was nearly losing both hope and patience, night was fast closing around, and I was beginning to think I should have to pass the night in the woods. I am not very superstitious, I believe; but the recollection of the bird so wantonly killed, haunted my memory just at that moment; like Coleridge's "Ancient Mariner," I had done "a hellish thing," in slaying that innocent bird. Was this entanglement the penance inflicted by the spirit of the woods? The certain ridicule of my comrades if I should not be at the meeting, again occurring to my mind, I was prompted to make another vigorous effort; and after toiling for about half an hour, I reached the highway, about half a mile from the Fort, with no more injury than torn and soiled clothes, and a few deep scratches from the prickly vines, across my face and hands. Glad to find it was no worse, I resumed my journey, and was home in time enough to be able to change my clothes, wash, and take some refreshment before making my appearance at the meeting, where I managed to acquit myself tolerably well to my own satisfaction, as well as that of my friends.

Our society existed about three months, a longer period than I had calculated on its continuance at its first commencement, and I believe that but for the choice of a subject for discussion of a rather injudicious nature, at least considering that the society merely existed by sufferance, it might have continued to flourish while we remained in that garrison. With a good deal of the absurd and ridiculous, there was occasionally a very fair display of talent and ability at these debates. The lawyer and the schoolmaster of the village, who attended one evening, attracted by curiosity and the fame of the discussions, were heard to express their astonishment and gratification at the skill which some of the members displayed in handling the topic of the evening. I am much mistaken if I have not seen more indifferent specimens of eloquence in the newspaper columns, as emanations of the legislative wisdom of the greatest nation in existence, than some of the speeches I have heard delivered in that society; and no mighty encomium either, the reader will perhaps think, if he has been in the habit of perusing one of the Washington daily or tri-weekly papers. The question which was commonly supposed to have extinguished our society was to the following effect, " Whether does the civil or military life offer the highest rewards and incentives to an honourable ambition ?" This question was propounded by Theoretical Davis, as Nutt called him, who was anxious to produce several very important facts bearing on the subject, which I am afraid are now lost to the world for ever. Whether the commanding officer had heard the subject proposed for discussion, and considered that it trenched on rather dangerous ground, we never correctly ascertained, though such was the current opinion. This much is certain, that a few days before our next meeting, he issued an order signifying his disapproval of these societies, as being contrary to the spirit of the regulations of the service; so, of course, there was no more to be said on the subject. A meeting of the members was called one evening for the purpose of deciding upon the best means of disposing of the surplus funds in the hands of the treasurer, when it was proposed, and carried without a dissenting voice, that as much whiskey as the money would procure, should be furnished and produced on the table forthwith. This was done accordingly, and an exceedingly convivial evening was the result of this spirited motion.

CHAPTER X.

General Scott—The Coast of Mexico—A jolly Captain—A Gale of Wind—The River—Tampico.

ABOUT the beginning of October, 1846, we received a large draft of recruits from Governor's Island, who were distributed between the two companies lying at Tampa Bay, increasing each to about eighty-six men; this we considered very like a hint to prepare for a move to Mexico. General Scott, at the commencement of the war with Mexico, had been accused of a want of skill, courage, and patriotism, by a large portion of the captain Bobadil editors of the "great nation." This abuse he had received principally, I believe, in consequence of declining to adopt the very simple and cheap method recommended by the said Bobadils; which was to march through every town in Mexico with a regiment of five hundred men, and wind up with taking deliberate possession of the halls of the Montezumas, where he should remain until the Mexicans were inclined to come to terms. General Scott, who knew how to "bide his time," had waited patiently, quietly digesting the hasty plate of soup, the bare mention of which had caused so much commotion among people of weak stomachs throughout the country generally. At last the President and his advisers, seeing no prospect of a speedy and successful issue to the war without putting his military talents into requisition, which they were quite willing to discover, or acknowledge, as long as they stood in need of them, began to think of employing him. The plan of marching through the country with five hundred men was now rarely spoken of, and the expedition preparing at the suggestion of General Scott, was being fitted out on a scale somewhat commensurate with the importance of the undertaking contemplated ; which was generally understood to be the reduction of Vera Cruz, and a subsequent march to the gates of the city of Mexico.

On the 10th of December arrived the order which we had been long expecting; we were to be in readiness for immediate embarkation, being required to join the present expedition fitting out for the reduction of Vera Cruz. Our place at Tampa Bay, which, on account of the Indians in its neighbourhood, could not be left wholly defenceless, was to be supplied by a body of Volunteers raised in Florida for the purpose, until the war in Mexico should cease. So desirous were we of escaping from the dull monotony of this place, of which we were exceedingly tired, that I believe many heard the orders to prepare for leaving it with much satisfaction. But the married men, whose wives and families were all to be left behind, were looking very dull; and as for the wife of our Lieutenant, who had four small children, she cried for a whole day, it was said, when the order came. Poor woman! if she could have foreseen that her husband was to fall mortally wounded, pierced in the body with three musket-balls, at the battle of Churubusco, about nine months after receiving that order, she would have cried still more bitterly. The wives and families of officers and soldiers were allowed by government to remain in the quarters they occupied when their husbands left; they were also furnished with rations until the conclusion of the war, when they were to be forwarded to those garrisons to which their husbands were sent.

About a fortnight after we had received the order to be

in readiness, a merchant brig, called the *John Potter*, arrived to take us to Tampico, a port about two hundred miles east of Vera Cruz, where the forces destined for General Scott's expedition were to be concentrated. We embarked on the 1st January, 1847, and on the morning of the 2nd we set sail, and having a fair wind, soon lost sight of the low-lying, sandy coast of Florida. We found our accommodation in the *John Potter* rather limited, there being nearly two hundred men on board a vessel not quite three hundred tons burden; but one comfort was that we were spared the annoyance which is usually caused in a crowded vessel by women and children, "there not being a single stick of a petticoat on board," as some one remarked. My comrade, Nutt, and two or three more of the soldiers, who had been sailors at a former period of their lives, were engaged, with the permission of our commanding officer, to help to work the vessel, which had left Charleston short of hands. One of the crew had also become partially insane since he had been shipped there, and they could not trust him to do much work. He had just been discharged from hospital at Charleston when he came on board, and his health had not been firmly established, it was supposed, as he had a pallid and dejected sort of look. His insanity was of a mild form, and he was perfectly quiet; but he insisted that the ship swarmed with a crew of horrible-looking old witches, numbers of whom he saw perched upon the rigging, and who he constantly affirmed would lead the vessel into difficulty. Nothing could persuade him that the *John Potter* was not a doomed craft, that would never leave the gulf; and though he sometimes took a turn at the wheel, steering as well as the others, yet he kept always eyeing the rigging with a troubled and suspicious glance. One of our recruits who had joined with the late draft in Tampa Bay, had also become insane a few weeks after he joined; he was named Hogg, and belonged to the north of Ireland. He had been in hospital for some time previous to our embarkation, but the surgeon was of opinion that he was only acting the character for the purpose of procuring his discharge, and he was placed in charge of a sentry when we went on board. One day, when the sentry having him in charge had his attention attracted elsewhere, Hogg, having climbed over the ship's side, got into the forechains, and stripping off his clothes, jumped into the water. The vessel was going at the rate of three or four knots at the time, and before we could get her hove-to, and a boat lowered, he had gone nearly a mile astern, and had he not been a very good swimmer, he must have been drowned. As sharks were numerous in those seas, and as there had been one reported alongside several times since we sailed, few questioned the fact of the poor fellow's insanity after that occurrence, and shortly after our arrival at Tampico he was discharged.

On the morning of the twelfth, after a pleasant voyage of only ten days' duration, the coast of Mexico was distinctly in view. We had the cable all on deck, and considering the voyage ended, we were congratulating each other upon the short and withal pleasant trip we had made. But we were rather premature, as it fell out, and our voyage was not to be over so soon as we anticipated. It is a very good old saw, the truth of which we fully experienced on this occasion, that " We should not halloo till we are out of the wood."

We had the clear bold outline of the lofty inland range of mountains, which the coast of Mexico there presents, in view for the remainder of the day; and at sunset we were said to be within twenty miles or so of anchorage. The first mate, who was an excellent sailor, and generally considered by the crew and soldiers to be the most competent of any on board, was very anxious that we should run into anchorage that nigh*. He was of opinion that, as we had good moonlight, and the wind light and answerable, we should run in during the night, and drop anchor a few miles from the mouth of the Panuco, when we would be ready for the steamer in the morning, which would tow us over the bar, and up the river to Tampico. But unfortunately the captain happened to differ in opinion with him, or rather, he had no very decided opinion upon the matter, it being said that he complied with the wishes of some of our officers, who thought there was danger in going in without good daylight. The captain, therefore, resolved upon tacking off and on during the night, and taking his chance of a change of wind in the shape of one of those violent gales called northers, which are prevalent at that season, and which was the contingency so much dreaded by the mate from former experience on that coast. It was also said that the captain had a capital stock of liquors on board, which he wished to dispose of before entering port; and to judge from the rubicund jollity of his countenance, through which his half-shut blue eyes twinkled with the peculiar silly-looking, though good-humoured leer of the toper, he must have been a staunch anti-teetotaller. During the whole of the voyage, up to the present time, he had seldom made his appearance upon deck, having left the sailing of the vessel wholly to the first mate, and being solely occupied meanwhile in carousing, and drinking bumpers to the success of the expedition, along with our officers, towards whom he apparently exercised an excess of hospitality that, under existing circumstances, might have been much better dispensed with. If our officers, as has been alleged, really influenced the decisions of the captain, causing him to keep his vessel off until morning, in place of leaving the matter in the hands of the mate, their ignorant and presumptuous interference was pretty severely punished by the result.

Having stood off and on, as it is called in sea phrase, by tacking at short intervals during the night, next morning we found with the wind we had, we could run in to an offing in four or five hours. The appearance of the morning was rather suspicious, being slightly cloudy and showery, but the breeze was in our favour, and we went steadily along at the rate of six or seven knots an hour, expecting to be in the river by noon. At eleven o'clock we were within a couple of miles of the anchorage, and the pilot coming off to board us was only about half a mile from our bows, when a heavy, dark-looking cloud which had been gathering ahead of us for the previous ten minutes, began to sprinkle the deck with a few large drops. At the same time the whistling and hissing sounds, amongst the running gear and shrouds, changing finally into the wild roar of the hurricane, as the vessel careened over nearly on her beam ends, showed that there was no time to be lost; the gale was on us, and our only chance was to "cut and run," as the sailors term it. Fortunately the storm had not come on unobserved, a number of the sails had been taken in previous to this, and as the gale came on, the vessel was speedily put about, and bounding with astonishing velocity from the harbour. As for the pilot he was close in shore, having run for the nearest point on the first burst of the gale. The captain, who, to do him justice, was a very good sailor when he was roused, and who now probably saw his error, and regretted that he had not taken the mate's advice on the previous evening, behaved with a great deal of energy and decision; both he and the mate showing by their example how a sailor can and ought to work in an emergency like the present. Indeed but for the extraordinary exertions of the officers and sailors composing the crew, I believe we should have been driven on the sands; and some days afterwards, when the gale had moderated, the captain confessed that we had a very narrow escape. In the meantime, under close-reefed topsails we were scudding through the water with fearful velocity, far more anxious now to get out from land, than we had been a few hours ago to approach it. For several hours the colour of the water warned us of our close proximity to the shoal sandy coast, fatal to so many gallant vessels, and it was evening before we were considered out of any immediate danger. The captain and mate were heard to agree while conversing together on the subject, that but for the superior qualities of the *John Potter* in sailing close to the wind, we should have been driven on a lee shore in spite of the best seamanship in the world. It was a knowledge of the frequency of these north gales at that season of the year, and the danger of being caught by one upon a lee shore, that made the mate wish to run in on the previous night. Had the captain taken his advice and done so, we should have been over the bar, and in the river at anchor, several hours before the gale came on before which we were now driving; but there was no use for unavailing regrets. During the whole morning's proceedings, the sailor who was wrong in his head, sat perched on the point of the bowsprit with his legs crossed, looking up at the rigging, and in towards the deck of the vessel. Amidst all the rain and wind, and the bustle of putting the ship about, he never stirred from his position; towards evening one of the men went out, and coaxed him to come down. "I'm blest if I know what to make of that unlucky beggar, and his strange lingo about witches and such like," said an old tar, "but if so be as how there is witches bringing ill luck on the vessel, it must be him they follow, for no one else sees them but him. At all events, if I was the skipper, the first day I went into port, would be the last day the unlucky beggar would ever put a foot on the *John Potter's* deck."

Steadily and without intermission for the next three days the cold bitter north blast continued to blow. I have never seen a gale last so long with such continuous and unmitigated fury. We had one comfort, however, in the midst of our misfortunes; this was found in the admirable qualities and excellent behaviour of the *John Potter*; these constituted a theme of universal praise. "She was not a very handsome built craft wasn't the *John Potter*," one of the old tars remarked, the same old fellow who made the remarks about witches, but blest if he ever seed a craft that seemed to understand what you wanted of her, or would do it more cheerfully than this same craft. "Why, bless your soul," he continued, "half of your fine Baltimore clippers would have been lying on the sands if they had been in our place the other morning; give me the craft that never misses in stays, and lies well to the wind." "Be the blessed bird of heaven! if she doesn't watch the waves coming and ride on the top of them like a duck," said Dennis Mulloney. "Yaw, dat is vat you call a wasser duck," said a phlegmatic-looking Dutchman, as the combing of a huge wave broke over the bulwarks to windward, giving the party a tolerable specimen of the *douche*, and thoroughly drenching their clothes from head to foot. While the gale continued very few of the men stayed upon deck, and as the vessel pitched a good deal, they with few exceptions lay in their berths nearly all the time it lasted, a period of nearly three days, during which time of course we never attempted cooking. With some of my comrades I managed to crawl upon deck, now and then, to have a look at the weather, and I shall not soon forget the appearance of the sea upon these occasions. The huge black inky looking masses of water, with their superb crests of snow-white foam, as they came rolling on, presented a spectacle at once grand, magnificent, and appalling. Three or four of these huge waves bounded the visible horizon, as the drifting spray prevented us from seeing more than two or three hundred yards on each side of the vessel.

At length the gale having fairly exhausted its fury, we began to entertain hopes of speedily regaining the port from which we had been so suddenly and unceremoniously driven. But our hopes were somewhat qualified by the intelligence that we would be fortunate if we could reach Tampico within a week, while our provisions would be wholly consumed in three or four days, unless we were put on short allowance. The reason of our provisions being short, was owing to the commissariat stores at Tampa Bay being nearly exhausted when the *John Potter* arrived. Had we waited for a supply from New Orleans, we might have been detained eight or ten days, and the officer in command, afraid of appearing too cautious, resolved upon taking the responsibility of proceeding with what we had. If we had been so fortunate as to get in before encountering this gale, we should have had enough, but it is extremely injudicious, to say the least of it, to send troops to sea, with just sufficient provisions to last, in the event of a fortunate voyage. In consequence of the shortness of provisions, we were accordingly supplied with eight ounces of biscuit a day, instead of a pound, as formerly. This was no great hardship, but as the wind died away, and we were lying idly becalmed for two or three days, serious apprehensions began to be felt, lest we should soon have nothing at all to eat. Besides, if we did not get the wind in our favour soon, the probability was that we should be caught by another gale, as at that period of the year, it was seldom that two or three weeks elapsed without one of these dangerous visitors. In this latter event our case would be hopeless indeed, unless we should have the good luck to fall in with some ship who might give us some assistance. One of our officers had brought a dozen hams from Tampa Bay; these were stowed down in the hold, and intended as a valuable reinforcement to the larder of the officers' regimental mess at Tampico. But some of the men having discovered the nature of the contents of the box in which they were packed, and acting upon the axiom that in cases of general emergency, private property may be lawfully seized, and appropriated for the general good, they contrived to make a very expeditious clearance of these comestibles. However, to preserve appearances, and prevent any unpleasant feelings on the subject while on board, they had the box made up in weight, by packing a sufficient quantity of ballast among the straw, in place of the hams; and having nailed on the lid, the damage was not discovered until the box was opened, after we went ashore.

Our short allowance had continued for five or six days, during which I cannot say that I suffered any inconvenience from hunger, though, like the rest of my companions, feeling sometimes a slight degree of anxiety as to our future prospects; but before being reduced quite to the starvation point, we fortunately met with assistance. On the morning of the 20th, we descried a steamer to leeward, and on making sail for it, and hoisting the American flag half mast, as a signal that we required assistance, we soon had the satisfaction of seeing that she had observed it, and was directing her course towards us. On her nearing us we found that she was a large propeller, in the employment of Government, called the *Massachusetts*. She was on her way to the Rio Grande, with dispatches for General Scott, who was there at that time, and consequently could not tow us into Tampico, as our commanding officer requested, but offered to supply us with provisions. This offer we were very glad to accept, so coming alongside, she gave us twenty barrels of biscuit, and a few barrels of pork; and her captain bidding us good bye, and wishing us " better luck next time," she was soon on her course, and in a few hours out of sight.

Although disappointed in getting towed into the river, we were now comparatively independent to what we had been a few hours previous, having provisions enough to last for several weeks on board, in case of emergency; and the wind, though light, continuing to blow steadily in our favour, in a few days after this event we were again in sight of, and rapidly nearing the harbour. When within about ten miles of the mouth of the river, the pilot came on board; this time he came in a six oared boat, rowed by Mexicans. These were the first Mexicans we had seen, fine tall stout looking fellows they were, but as we afterwards found considerably above the average of their countrymen in height and physical condition. As we expected to meet some of their countrymen soon, in the "tug of war," of course their personal appearance excited considerable interest, and remark. " By the hokey," said Mick Ryan, " I don't see that thim Mexicans is the weeny yaller atomies they do be telling us, afther all." " Faith an it's no lie for you, Micky, anyhow, barrin the ignorant crathurs don't know the beauties of the shillelah, they look like boys that could empty a fair in less than no time, and a fistful ov minutes to spare; but with the help ov the blessed Vargin, we'll soon see how they behave in front ov their betthers," responded Paddy Byrne. " By my conscience, Geordie, they're a strong, supple, treacherous looking set of deevils; od gin they hae a trifle of courage, wi' the defensible nature o' their kintra, an their ain d—d cleemate to back them, I'm thinking we may consider ourselves in a pretty considerable bit of a fix, as Jonathan says," remarked Tom Mathieson. In the meantime, the Mexicans had come on board, and were jabbering and laughing to one another in their own language, in the most free and easy manner apparently, and making use of their two or three English words, while offering to shake hands with any of our men who approached. But none of our men could talk Spanish, and their English consisted merely of a few of those epithets, and phrases, "not calculated for ears polite," the universal introduction to the English language, at those foreign ports, where the schoolmaster abroad is the sailor or the soldier. The pilot, a little withered looking old fellow, and a true *Castilliano*, as he repeatedly endeavoured to make us comprehend, by repeating the term, and pointing to himself at the same time, had now taken charge of the vessel. The morning was delightfully clear, and we had a beautiful view of the romantic scenery of the wooded mountain range, that bounds the prospect round the bay of Tampico. The shore round the bay is low and sandy, and covered with groups of cactuses, and other thorny shrubs; but a short distance inland the soil is rich, and clothed with vegetation of a more valuable and pleasing character, abounding in good natural grass, and a variety of wild fruits and flowers. About ten o'clock on the morning of the 25th we dropt anchor about two or three miles from the mouth of the river, and about an hour after a steamer arrived to tow us in.

The entrance to the river Panuco is very difficult to sailing vessels, being obstructed by a dangerous sandbar at its mouth, and at the time we entered, the skeletons of two large craft, and several smaller ones, bedded in the sands at the entrance, gave significant warning to the careless navigator. It is only at particular favourable conjunctions of wind and tide, that a pilot will risk bringing a sailing vessel over, but the necessity of waiting for a fair wind was at the present time obviated in the case of American vessels, by the government having stationed steam-tugs there, to take vessels over the bar, and up and down the river. We were towed over the bar by the steam-tug, without any difficulty, but the tide not answering to go up to the town of Tampico, which is about ten or twelve miles up the river, we again let go our anchor. Our vessel was now immediately surrounded by a whole fleet of canoes, with fruits and vegetables for sale, which they sold exceedingly cheap; and finding plenty of eager purchasers among our men, their stock of oranges, pine-apples, plantains, bananas, etc., was speedily disposed of. Towards evening, the tide serving, the steam-tug arrived to take us up to Tampico. As we sailed up the river, which here seems a sort of miniature Mississippi, being a dull, broad, coffee-coloured stream with a strong current, its banks clothed with luxuriant vegetation, and its muddy line of water-mark covered with a debris of the trunks of trees, of the genus *snag*, the interesting features of the landscape were gazed at with intense curiosity. The palmetto-thatched hut, the tall cocoa-nut tree, with its slender and graceful trunk, and its huge fan-like leaves, relieved so distinctly by the deep azure of the blue sky; the tropical looking banana with its immense bunches of delicious fruit; the orange trees with their fruits of golden hue, gleaming so temptingly through the deep dark green of their thick foliage; all these in turn elicited our admiration and excited our curiosity. The left bank of the river especially attracted our attention: the mountains which there ascend gradually from within a short distance of the river are very lofty, and covered to their summits with trees, and evergreen vegetation of every varied and contrasting shade and hue; and each new turn of the serpentining river presented some fresh combination, from the changed point of view; producing the most delightful panoramic variation of scenery imaginable.

This town of Tampico has a very pleasing and lively appearance viewed from the river, the houses and stores facing which are painted red or white; nearly all have porticos in front, supporting balconies or verandas, and the open space between them and the river is wide and well paved. Sloping up from the wharf is the market place, which, like all Mexican markets, presents a very busy and animated picture; game, fish, fruit, and vegetables were the principal commodities in the market on the next morning after our arrival, and these were all remarkably cheap, a brace of wild ducks being sold for a real (about sixpence), and other articles in proportion. The town is principally built on a hill which has a gradual ascent for about half a mile along the right bank of the river; the highest part of it is near the house of the British Consul. A little way above, the hill ends in a precipitous bluff, from which there is an excellent view of the river and surrounding country. We had no sooner dropped anchor in the stream, than we were boarded by several boatloads of men belonging to those companies of our regiment from whom we had been separated on leaving Pensacola. They congratulated us warmly on our safe arrival, the current report having been for some days previous, that the *John Potter* had been wrecked, and all hands lost. They told us they had been lying in camp in the suburbs of the town for the last month; that about a third of them had the fever and ague; that there were five or six thousand troops in the town, and in a few days as many more were expected: that tobacco was sold for a dollar a pound, and a poisonous description of liquor, under the denomination of brandy, for a shilling a glass; and a few more items of that sort, comprising the current gossip of the camp.

It was near sunset when we dropped anchor, so we had to content ourselves for another night on board; but boats came alongside bringing their welcome supplies of fresh bread, cheese, fruits, and other tempting luxuries; and there were few on board the *John Potter* who did not indulge in at least one ample meal as a counterpoise to the hard and unpalatable fare, and forced abstemiousness of the voyage. Early next morning a steamer came alongside and took our baggage, which was landed in a very expeditious manner, and placed in the commissary waggons waiting on the wharf for its reception; after which we were all landed by the steamer. Having left a small guard to escort the baggage, we were formed into companies, and preceded by the lively notes of the ear-piercing fife, and the beat of martial drum, we marched through the principal streets of Tampico to the camp, which lay nearly a mile down the river.

On arriving at the camp, after piling arms, and taking off our knapsacks, we were shown, by the adjutant of the regiment, the ground our companies were to occupy, and immediately proceeded to pitch our tents. This was soon done, and then we commenced cleaning our arms and accoutrements. The other companies stationed here before us had all their things in the most perfect order; and as there were parades and inspections every morning, our lieutenant hoped we would try to uphold the credit of company I. All our clothes also required to be washed after our voyage, but as there were plenty of poor Mexican women coming to our camp and asking for clothes to wash, which they did very well, and cheap, Nutt and I got one of them to wash for us while we stayed there, thus saving a great deal of very disagreeable labour at a trifling expense. For the purpose of allowing us to rest a little after the hardships of our voyage, and also to give us an opportunity to clean our accoutrements and clothes, the commanding officer excused us from going to parade for two days after our arrival, during which time we contrived to get all our things into good condition.

CHAPTER XI.

The Town and its Population—Reinforcements—General Shields—
Bill Nutt as Orderly—Expedition to Vera Cruz.

I SAID the town of Tampico had a pleasing appearance when viewed from the river, but a closer inspection dissipates the favourable impression made by its first appearance. The streets nearest the river are composed of good substantial stone buildings, inhabited by the wealthiest part of the population; but in the suburbs, and a number of the back streets, are rows of the most wretched-looking habitations, containing the most squalid population which the imagination can conceive. I had seen misery in Ireland which I thought unsurpassable, but some of the poor wretches in the suburbs of Tampico, presented a squalor of appearance more abjectly miserable than anything I had seen even there. The huts of the poor are built either of mud, or bamboos, stuck as close together as possible, and placed upright in the ground; they are covered with palmetto leaves, which are also interwoven with the bamboos to exclude the cold wind of the north gales which blow during the winter. The interior of these huts presents as forlorn and wretched an aspect as the exterior; they are mostly destitute of furniture, save a few earthen pipkins used as cooking utensils, and a mat of grass or rushes, used as a bed. The only bed the bulk of the labouring population of Mexico ever think of sleeping upon, is a mat spread down on the floor, on which they sleep without ever taking off their clothes—a practice

which is quite sufficient to account for the charges of dirt
and vermin brought by most travellers against the Mexicans;
charges of the truth of which, while I was in Mexico, I had
frequently too abundant proof.

The gentry and respectable portion of the inhabitants kept
very retired while we lay in the vicinity, many of them shut-
ting themselves up in their houses, as if in a state of siege.
Indeed it was no great wonder though they should be a little shy of the strange, wild-looking, hairy-faced savages of the
half horse and half alligator breed, who galloped about the
streets and plazas mounted on mules and Mexican ponies,
and armed with sabres, bowies, and revolvers, and in every
uncouth variety of costume peculiar to the American back-
woodsman. The senors or caballeros, masters or gentlemen,
the Mexicans called them when addressing them, but when
speaking of them in their absence, it was "Malditos Volun-
teros," which they enunciated with a bitterness of tone, that
showed the intensity of their dislike. In fact I believe they
had no great love for any portion of the "hereticos Americanos," though the volunteers seemed to be objects of their
special detestation; and I imagine they looked upon us all
with similar complacency, to that which the Spaniards looked
upon the army of France, during its usurpation of the Peninsula.

About a week after our arrival, a strong reinforcement
arrived from General Taylor's army at Monterey. These
were principally volunteers, and one regiment called the Ten-
nessee cavalry, were a fine looking set of stout fellows, well
clothed, armed, and mounted, at least for volunteers; and
they were said to have behaved very well in action. But
they had only been raised for one year. A few months after-
ward, when their time expired, great exertions were used to
induce them to remain, but with no effect; the poor fellows

had "seen the elephant," and were perfectly satisfied with the exhibition. A considerable number of regular troops, both infantry and artillery, were also withdrawn at this time from General Taylor's army for the Vera Cruz expedition, weakening his force exceedingly. This, it was thought, had suggested the idea to Santa Anna of overwhelming him by superior numbers, and taking him and his whole army prisoners, which resulted in the battle of Buenavista; where the Mexicans, in a fair field, and with a numerical force of at least four to one, were so shamefully defeated.

The town of Tampico had a bustling and animated appearance while the troops remained in the vicinity, a band of music furnished by each regiment in succession playing in the main plaza for a few hours each evening; and the streets and houses of entertainment being thronged with officers and soldiers. The troops received two months' pay while we lay here, being paid up to the 1st January; there was consequently a good deal of money amongst the men for a few days. The larger portion of this soon found its way into the hands of the army followers, a sort of human vultures who followed the army all through the campaign, keeping hotels, called by the popular cognomens of "The Palo Alto House," "The Rough and Ready Restaurant," "American Star Hotel," &c.; the whole stock in trade of said restaurants and hotels mostly consisting of a piece of villanously tough roasted or fried *carne* (beef), and a few dollars' worth of an abominable spirituous liquor called aguardiente. The Mexican shop-keepers were prohibited from selling spirits to the soldiers under the pain of a heavy penalty, but these camp followers were winked at by some means or other, and the scoundrels had a complete monopoly of the sale of liquor, and were permitted to poison and plunder the soldiers with impunity. In most of these houses gambling was incorporated with the business of selling liquor, two or three professional gamblers being usually the joint proprietors of these low concerns, where the most brutal riots, frequently resulting in loss of life, were of frequent recurrence. It would have considerably improved the *morale* of the army if these shops had been prohibited, and all citizens not in the employment of government packed off to the States.

A company of theatrical performers, who had been with General Taylor's army in Monterey and Matamoras, came down with the division of troops which had just arrived, and were performing to good houses in town, the officers and soldiers crowding the theatre every night to overflowing. A newspaper, called the *American Star*, was also published once a week, and sold at six cents. As it was only purchased by the army, of course its circulation must have been rather limited; but it usually contained a good many items of army intelligence, and a considerable number were bought to send home to friends in the States, both by officers and soldiers.

For some time after our arrival at Tampico, our regiment furnished an orderly to General Shields, who was selected by the adjutant, at guard mounting, from the men paraded for that duty. One day my comrade Bill Nutt having been selected for the office, a rather amusing occurrence happened to him. It appeared that Nutt, who had never seen the general, had taken him for a servant, as he had opened the door for him, and also from his wearing plain clothes, and his free and unassuming manners. The morning was cold, and he had asked Nutt to sit down at the fireside, sitting down himself on the opposite side, and entering into conversation with him. Nutt, who laboured under a false impression with regard to the identity of the person he was dressing, had spoken his sentiments very freely on some of the topics connected with the present war, condemning the aggressive sort of policy that seemed to actuate the democratic party of America. In the midst of a discussion on the question at issue, an officer in uniform entered from an adjacent apartment, and bowing to Nutt's opponent, who was calmly listening at the time to his views of the subject, addressed him by the title of general. Nutt, who felt quite shocked at the discovery, made a hasty and unceremonious retreat into the ante-room, and though the general resumed the subject after the departure of his guest, he confessed that the general soon had the best of the argument, as he could not speak with the same freedom as before. Nutt often alluded afterwards to the urbanity and gentlemanlike manners of General Shields, allowing that a few gentlemen might be found among the citizens of the enlightened republic, and quoting him as one example, at least, that he had met with in his travels.

Our troops, a large proportion of whom were raw recruits, were kept closely at drill while we lay in camp at Tampico, and by the end of February they were considered in good order for active operations. General Scott's arrival about the 20th was a signal to be ready for a move, and in a day or two after, the army received orders to embark; the first of the troops going on board on the 24th.

Several days were occupied in getting all the men and horses on board, but on the 27th of February all were ready to sail. The regiment to which I belonged, being in the last division, had no delay; and getting into a steamer at the wharf at Tampico, we were taken down the river and put on board the barque *Caroline*, with all our baggage, in a few hours. We were no sooner on board than we began to weigh anchor, and in a very short time all our transports had spread their canvas to the breeze. Our fleet, comprising nearly a hundred sailing vessels, fifty or sixty of which were large ships and the remainder brigs and schooners, presented a very imposing appearance during the afternoon. The change of position perpetually occurring in the different vessels, caused by the difference in their rates of sailing, created excitement among the men, and added variety and animation to the scene. The number of large ships filled with troops, stores, and ammunition, and the strength of our whole armament, as compared with anything which Mexico could furnish, inspired our men with the certainty of success in the reduction of Vera Cruz. As to the cost of life involved in the undertaking, that was left to the chapter of accidents; in reckoning the probable contingencies of a coming engagement, the soldier seldom includes himself in the list of the killed and wounded. Our destination for the time was the island of Lobos, that being the place appointed for the whole vessels belonging to the expedition to rendezvous, preparatory to sailing for the harbour of Vera Cruz. We had a smart gale of wind during the night, and next morning we could only discern two or three vessels in the horizon out of the large fleet which had sailed with us on the previous day. We arrived at Lobos about five o'clock of the same evening, and came to anchor; having beaten every vessel of the expedition. The others continued to drop in by twos and threes until the middle of the day, by which time they had all come to anchor.

Lobos is a small sandy island not far from the coast, between Tampico and Vera Cruz. It is not seen until the voyager is close upon it, as it is very little above the level of the sea. While we lay there, as there was a slight gale of wind, the sea broke in a heavy surf on the barren and desolate spot, on which the only signs of vegetation were a few stunted shrubs, evidently struggling hard with the difficulties of their situation for a bare subsistence. Three or four vessels from New Orleans were lying here on our arrival; they formed part of the expedition, and were waiting for us; a few of their passengers had gone ashore and pitched tents, preferring to sleep on the solid sand to the pitching of the vessel. All our fleet having arrived, on the morning of the 1st March we again set sail for Vera Cruz, which we reached on the evening of the 2nd, and came to anchor about eight miles from the castle of San Juan de Ulloa, the name of the fortification at Vera Cruz, about four miles from Sacrificios, a small island near the castle, where "men-of-war" anchor.

On the morning of the third, General Scott summoned the city and castle of Vera Cruz to surrender; and after a delay of several days, consumed in discussion by the military governor and the civil authorities, the latter of whom were in favour of a surrender, a definitive answer was returned to General Scott that he might come and take them if he could. San Juan is a very strong fortification built upon a small island in the bay, about three quarters of a mile from the pier at Vera Cruz. It had a garrison of between five and six thousand men, was well supplied with ammunition, and bristling with cannon, of which it had about a hundred, some of them of very heavy calibre. The buildings in the castle are all bombproof, and with the sea wall, are built of a soft species of coral, in which cannon balls are imbedded without producing the usual shattering and crumbling effect of these missiles on stone of a harder quality, and which is necessary to cause a breach. It was generally considered impregnable, and could only be approached by vessels on one side, a coral reef stretching round it on every side except the one facing the town. The city of Vera Cruz is surrounded with a wall about twelve or fifteen feet high, but which could be easily breached, and there are a number of half moon batteries round it well manned with guns; it is about three miles in circumference.

Having received the answer of the governor refusing to surrender, on the evening of the 7th General Scott issued an order for the troops to prepare for landing next morning. Commanding officers were directed to see their men furnished with two days' provisions in their havresacks, and that they had their canteens slung, and filled with water. Each man was also to take either his great-coat or his blanket with him, leaving the remainder of his clothes and necessaries, packed in his knapsack, on board. On the morning of the 8th, however, a stiff breeze having commenced to blow, the surf was too heavy for landing, and the order was counter manded. On the evening of the 8th the order of the previous evening was re-issued for the next morning, which having turned out fine, shortly after sunrise we began to get into the boats.

CHAPTER XII.

Sacrificios—The debarkation—A bivouac—A night alarm.

THE surf-boats used for our disembarkation, had been expressly made for the purpose, for which they were admirably adapted, being strong, light, and roomy, and carrying about a hundred men with ease. The whole of the troops had been told off into three divisions, which had to be transferred from the vessels they were in, to those denominated in the order. When all were ready, at a signal from the vessel in which General Scott was, we were to get under weigh for Sacrificios, where we were to drop anchor and disembark at a distance of four miles from the city of Vera Cruz. The regiment to which I belonged was transferred to the deck of the Porpoise man-of-war brig. Between ten and eleven o'clock, A.M., the troops having been all arranged on the vessels, on board of which they had been ordered to proceed, we got under weigh; but as the breeze was against us we had to beat up, and a number of the vessels were towed up by steamers. It was nearly four o'clock before we had all dropped anchor at Sacrificios.

Of vessels of foreign nations lying at anchor at Sacrificios, there were an English man-of-war brig, a French ditto, and a Spanish sloop of war. The officers of these vessels were all on the poop, or quarter-deck, and their crews on the rigging, all apparently eyeing our proceedings with much curiosity, as we came up and successively dropped anchor, our nearest vessels about a cable's length astern of them.

The order of landing was to be as follows: General Worth was to land first with his division; General Twiggs was to land with the second division as soon as the boats returned from landing all of the first; General Scott with the third division was not to land until the following morning. As our regiment belonged to the second division, we had an excellent opportunity of witnessing the landing of the first party—an interesting spectacle, as we fully expected they would receive a warm reception from the Mexicans, who we imagined were stationed behind the sand-hills. A little above high-water mark, on the coast, in the neighbourhood of Vera Cruz, there is a series of sand-hills, formed by the drifting of the fine sand by the violent north gales that blow during the winter months. These sand-hills are thirty or forty feet to a hundred feet in height, the highest being in the vicinity of the city. It was on the highest of these that our batteries were erected for its bombardment. Immediately opposite where we were to land, they formed a sloping acclivity, varying from thirty to fifty feet in height, covered with short scrubby brushwood, and the prickly pear cactus. While the troops were getting into the landing-boats, an operation which, though using all possible despatch, occupied about half an hour, the gun-boats sailed as close as they could to the shore, throwing an occasional shell into the brushwood, for the purpose of ascertaining if the Mexicans had any masked batteries erected, as we supposed. There being no indication of any enemy in the vicinity, and the boats being now filled, everything was ready for landing the first party.

I cannot say that I felt in the slightest degree inclined to earn high fame or distinction, by any very decided demonstration or extraordinary exhibition of personal prowess and heroic valour on the present occasion; neither did I overhear any very strong expressions of regret amongst my comrades, at the circumstance of our regiment not being the first party who were landing. In a short conversation which the sur geon held with the hospital attendant a few minutes before, we could overhear him ask if the lint and bandages, and his case of instruments were close at hand and immediately under his eye. An inquiry, just at that particular juncture, horribly suggestive of thick-coming fancies, and exceedingly well calculated to cool down any dangerous excess of enthusiasm and martial ardour entertained by those who overheard it. Still, when the boats, which contained fully two thousand men, were drawn up in line and ready to start, so strong was the feeling of contagious sympathy elicited and communicated by the sight, surrounded as it was by all the glorious pomp and circumstance of war, that I believe there were few of the army who did not envy their position, or would not gladly have incurred the hazard of the enterprise, for the shadow of glory which the distinction conferred. The scene was certainly exciting and imposing: the military bands of different regiments stationed on the decks of the steamers, transports, and men-of-war, played the national airs of "Yankee Doodle," "Hail Columbia," and the "Star Spangled Banner." Ten thousand of our own troops were anxious and eager spectators, and the English, French, and Spanish fleets, had each their representative, scanning our operations with critical eye, and all looking with curiosity to see the issue of the exploit.

At a signal from the vessel having General Scott on board, the boats simultaneously gave way for shore, leaving a considerable space vacant in front of our men-of-war, who were anchored next the shore, and had their guns double shotted, ready to open upon the enemy, should they make their appearance. The gun-boats, meanwhile, continued to tack backwards and forwards, almost close to the shore, for the same purpose. Under the circumstances, it was plain that the Mexicans could not prevent us from landing, but, by waiting until the first party were fairly on the sands, they might assault them with a very superior force, when our gun-boats and men-of-war would be prevented from firing, by the fear of injuring our own men. This was the event we almost expected to witness, and, as the boats neared the shore, all straining their energies for the honour of being the first to land, we watched the result with intense anxiety, expecting each moment to see a body of Mexican cavalry charge over the sand-hills. But no such event occurred; on coming to within about a hundred yards of the shore, the boats grounded on a small sandbar. The men and officers immediately leaped into the water, the former carrying their muskets on their shoulders, and holding their cartridge boxes well up, as the water reached to their hips while wading ashore. As the boats successively arrived, the men were formed on the beach; the boats making all expedition back to the vessels for more men. All of the first party having formed into line, several regimental colours were displayed, and a charge made to the heights in front, but not a single Mexican was to be seen. The American flag was immediately planted amidst loud and prolonged cheers, which were enthusiastically echoed by the troops on board. All idea of there being any fighting for that day, at least, was now at an end, piquets were thrown out, and sentries posted on the most advantageous points of the heights to guard against a surprise; the men began to make themselves at home; we could observe fires were kindled, and camp kettles swinging on them, in less than an hour after they had landed, and before evening the beach had all the appearance of a camp.

The captain of the Porpoise brig, who seemed a jovial and good-hearted fellow, proposing to act hospitably to the soldiers whom he had on board, ordered the steward to furnish an allowance of grog to each, the same as the sailors were in the habit of receiving; but our officers put a stop to the exercise of his generosity, for which extreme shabbiness they had the contempt of the captain, and the discontented murmurs of their own men. Their conduct, on this occasion, was the more freely commented on and censured, as it was well known that they had all partaken of the captain's hospitality, without stint, themselves, and it was utterly absurd to imagine that a single allowance of grog could injure any person, however unused to spirits. We had been standing on deck all day in the hot sun, with our muskets in our hands, for there was neither an awning nor room to sit down anywhere, on account of the crowded state of the deck. It would probably be nine or ten o'clock that night before we got ashore, when we should have to lie down and sleep on the beach without taking off our accoutrements, which we should have to wear for days, perhaps for weeks to come. But all these disagreeables, as they were the natural and unavoidable consequence of our position, were as dust in the balance, compared with the reflection, that our officers grudged us the slight degree of sympathetic consolation, implied in the good-natured captain's offer of a glass of grog. "The dirty miserly nagurs," audibly grumbled Micky Ryan, "faith, an' six allowances some of the customers have in their own insides; may the Lord look down on us, for we've happened badly on them for gintlemin; shure there's not one of the miserly crathurs has a heart as big as a grasshopper's."

About ten o'clock at night the boats came alongside to take our regiment ashore, being the last of the second division. Two or three lanthorns were held over the ship's side, and, the water being smooth, we were soon all in. We were then rowed ashore till, the boat striking the sand, we had to jump in and wade up to the middle for about a hundred yards, as the others had done. This was a bad preparation for going to sleep on the beach, but, except when there is a north gale blowing, which was not the case that night, the night air is warm on the beach of Vera Cruz, and we suffered little inconvenience from our wetting. We were met by an officer on shore, who said he would show us the position our regiment was to occupy; and, after being formed into companies, we were marched along the beach through a number of rows of small oblong heaps, which, in the dim starlight, the sky being partially obscured by the drifting clouds, bore a striking, and I could scarce help fancying, ominous resemblance to an extensive and over-populous graveyard. At length we arrived at a vacant spot in the line which had been reserved for our occupation, and, having been directed to pile arms, we were told we might lie down when we pleased, but in the immediate vicinity of our arms, which each man was to be ready to grasp at a moment's notice. This was the first time I had ever seen a bivouac, and, certainly, it seemed a very primitive and cool way of lodging; as my comrade Nutt remarked, it did look rather like taking actual possession of the soil. After enjoying a comfortable smoke, we prepared for taking a warrior's rest, by wrapping our martial cloaks around us, or pulling the capes of our great-coats over our heads, to exclude the sand and night air; we tumbled over on the beach, and were soon several fathoms deep in the land of dreams.

But the Mexicans were not disposed to allow us the undisturbed possession of our first night's quarters, indifferent though they were, without giving an intimation, at least, of their sentiments towards us. It was between twelve and one o'clock, and only about an hour after we had fallen asleep, that we were roused by the report of musketry, and found the whole camp a scene of the utmost confusion and commotion. A number of the men, owing to the fatigue of the previous day, and having slept little the previous night, were so sound asleep, that it was only by violently shaking or kicking them, that they could be roused. At last they were all got up and formed into line, when we were directed to examine the priming of our muskets, and see if they were ready for immediate use. In the meantime the balls flew over our heads, with their peculiar metallic ringing sort of whistle, in quick succession; and, though high enough fortunately to do little damage, yet quite near enough to make nervous persons feel rather uncomfortable. The firing continued for about ten minutes, in as quick a succession of reports as would be made by the irregular file-firing of two or three hundred men; and, if it had been well directed, as it easily might have been, by an enemy well acquainted with the surrounding country, and the position we occupied, we might have paid dear for our "lodgings upon the cold ground." A few rounds from a division of infantry ordered out for the purpose, having caused these night disturbers to scamper, we soon piled arms, and in a few minutes were again fast asleep; and, thanks to the vigilance of our out-lying piquets, who gave and received a dropping fire until near morning, we enjoyed our slumbers unmolested during the remainder of the night. Next morning, we learned that the firing of the previous night had proceeded from a body of lancers from the city, who had been quickly driven in by a regiment of General Worth's division. The casualties of the night were five or six wounded, one or two of whom were, report said, dangerously hurt; but there had been none killed.

CHAPTER XIII.

General Scott—The Shell—Naval sporting—Investment of Vera Cruz—Vergara—Spoiling the knapsacks.

EARLY next morning, the third division, with the Commander-in-Chief, General Scott, landed; and our army having been formed into column, we moved to a position a mile or two nearer the town, and covered from observation by the sand-hills. Here we bivouacked in the vicinity of a small stream—General Scott and his staff had tents pitched—the remainder, officers as well as men, crept under the shade of the bushes to screen themselves from the 'scorching rays of the sun, or sticking stout branches upright in the ground, cut a quantity of leafy twigs to serve as a roof, and thus made a tolerable sort of a bower. In the meantime, one of our light batteries was out skirmishing with the enemy's outposts, which offering slight resistance, were successively driven in with little difficulty. From the landing of siege material and heavy ordnance, which had busily commenced, we now perceived that the intention of General Scott was to bombard the city.

A great deal of virtuous indignation has been exhibited by the English press on the subject of the bombardment of Vera Cruz, which it has generally stigmatized as a barbarous slaughter of women and children, having no parallel in modern history. It was asserted that Wellington, or any of his generals, had never bombarded an open city, and a great deal more of a similar tendency, all calculated to show that war is carried on in a highly humane and civilized mode by the enlightened nations of Europe ; and that the Americans, and General Scott in particular, had behaved in a very barbarous manner. Now all that sort of twaddle seems excessively weak to any one at all acquainted with the circumstances ; the truth being notorious that General Scott, besides being one of the most skilful and scientific generals of modern times, is also one of the most humane men in the world. For my part, I have not the slightest doubt that his character, in respect of the noblest attributes of humanity, may bear triumphant comparison with that of the most praiseworthy and philanthropic members of any society, order, or profession, in the world. The real fact being, that his humanity, and a desire to spare a needless effusion of blood, caused him to adopt the method he took for the reduction of Vera Cruz; being anxious to avoid a repetition of the horrible and savagely barbarous scenes consequent on the storming of a city, of which the history of the Peninsular war may furnish a few examples illustrative of the humane practices of European armies. To understand this apparent paradox, one should know a few of the facts of the case. In the first place, Vera Cruz, so far from being an open city, is very well fortified, having a wall and ditch all round it, and a series of half-moon batteries, not deficient in the requisite ordnance to make a stout resistance. These batteries sweep a perfectly level plain, extending from half a mile to a mile between the walls and the sand-hills, and would have proved very destructive to an assaulting party. Now, if the inhabitants, receiving, as they did, two or three weeks' previous notice to quit, preferred remaining in the city, General Scott having plainly signified that, for certain economical reasons, he declined taking their batteries with the bayonet, and intended to try a game at the long bowls, which the Mexi-

7*

cans are so fond of themselves—if, being duly warned, they chose to remain and be killed, I do not see how General Scott should be blamed for the result. But let us suppose that, with the intention of sparing the lives of the inhabitants, by the very disinterested sacrifice of the lives of a few of the troops under his command, he had decided on carrying the place by assault, which would probably have cost the assaulting force from 1,000 to 1,500 men; does any person, in the possession of sound intellect, imagine that, in the latter event, General Scott could have prevented scenes of plunder, the resistance of inhabitants, and the commission of deeds of crime and horror, fearful to contemplate? Those who think that troops, even of well-disciplined armies (a character I would by no means claim for the army under General Scott), can be held in subordinate check by any amount of exertion on the part of their officers, on an occasion of the above nature, are not likely, I apprehend, to form a correct idea on the subject. But to any impartial person, taking an unprejudiced view of the case, I think it will appear tolerably obvious, that the method adopted by General Scott was the most humane even for the inhabitants.

A few days after landing, the various divisions were ordered to the positions which they were to occupy during the progress of the siege. The division to which I belonged, that of General Twiggs, was ordered to Vergara, a small village close to the sea-beach, and on the north-west side of the city, from which it was distant about four miles. In crossing a high sand-hill behind the city, our men being exposed to the view of one of their batteries, they kept up an incessant fire of round shot and shell while our division passed, which, being in file, occupied a considerable time; but they showed no great proficiency in gunnery on this occasion, as very few of their shot took effect. It was here that I heard, for the first time, the singular and diabolically-horrific sound which a large shell makes when passing within a short distance ; I don't mean when it explodes (as that exactly resembles the noise made in firing a gun), but when it passes within a few, or it may be fifty or a hundred yards; the noise seeming equally loud and discordant in either case. I recollect a reply of honest Mick Ryan on being asked if he had ever heard a sound like that before. " No," said Mick, " one can both hear and feel that sound— by the Eternal, I felt it all over." There is no earthly sound bearing the slightest resemblance to its monstrous dissonance ; the angriest shriek of the railway whistle, or the most emphatic demonstration of an asthmatic engine at the starting of a train, would seem like a strain of heavenly melody by comparison. Perhaps Milton's description of the harsh, thunder-grating of the hinges of the infernal gates, approaches to a faint realization of the indescribable sound, which bears a more intimate relation to the sublime than the beautiful. However, the Mexicans did very small damage by their practice; the only result was to make our men fall flat on the sand; which they did every time a shell came, and which I have no doubt saved a few limbs from damage. It was amusing, even amidst the danger from these horrid missiles, to see an officer, after getting up and anathematizing his men emphatically for lying down on the sand, drop as suddenly and as flat as any of them, when the next shell came whizzing rather close to him. The only victim to this ball-practice of the Mexicans in our regiment was a little drummer-boy, about thirteen years of age, named Rome, who had one of his arms shot off by the fragment of an exploding shell. He was one of the most quiet and obliging boys in the regiment, and we were all very sorry for him; many of the men saying if· it had been such a boy (naming one of the others), it would have been no great matter, bu* it was a pity for poor little Rome. The little fellow cried very bitterly at the time, but the surgeon having carefully amputated it, he soon recovered, and on our regiment returning to New York in August, 1849, he came over to Governor's Island to see us. He was then living with a gentleman in New York, who employed him to carry messages and do light work for him. A captain of a volunteer regiment had his head taken off by a cannon-ball the same afternoon; but considering the immense amount of their practice, and the quantity of ammunition fired by their various batteries, the smallness of our loss in killed and wounded is astonishing: the total American loss including those killed and wounded in skirmishes in the vicinity of the city, during the whole siege, only amounted to seventeen killed and fifty-seven wounded.

We bivouacked near the edge of a thick *chaparral*, about four or five miles from Vergara, the position our division was to occupy; but which, for some reason or other, we did not move to for the next three days. We were amused with a volunteer whom we met here, coming out of the chaparral loaded with two muskets and a turkey. He had followed the turkey, a tame one, into the chaparral, and having strayed too far off the road, he was seen and fired at by a Mexican piquet—they exchanged a few shots, he said, when he killed the yellow beggar by shooting him through the body. He had brought the Mexican's musket as well as the turkey, a fine fat one, and decidedly the most valuable prize in general estimation; he spoke very contemptuously of the Mexican's skill in the use of fire-arms, none of his shots having come within yards of him. On quitting us, he added, that there were plenty more in the chaparral, and he guessed he would shoot another before sun-down; whether he meant turkey or Mexican was difficult to comprehend, but, as he seemed to enjoy the sport of shooting the one biped about as much as the other, I have no doubt he considered them both equally fair game. As usual, we were aroused during the night by the firing of musketry, and fell in under arms until the alarm was discovered to be false. These nocturnal alarms were very annoying for the first week or so after landing, as we never passed a night without being roused from our sleep, and ordered to fall in under arms, and this too, twice or thrice during the course of the night sometimes. At last, as they were found, except in one or two instances, to be caused by the blundering of sentries, a number of whom were Germans, and not sufficiently acquainted with the English language to clearly comprehend their orders, our officers ceased to mind these alarms; and when wakened by the report of a few muskets we only turned over to sleep again, grumbling a curse on the stupidity originating the disturbance. Bodies of the enemy, principally lancers, were known to be in the vicinity; but, owing to the nature of the country round Vera Cruz, which is covered with chaparral, no body of the enemy could approach our lines at night by any other mode than the open road. These keys of the position were well watched by our piquets, and being defended by a few field-pieces, there was little danger to be apprehended from an enemy like the one we had to contend with. A few desultory skirmishes took place between part of General Worth's division, consisting of volunteers, and Colonel Harney's dragoons, and a body of Mexican lancers; but the Mexicans fought very shy on these occasions, and soon gave up the idea of being able to effect anything like a bold stroke in favour of the besieged. For two or three days after moving from where we landed, all our provisions had to be carried from the beach, a distance of three or four miles through heavy sands, and under a scorching sun ; and as the men who carried them had to take their arms at the same time, to defend themselves in case of an attack, the duty was excessively fatiguing. Several of our men who died shortly after, assigned as the cause of their illness, the over-exertion they had used when on these harassing fatigue duties.

Our supply of water while lying here was scanty and bad, being only procurable by digging holes in the sand to the depth of four or five feet, and then waiting until the muddy-looking fluid oozed up to a sufficient depth to enable us to dip it with the tin cups which we carried. We were all very glad, therefore, when we moved to Vergara, as we were told that there, at least, we should have plenty of good water. Our road at first wound through chaparral and tangled thickets of *cacti* and other war-like vegetables of the *chevaux de frise* order, along the edge of a marsh, where we halted in order to drink and fill our canteens with the water which it contained. As we had all been suffering considerably for the previous two days from the effects of thirst, few were inclined to criticise too nicely the quality of this water, which, though not exactly transparent, yet to observe the apparent gusto with which almost all quaffed repeated draughts of it, one might have fancied it to be exceedingly like nectar, indescribably sweet. "Hunger is a good sauce," says the proverb, and thirst is equally remarkable as a filter. We had a Mexican guide with us who was well acquainted with the country in the environs of the city, and who rode beside General Twiggs. In all our marches in Mexico, the guide always rode along with the commander of the division, acting as interpreter and guide both, upon occasion. When we approached within two miles of Vergara, our road led through a rich and fertile soil, partially cultivated, and containing a number of very large and venerable-looking trees. We also passed several *ranchos*, but all deserted by their owners, the poor creatures having been the first to suffer from our invasion. We soon reached Vergara, a few straggling huts on a road leading down to the beach. A beautiful clear stream emptied its waters into the sea close to the village, so clear that every motion of the small fish playing in its pellucid pools, was as distinctly visible as those of the unfortunate goldfish one sometimes observes pensively circumgyrating in the interior of its enchanted globular ball in the shop-window. The banks of the stream were shaded for miles by magnificent trees, and in the adjacent thickets a variety of wild fruits were found growing; but the only ones I found ripe were lemons and limes, of which I plucked quantities to squeeze in water, an acidulous drink being exceedingly refreshing with the thermometer upwards of ninety. When returning in July of the following year, I found some delicious guavas and sour sops in these thickets. The timber and the fertility of the soil are unusual features in the face of the country in the vicinity of Vera Cruz; for a considerable distance round which sandy hillocks and swampy morasses, varied by a section of dense chaparral, are the general rule. The chaparral, or natural thicket, of Mexico, is totally unlike any other thicket I have ever seen—a great portion of it being completely impenetrable. All the shrubs and trees of the dense chaparral bear clusters of thorns, sharp as the stings of bees, and as stubborn as bayonets. The various tribes of the cactus nation, with their innumerable needles—trifles in comparison to the thorns before mentioned—fill up the intervals between the thorn-bearing trees, rendering the whole a complete series of impregnable natural defences. The foregoing description applies to thick or dense chaparral, which is utterly impassable—of course, there are portions of it more open, where thorny shrubs are less frequent, and which may be traversed with ease.

We found a waggon loaded with barrels of Madeira wine in the village—it had just arrived from Jalapa, and was destined for the garrison at Vera Cruz. General Twiggs ordered the wine to be distributed amongst the men, and we each received a small measure containing about half-a-pint. General Twiggs and his officers found good quarters in the huts of the village—the different regiments bivouacking in the vicinity. In the evening a report was current that a body of lancers meant to attack us during the night, and the piquets had orders to be on the alert. The road, at the distance of about a mile from our encampment, was defended by two field-pieces, and a few trees were felled and laid across the road, but the lancers declined making their appearance.

Next day a schooner arrived loaded with provisions, saving the men a very laborious task of carrying them round from the beach. Still the duties of guards, piquets, and fatigue parties, harassed the men greatly; and many of them were soon prostrated by disease—especially with that scourge of armies on a campaign, diarrhœa. About a week after our arrival, we also got tents pitched—our regimental baggage having been brought round from Sacrificios by light sailing vessels. Our knapsacks also arrived at the same time; but the plight in which we received them, was the cause of loud and general complaint; many of them being rifled of their most valuable contents, and some completely gutted, while but a small number had escaped untouched. They had been left on the beach, at the place where we had landed, for the previous eight or ten days, during which time they had been in charge of different hordes of volunteers, who, as might have been expected, had made rather too free with their contents. But there was no help for it; and the bursting choler of many found vent in a storm of imprecations and maledictions, while the more cool and reflective only hoped they would have an opportunity of serving out a volunteer before the end of the campaign.

CHAPTER XIV.

A prophecy fulfilled—The bombardment—Visit to Vera Cruz.

A SINGULAR coincidence with the prediction of the insane sailor who came to Tampico with us in the John Potter, occurred while we lay at Vergara. This was the total loss of that brig, which, with two schooners sent round from Sacrificios with stores and provisions, was driven ashore by one of those violent north gales which blow so frequently on this coast during the winter. There being no practicable means of getting them off, without incurring more expense than they were worth, they were left to their fate; and when we returned in the summer of the following year, their upright timbers protruded from the sand, where they lay firmly imbedded. Several of our men considered the occurrence ocular demonstration of the existence of witchcraft, or some species of demonology, and some whom the march of intellect had rendered sceptical on these points had their faith in these ancient doctrines revived and confirmed.

The preparations for the bombardment of the city meanwhile went on vigorously, but many of the men appeared to think that General Scott was only losing time, and that a rush on the city at all points, to carry it by a *coup de main*, would be the only proper and effectual plan of proceeding. General Twiggs himself had been heard to express his disapproval of losing so much time, after the following manner, " Ugh! my boys 'll have to take it yet with their bayonets." As a short description of General Twiggs may not be altogether uninteresting, I will give it as it struck me at the time. In height the General is about five feet ten inches, very broad shouldered and bull-necked, and is altogether a very stout and robust-looking man, though verging on sixty years of age. His face is large and red, with blue eyes, and rather coarse and heavy-looking features; an exuberant mass of tow-white hair, with long beard, and whiskers of the same colour, give him a gruff appearance, quite in keeping with his character, in which the disagreeable and the unprepossessing are the preponderating qualities. But he was a great favourite amongst the men, who admired him principally, I believe, for his brusquerie and coarseness of manner, and a singular habit he had of swearing most vehemently, and flying into a passion on the most trifling occasions. But though General Twiggs had the most republican contempt for etiquette, and even the common courtesies of civilized life, in his intercourse with others, he was furious if a soldier happened to omit paying him the customary military salute in passing.

The erection of the batteries on the sand hills, and the conveyance of so much heavy ammunition to places convenient, was a very laborious task for our army in such a warm and exhausting climate. But all the troops took their share of the duty, each regiment working so many hours in succession, under its officers. At last, by dint of prodigious and untiring exertion, parties of our men having been employed in working day and night ever since our landing, on the 22nd of March, all being ready for operations, the town was formally summoned, and the governor having refused to surrender, the work of havoc and destruction was ordered to be commenced. For three successive days and nights, with short periods of intermission, the thunders of our guns and mortars, and the enemy's batteries in the city, were most deafening and incessant. On a height near our camp at Vergara, a number of our men frequently stood watching the shells at night; their appearance resembled that of the meteors called shooting or falling stars; and they were distinctly visible from the time when they began to ascend in their circling course until they disappeared among the roofs of the buildings. At length, on the 26th, after shot and shell to the number of seven thousand of those destructive missiles had been poured into the unfortunate city, they displayed a white flag, and after a day or two spent in negotiating, the following terms were finally agreed on. The town and castle were to be surrendered on the 29th, the garrison to march out of the central city gate and lay down their arms, and to be furnished with four days' provisions. The officers to be allowed to retain their arms, and to have five days to return to their native homes; all public property and *matériel* of war to belong to the American forces, the sick and wounded to be allowed to remain in the city, and no private property or building to be taken possession of by the Americans. On the 29th, the Mexicans, amounting to between four and five thousand, marched out of the city, and deposited their arms in front of a strong body of the American army drawn up to receive them. A brigade under General Quitman marched in and occupied the garrisons forthwith, and the American flag floated over San Juan d'Ulloa and the city of Vera Cruz.

Having procured a written permission from the officer commanding our regiment, a few days after our troops had taken possession of the city, I visited it in company with Sergeants Lear and Beebe, of ours; being curious to observe the effects of the bombardment, and also to gratify our curiosity with a view of the interior of a city which at a short distance presents a very grand and imposing appear ance. The city of Vera Cruz is very well built, the houses being of stone, and the walls of the most substantial thickness, an excellent thing in a warm climate. The streets are wide and well paved, and its general appearance is that of a clean, neat, and compactly built city. It contains a number of very handsome churches, the painted and gilt domes of which give a highly imposing effect to the view of it from a short distance. The interiors of several of these churches which we visited were highly ornamented with shrines, and all the profusion of carving, gilding, and painting, usual in these places; the most of it tawdry and vulgar-looking I imagined. One of the churches which we entered near the centre of the city, the most richly decorated we have seen, having a fine marble-paved floor, a magnificent dome, and some very good pictures, had been converted into an hospital for the wounded, and contained upwards of a hundred male patients at the time we were in it. Several shells had fallen through the dome, on the marble floor, the fragments of which had made sad mutilations of the pictures and effigies of the saints and virgins of the various shrines round the building. And what seemed to us heretics far more pitiable, though doubtless of minor importance in the eyes of a true Catholic, one of these shells had killed and wounded about twenty of the unfortunate inhabitants who had fled to its shelter as a sanctuary of safety during the bombardment. The whole of the south-west side of the city, which, lying nearest our batteries, was most exposed to the storm of destructive missiles, was a scene of desolation calculated to make the most strenuous advocates of physical force pause and reflect. For my own part, while ready to admit the whole weight and force of such powerful arguments, I felt strongly inclined to doubt the justice or propriety of having recourse to them. Whole streets were crumbled to ruins, and they told us the killed and wounded inhabitants amounted to between five and six hundred, while the soldiers who had been employed at their batteries during the whole time of the bombardment had as many more; the entire killed and wounded being over a thousand.

CHAPTER XV.

Sickness—March on Jalapa—Position of the enemy—Order to attack—The counter-order and its effect.

A GREAT deal of sickness prevailing among the troops, General Scott wisely determined to lose no time in removing the main body to Jalapa, where it was said to be his intention to wait for further reinforcements from the States. General Twiggs with his division was to march on the 7th of April, the other two divisions following in succession. As an engagement with the enemy was anticipated before we reached Jalapa, and as the means of transport were too limited to admit of our carrying much of our baggage along with us, all the heaviest of it, together with our tents, was directed to be packed up and left in the quartermaster's stores at Vera Cruz. A great number of sick were left behind, few of whom ever joined again, as most of the poor fellows soon fell victims to the unwholesome climate and the careless treatment soldiers receive in over-crowded hospitals during a campaign. Among those early victims for whom we were especially sorry, were Davies and Bob Madden, formerly mentioned, who were left behind with several more of our company, and of whose deaths we received intimation shortly after we arrived at Jalapa.

On the morning of the 7th, about seven o'clock, our division, consisting of about 3000 infantry, a light battery, consisting of two six-pounder field pieces and two twelve-pounder howitzers, and a small body of cavalry, proceeded on our march to Jalapa. For the first six or seven miles our progress was very slow and painful, the road being a loose sand, in which we sank to the ankles at every step. A great many of the men, myself among the number, were ill with diarrhœa; but being of opinion that small chance of renewed health awaited those who stayed behind in the hospitals at Vera Cruz, we were all glad to get away from it; trusting for a renewal of our exhausted vigour to the purer air of the mountains, which a few days' march would enable us to breathe. After marching about three miles, we halted at a bridge thrown over a small stream which crossed the road, and many of the men taking off their knapsacks, began to select those articles which they resolved to carry, throwing the remainder away. Numbers of them reserved only a great-coat or blanket, deliberately sacrificing the rest of their effects, and before we reached Santa Fé, a small village about eight miles from Vergara, the road was strewn with articles of clothing thrown away by the men.

We halted in the village of Santa Fé, for a short time, and General Twiggs and the officers of his staff entered a house where they sat down to rest, sheltered from the scorching heat of the sun. Some of the men in the meantime had discovered an apartment at the other end of the building, containing some barrels of aquadiente, or Mexican brandy, and an entrance having been effected, a considerable portion of the liquor had found its way into the men's canteens, before a knowledge of their proceedings had been communicated by the Mexican to the General. The anger of General Twiggs as he rushed to the scene, and the celerity with which the marauders " *vamosed the ranche,*" as they heard the ominous alarm of " here's old Davy," transcend description. Two or three of the unlucky wights, however, he met on the threshold of the door, on their way out; these he seized by the collar and swung round till he had an opportunity of administering a sound kick to their posteriors. None of them, however, stayed to remonstrate on these rather unpleasant demonstrations of the old General's love of justice, being only too happy to get out of that fix so easily, and the bugle having been ordered to sound "The Assembly," we were formed into our ranks, and the march was immediately resumed.

General Twiggs, who rode at the head of the division, committed a great error in permitting the men in front to walk too quick on this day's march. The consequence of this was that a great many of the men being weak from the effects of diarrhœa could not keep up, and slipped off the road into the thickets, which after leaving Santa Fé began to offer an inviting shade, and in which many of them lay down and deliberately resolved on staying behind the division. When we reached the place where we were to encamp for the night, a small stream about five miles from Santa Fé, the rear of the column was several miles behind, the men straggling along the road at their own discretion; and when the rolls were called at sunset, about a third of the men were absent, not having come up. We bivouacked under the trees by the roadside, the grass was deliciously soft and elastic, and, after a supper of coffee, biscuit, and pork, Nutt made us some aquadiente punch, after quaffing a bumper or two of which, we lay down, and slept very comfortably until roused by the *reveille* next morning about four o'clock.

We had warm coffee before starting in the morning, our cooks, who had no other duties to perform on a march, except cooking, always getting up sufficiently early to have coffee ready before the hour of starting. On the rolls being called this morning, there were between three and four hundred men still absent, according to current report. Although there was no great danger for these men, as they would go in small bodies, for mutual protection, and each man, besides being well armed, had three days' provisions in his havresac; yet one could scarcely help thinking that it was a strangely irregular system of marching, which, carried on to much greater extent, would have a fatally destructive effect on the discipline of an army. We marched considerably slower to-day, resting more frequently, and taking care that none of the men straggled to the rear. Our road to-day was over a level tract of country, containing some good rich soil, and for a distance of eight or ten miles we had a wood of very fine looking timber on each side of the road. Fantastic draperies and festoons of flowing creepers and vines, hung from the branches, and numerous beautiful parasitic plants climbed the trunks of trees in these woods. Many of the trees also bore magnificent flowering blossoms, and the whole air was redolent of their rich perfume. I was almost sorry when we emerged into the light and air of the open country again, though knowing it to be infinitely more healthy than the heavily-loaded and poisonous atmosphere of these delightful shades, in which, on account of their beauty, I could have lingered a little longer with pleasure.

We arrived at one o'clock, and bivouacked that night at a small stream, which had the appearance, from its broad pebbly channel, and a number of deep pools which it contained, of a river of considerable size at certain periods of the year. My comrade Nutt, and I, bathed in one of these pools, and found ourselves considerably refreshed by the operation. One of the greatest luxuries which I ever enjoyed, is bathing in a clear river after a hot and dusty day's march. On these occasions, of course one should not go in until rested and cooled a little, nor stay too long in, especially if the water is cold; but with the precautions which common sense may teach one, besides being a luxury of the highest order, I have always found it a most valuable and powerful auxiliary to health.

Some of the men who had fallen behind came up with us this evening. They said the rest of the stragglers had determined not to come up with the division for a few days. They had shot some cattle, and were plundering the houses of those who sold aquadiente of that article, as they came along; and upon the whole they seemed to be taking pretty good care of themselves; at all events these demonstrations seemed tolerably vigorous for sick and delicate persons unable to keep up with the division. Most of them came up with General Patterson's division, which was only one day's march behind us, and except a few who were killed by the peasantry, they had all joined before the battle of Cerro Gordo.

We commenced the next day's march about an hour before sunrise, as we wished to have the most of it over before the extreme heat of noon. The road was up hill, rocky, and very bad travelling for man or beast; it also lay through a barren tract of country, and water was not to be procured. Those men who had neglected to fill their canteens with water before starting, found great difficulty in procuring a drink when thirsty to-day; as the others who had been more provident, considered it sufficient hardship to carry enough for themselves. At length, about 11 o'clock, on winding down a steep hill, we came in sight of the *Puente Nacional* (National Bridge). This was the first scene since we had entered Mexico, that by its picturesque beauty called forth a spontaneous burst of admiration. "Scotland or d——n me," was the exclamation of Jock Whitelaw, a Glasgow callant, as the scene opened on his delighted vision. The precipitous banks of the river, rocky, and ornamented with tufts of flowering shrubs, shooting out from its fissures, and suggestive of broom and breckan, blue bells and heather, render the scene exceedingly like the section of a Scotch river glen. Indeed, I believe the most unimaginative Scotchman will hardly pass the National Bridge without feeling his native land suggested to memory by the similar characteristics of the scenery. The bridge is a very substantial and magnificent-looking structure, built of stone arches through which rushes the clear and rapid stream over a fine pebbly channel. We halted here a considerable time, for the purpose of allowing the men to refresh themselves with the delicious sparkling water of the *Rio Antiqua* (Old River). We then marched through a village of huts which stood on each side of the road at the end of the bridge, the walls of which were canes, and wooden poles, made into a sort of hurdles, and the roofs thatched with palm leaves. The village was shaded by some very fine mimosas, and on a plain at the end of it we encamped for the night. The weather had been fine since we left Vera Cruz, and we had suffered no inconvenience from sleeping on the grass; my health had also materially improved, a result I had anticipated from the exercise of marching, which had always agreed with me. In the afternoon, my comrade Nutt and myself went down to the river and bathed, after which we washed our shirts and stockings, which soon dried in the hot sunshine. We remarked, while going through the village, that all the huts except two or three containing a few old women and children, were empty and deserted. This was considered a proof that a force was collected at some point farther on the road, and between us and Jalapa.

We commenced our march before sunrise next morning as usual, and after a fatiguing march over a tolerably good road, but mostly up hill, and with thick woods on each side of it, which obscured the view and prevented the circulation of air, we arrived about twelve o'clock at *Plan del Rio* (The River of the Plain). At the entrance to the village, wu crossed a fine bridge of hewn stone, thrown over a broad and rapid, but shallow stream, with broken and precipitous banks, covered with a rich and luxuriant vegetation. The village, a wretched collection of huts, of similar construction to those at the National Bridge, was also deserted by its inhabitants. A party of lancers who were there when our advance guard, composed of a troop of dragoons, arrived, were very near being surprised and made prisoners. They had barely time to ride off pursued by our dragoons, with whom they exchanged a few shots, but owing to their horses being fresh, while our men's were tired with a long march, they soon increased the distance between them. These were an advanced piquet of the enemy, and we now knew that we were approaching close to their position. We encamped at the end of the village, and in the evening strong piquets were posted on the road in the direction of the enemy, ascertained to be only a few miles from Plan del Rio on the highway to Jalapa, which ascended a steep hill near the bottom of which we were encamped.

Our reconnoitring parties soon discovered that the enemy, who were in strong force, were in a position exceedingly well fortified, both by nature and art, to oppose our hitherto triumphant progress. On the highway to Jalapa, about four miles from Plan del Rio, the road enters a gorge between two heights, which the enemy had strongly fortified. About three quarters of a mile further, on the right-hand side of the road, rises the steep conical hill of Cerro Gordo, the key to the seemingly impregnable pass; as, in the event of our succeeding in forcing the other batteries, it, from its position and elevation, commanded both them and the intermediate road. This hill of Cerro Gordo, the Mexicans had also strongly fortified, and with the redoubtable Santa Anna commanding in person, and a force supposed to be at least fourteen or fifteen thousand strong, we all looked for some rather serious work, before luxuriating on the delicious fruits of Jalapa. To say that I felt no apprehension of personal danger at the prospect of an engagement likely to prove a severe one, would be ridiculous affectation; as I believe no man, possessing a particle of reflection, ever contemplated a similar position with perfect indifference. Be that, however, as it may, it seemed sufficiently evident to me on the present occasion, as well as on subsequent ones of a similar kind, that on the night before the expected engagement the camp wore an air of stillness unusual at other times, the men generally appearing more thoughtful, and conversing less, and in more subdued tones than usual.

On the evening of the 13th, General Twiggs, who, during the sickness of General Patterson, commanded the forces at Plan del Rio, after having spent two days in reconnoitring, gave the order for an attack on the enemy's batteries, which we were to take at the point of the bayonet by assault, early next morning. The bugle having sounded for the troops to assemble a little before sunset, the captains of companies addressed their men, informing them of the General's intention, and explaining as much of the plan of the meditated attack as would tend to facilitate its execution. They concluded with a hope that all would do their duty gallantly, and required us to give three cheers, an invitation which was very faintly responded to. The want of enthusiasm displayed by the men, arose, I am persuaded, from a want of confidence in the judgment of General Twiggs, and not from any deficiency of the necessary pluck required for the occasion. But that General, though always admitted to be a brave old cavalry officer, was considered, from his peculiar temperament, and previous school of education and discipline, to be totally incapable of successfully directing an operation of such magnitude as the present, which any person might easily see required both military talent and skill. Perfectly aware of the enemy's overwhelming force, and the strong nature of his position, and also of the inconsiderate rashness of General Twiggs and his advisers, we felt that we were in danger of a defeat, or a victory purchased by a lavish and useless expenditure of life. And as we knew that General Scott with a division of the army was only two days in rear, no one could perceive the least necessity for either of these alternatives; from either of them, however, we were fortunately saved.

It coming to the ears of General Patterson that an attack was ordered next morning, he immediately resumed the command of the troops by having his name erased from the sick returns. He then issued an order countermanding that of General Twiggs, and stating that all active operations against the enemy's position were suspended until the arrival of General Scott. This turn of affairs gave universal satisfaction, as General Scott deserved and possessed the confidence of both officers and men in the highest degree. We had received a pint of flour each man for our next day's bread, the biscuit having all been consumed which we had brought with us; and it was considered better to make cakes and toast them on the ashes, than to go without bread all next day. When the news of General Patterson's order came as late as 11 o'clock at night, various groups of anxious-looking faces might be seen by the flickering light of the bivouac fire, gloomily watching their unleavened cakes, and thinking bitterly of the morrow. The announcement produced one of the most sudden illuminations of the human countenance divine among these groups, which I ever recol lect to have seen; the cakes were either abandoned, or carried away half baked, to be finished at some other opportunity, and all retired to sleep, carrying the news to their dreaming comrades, that the attack was deferred until Scott came up.

CHAPTER XVI.

Arrival of General Scott—Ascent of the ravine—The charge—The loan of a pipe—Colonel Harney—General Pillow—Bill Crawford—Victory.

ON the 14th about noon, greatly to the satisfaction of us all, General Scott arrived with the rear division. We now expected that something would soon be done, and all seemed to feel a revival of confidence and anticipations of success. The gallant old General was loudly cheered on his arrival, and without waiting for rest or refreshment after his toilsome march, he immediately proceeded to reconnoitre the enemy's position. The result was the discovery of a ravine leading to the right of the enemy's batteries, by which it was resolved that the main attack should be made. At the bottom of this ravine was the celebrated hill of Cerro Gordo, of a conical form, and rising to a height of about two hundred feet from the plain. It had about a dozen brass guns, of small calibre, being principally six and nine pounders. Bounding the ravine on the left, there was another hill about as high as Cerro Gordo, the summits of the two hills being not more than half a mile distant. This hill, which General Scott determined to possess, was only covered by a piquet of the enemy, and could be easily obtained when required.

The 15th and 16th were occupied in a strict scrutiny of the enemy's works, and in removing obstacles to the passage of guns, ammunition, and troops, by cutting the obstructing trees and bushes. This was done by the pioneers, protected by a strong skirmishing party. On the evening of the 16th. we were ready for commencing serious operations.

It was a beautiful night at Plan del Rio on the 16th of April, 1847, and though on lying down to sleep one could see the lustrous stars shining in the blue canopy over head, yet we were in the "*Tierres calientes*" (the warm country), and one can sleep out of doors there very well in dry weather. Comfort, like everything else, has many degrees of comparison; for two or three nights previous we had a little more rain than was agreeable, one advantage of which was, that we now actually enjoyed a good night. "Sweet are the uses of adversity." Most of us therefore slept soundly until roused next morning from our slumbers by the reveille, which sounded about half-past four o'clock. Having taken a good breakfast of our usual camp fare—biscuit, beef, and coffee—the last meal for many a poor fellow, we prepared for the march by falling into our places in the ranks.

The division to which I belonged, consisting of about 3000 infantry, had orders to proceed under the command of General Twiggs, to take possession of the hill at the bottom of the ravine, and opposite Cerro Gordo, which General Scott had previously decided upon taking. It was covered by a piquet of the enemy whom we had orders to drive in, and retain the hill in possession, as upon it was considered to depend our best chance of success in our attack upon Cerro Gordo.

Having stowed away our knapsacks in the waggons which were left behind in the camp, with the other two divisions, we began our march up the hill. We expected to be engaged in a slight skirmish with the enemy's piquets, but did not expect to get into the thick of a regular engagement until next day. Still a sort of chill was thrown over the spirits of most of the men; jests which yesterday would have elicited roars of applausive laughter, somehow seemed to hang fire this morning; and one or two of our regimental wits being snubbed by meditative officers for talking in the ranks, gave their vocation up in disgust, and became as gloomy and as taciturn as the others. It was no great wonder either that the men were rather more reflective than usual, considering that very few of our number had ever been close in front of an enemy before, and we were approaching fortifications which we should have to carry by assault, at whatever sacrifice of life.

On coming to the head of the ravine, we were ordered to form in file, trail arms, and keep perfect silence, the staff and field officers dismounting and leading their horses. One of our men happening to stumble over a stone, and his musket making a loud clattering noise against his tin canteen, a captain rushes up to him in the utmost fury, and bawls out loud enough to be heard along the whole line, "You infernal scoundrel, I'll run you through if you don't make less noise." As Blunderbore, for that was a sobriquet the men had conferred on the captain, stood flourishing his sword in a striking and theatrical attitude, while the poor fellow seemed terrified lest he should put his threat into execution, the scene presented such a ludicrous aspect, that in spite of our proximity to the Mexican batteries, all of us within sight and hearing burst into a hearty and simultaneous laugh.

Since 7 o'clock in the morning, when we first began to ascend the hill from Plan del Rio, we had only gained three or four miles, and it was now past noon. But we had moved very slowly, every now and then halting half an hour or so, while the rifles, as skirmishers, cautiously felt the way through the chaparral in advance. The regiment to which I belonged, the 1st Artillery, was at the head of the column; we should therefore have the precedence in the series of military balls about to be offered us by the Mexicans—a distinction I dare say not much valued by ourselves, or greatly coveted by others; the post of honour is sometimes the post of danger.

It was about 2 o'clock when we heard a few musket shots in front, followed by the sharp crack of our rifles, who had got within range of the advanced line of piquets. We immediately got the word to close up, and move in quick time to the front, and in a few minutes we were at the bottom of the hill occupied by the enemy. "First Artillery and Rifles form into line, and charge up the hill," was the word of command now given by General Twiggs. "I beg pardon, General, how far shall we charge them?" I heard one of our captains ask, as we hastily scrambled up. "Charge them to h—ll," was the reply of the rough old veteran, who remained with the rest of the division at the bottom of the hill. The balls came whistling in no very pleasant manner as we made our way up the steep hill, helping ourselves occasionally by the branches of the bushes; but the Mexicans are bad shots, and besides they were afraid to expose themselves by coming forward to take deliberate aim; so that all their balls went whistling over our heads, doing us no damage whatever. In the meantime on we went, shouting and hurrahing as if we were going to some delightful entertainment, every one in a state of the highest excitement, and nearly out of breath with hurrahing and running up the steep hill, but at the same time disdaining to think of stopping to recover it.

Before we reached the top of the hill, which we did with very trifling loss, the Mexicans quickly retreated down the opposite side of it, and now were experienced the bad effects of General Twiggs's expression, "Charge them to h—ll." After obtaining possession of the hill, our object, I suspect, should have been to retain it in possession with the least possible amount of loss—General Scott having resolved to plant two twenty-four pounders on it during the night, and to open a fire early next morning on the battery at Cerro Gordo, and upon that side of the hill which he intended we should carry by assault. The summit of the hill is nearly half a mile distant from that of Cerro Gordo, and they are separated by a deep and rugged ravine. Our men were extended about half-a-mile along the face of the hill, firing upon the retreating Mexicans, with whom, in the eagerness of pursuit, we had become almost mixed up as we pursued them down the ravine. But when the enemy had got halfway up the opposite hill of Cerro Gordo, we saw the error we had committed in pursuing them, being now caught in a complete fix.

To attempt to retreat up the hill in the face of the continuous fire of some thousands of Mexican infantry, and that of their batteries, who now opened a crossfire (those to the left sweeping the side of the hill with round shot, and that of Cerro Gordo opposite pouring in volleys of grape and canister), would have been instant and total destruction. We were forced to remain therefore under the cover of rocks and trees, firing an occasional shot at the enemy only, who kept up an incessant, though fortunately for us a very ill-directed fire until near sunset. Indeed the loud and incessant roll of musketry all that afternoon, exceeded anything of the kind I ever heard. At length, towards sunset, the enemy seemed preparing for a grand charge; there was a cessation of firing nearly; we could observe their officers forming their men into the ranks, and with colours displayed, and a band of music playing in front, they at last advanced towards our position, which at that moment seemed sufficiently perilous. We had a small howitzer, of the kind called mountain howitzers, from their peculiar convenience in mountain warfare, for which they were expressly made; being light, and easily dismounted and carried up a hill. This was prepared for their reception, being well loaded with grape, and we waited with some anxiety to see its effects. On they came till near the bottom of the ravine, and within two or three hundred yards of us, when the howitzer sent its murderous contents among them. I never saw such sudden havoc and confusion caused by a single shot. It swept right into the head of the advancing column, killing and wounding a great number of those in advance, among others several of the band, who ceased playing the moment the shot struck the column, which halted almost instantly. " Arrah, more power to the hand that fired you, my jewel of a *how-its-yure;* it's yourself sure that knows how to pay the piper; that'll make you change your tune any how, you yellow pagans," cried Mickey Ryan. The Mexicans were thoroughly taken by surprise by this shot, and had quickly resolved not to risk another, for taking up their wounded they immediately began to retire to their former position. Except a straggling shot now and then, the firing on both sides soon ceased; it was getting dusk, and our men began to make their way to the main body by circling round the hill. Parties were now sent out to search for and carry in the wounded; but owing to the nature of the ground, and the darkness of the night, with a share of culpable neglect on the part of those whose duty it was to see the search more carefully prosecuted, I am afraid a number of the wounded perished, who might have recovered if they had been promptly attended to. I saw one poor fellow brought in after the battle next morning, who had been wounded and left on the field on the previous night, and who affirmed that there were groans of wounded men in all directions round him during the night.

I was witness to an incident this afternoon during the action, which for the diabolical spirit displayed by one of its actors exceeds anything of the kind I ever saw. An orderly sergeant named Armstrong, having received a wound in some part of the body, sat down seemingly in great agony. One of the men belonging to his own company came over to where he was sitting, and asked him if he was wounded; on his answering that he was, very badly, " Arrah, then may the devil cure ye, you black-hearted rascal," was the unfeeling rejoinder. The sergeant was not popular, and I believe his conduct was not calculated to inspire much sympathy for his misfortunes; but the wretch who could thus triumph in his physical sufferings and agony, must have been a fiend, and his conduct was very severely reprobated and commented on by his comrades. This diabolical spirit was engendered, by what is singularly enough called religious hatred; the sergeant having been an *Orangeman*, and the man addressing him a Roman Catholic. The sergeant died on the field that night, his watch and a purse containing some money, which he had on his person, were missing, and there were several bayonet wounds in his body. It was generally supposed that the Mexicans had killed and plundered him, as he had been left near their lines; but some did not hesitate to express their suspicions of foul play, and plainly intimated their belief that some of his own company had killed and robbed him.

When the action commenced, as we were scrambling up the hill, and while the balls were whistling rather thick in our vicinity, I felt a rather smart blow on the right temple. On the instant I imagined I had received a *quietus*, but a moment's reflection showed me that I was happily mistaken. The false alarm had arisen from the sudden recoil of a branch caused by a man a pace or two in advance, who was crushing through the brushwood, a branch of which in recoiling had struck me on the temple. The impression only lasted for a second, but I shall not soon forget the singular, and by no means pleasant, sensation caused by this simple occurrence.

Some men have blamed General Twiggs for leaving the remainder of the division inactive, while the small body sent to drive in the piquets were in such a dangerous predicament; but there I think he acted with good judgment. Had he engaged the whole division, he might have extricated the first party, but assuredly with a far greater sacrifice of life. Nothing but the paucity of our numbers, paradoxical as it may seem, saved us from a general slaughter on the occasion, enabling us to obtain the cover, of which a large body could not have equally availed themselves. The great fault which I, in common with all my comrades with whom I have conversed on the topic, think he committed, was that he did not give more explicit instructions to the officers in command of companies sent out on that occasion. Perhaps he did not clearly comprehend the instructions he had received from General Scott himself. At all events that a blunder had been made was evident, that it had cost us nearly two hundred men equally so, but no one thought of General Scott in connection with it. General Twiggs has all the credit of the first day of the battle of Cerro Gordo.

It was now dark, with a slight rain, and amidst the groans of the suffering wounded, who were having their wounds dressed, and amputations performed until late at night, the most smooth and soft piece of turf having been selected for their accommodation, tired and weary, we lay down to seek repose, and recruit our strength for the struggle of next morning. I had the bad fortune to be on a piece of ground which was full of small stones, but as we were ordered to keep our places as if in the ranks, in case of a night attack,

I could not better it by shifting my ground. Still I managed to pick up a considerable number of them, and at last I found that it was somewhat more endurable. There was not much conversation amongst us this night, but taking a few mouthfuls of biscuit, a drink of water, and a smoke, we made ourselves as comfortable as, under the circumstances, was possible. As tending to show the effect of hardship and danger in blunting that feeling of subservient humility usually shown by the private soldier to his officer, I recollect an incident that occurred in the vicinity of where I was lying. One of our lieutenants sent a sergeant to a man of the name of Rielly whom he saw smoking, with a request for a smoke of his pipe. "Arrah, sweet, is your hand in a pitcher of honey, my jewel?" said Rielly; "the lieutenant is mighty condescending. May be you would be pleased, sergeant, to inform the lieutenant, along with Rielly's compliments, that if he will wait till Rielly has his own smoke— may the holy Virgin be near us, may be it's the last smoke ever the same Rielly will take—and tell Mickey Ryan, who axed the pipe afore him, has had a turn of it, I'll not be agin lending him the pipe." "Faith ye hae sent the sergeant aff wi' a flea in his lug," said a broad-spoken countryman of mine of the name of Findlay. "Bad luck to the impidence of the rapscallions, sure it's a gag they would be after putting in my mouth in the place of a pipe, if I was to ask one of themselves for a loan of the same thing," was the rejoinder of Teddy Rielly.

There was no disguising the fact that we had an ugly job before us next morning; but we had strong ground for hope in the positive cowardice of the Mexicans, our own comparative courage, and the superlative skill of General Scott. Besides, we had come through the baptism of fire that day, and were still unhurt, and perhaps we should be equally fortunate the next.

During the night, while we slept, the guns (two twenty-four pounders, with a complement of ammunition) had with incredible exertions been got to the summit of the hill, and placed in position for opening upon Cerro Gordo next morning. A temporary breastwork of stones and earth, capable of affording considerable protection to the men who would work them, had also been thrown up. I slept most uneasily all night, being cold and sore with lying on the stones; we had left our blankets and great-coats in the baggage waggons, and it had rained a little. I was not sorry therefore that when day broke, we immediately fell into the ranks, and began to ascend the hill. Motion is highly desirable to promote circulation and supple the joints after a rather cold night on the ground, (as I frequently had an opportunity of remarking while in Mexico,) and before we were half way up the hill I began to feel rather more comfortable. As we marched by a circuitous path, some of us turned occasionally to admire the appearance of the sky, which was tinted with a surpassing brilliance by the rising sun, while spread out beneath us, as far as the eye could reach, was some of the most picturesque and romantic scenery imaginable. But we were soon recalled to another sort of contemplation. A shot from the enemy's batteries, who had now caught a glimpse of us, followed by another and another in quick succession, soon dispelled any disposition to sentimentalize which we might have previously entertained. And having been cautioned to close up and quicken our steps, in a few minutes we gained the position we were to occupy, until the signal should be given for the charge.

There was a slight hollow in the top of the hill near where our twenty-four pounders were placed, and opposite Cerro Gordo; this was the position we ought to have maintained on the previous afternoon in place of following the Mexicans so rashly. In this hollow the rifles, a regiment of infantry, and our regiment, were ordered to lie down on the grass, in which position we were completely sheltered from the fire of the enemy's batteries. While lying thus, we could watch the effects of the grape shot passing a few feet above us, with its peculiar harsh and bitter whistle, to the opposite bank, where the saplings and branches crashed, under the withering influence of these unseen messengers, as if by magic. But soon our 24-pounders opened on the Mexicans with most terrible effect, as they were in a dense mass on the top of the opposite hill, where some thousands of infantry were crowded, to repel our anticipated assault. We now received orders to prepare for a charge. While the rifles were forming in the bottom of the hollow, one end of their line had incautiously gone a little way up on the opposite bank, or side of the hill. A shower of grape, that killed and wounded at least a dozen of their number, was the result of this exposure, and a volley of oaths from Colonel Harney, at the stupidity of the officer who had formed them in that position, seemed to grate as harshly on one's ears as the missiles showering over us.

While this was going on, a division of volunteers under General Pillow, had assaulted the batteries on our left, but were repulsed with considerable loss, General Shields being amongst the severely wounded. The moment had now arrived when we were to face the horizontal shower which for the last hour and a half had been flying almost harmless over us. But the twenty-four pounders had done wonders, and Cerro Gordo was getting rather thinned of infantry by the panic created by their deadly discharges. The activity of the Mexican artillery was also rather slackened, they were evidently getting paralysed, and discouraged, at seeing the effects of our shots. Now was the time for the charge, and pausing for a few breathless moments till the next shower of grape hurtled over us, the bugle sounded the charge, and with a loud hurrah we leaped and tumbled down the ravine, opposite the enemy's battery of Cerro Gordo.

A brisk fire of infantry opened upon us as we descended, and a few of our number dropped by the way; but we were in too great a hurry to stay and assist, or sympathize with wounded men just at that time. Bill Crawford, a Scotchman, and an old British soldier, with whom I had become acquainted at Vera Cruz, was going down the hill with me; we were within a few yards of each other, when recognising me he called out, "Ha! Geordie man, hoo are ye this morning, this is gey hot wark, how d'ye like this! Faith, Geordie; I doubt they've hit me," he continued, as he sat down behind a rock, a musket ball having entered the calf of his leg. I asked him if he was badly hurt. "I've gotten a scart that'll keep me frae gaun on; but gudesake, man, dinna mind me, I've shelter here; an I ken ye'll no like to be the last o' gaun up the hill." I had just jumped down four or five feet, when a rattle of grape that splintered a ledge of rock where I had stood while talking to Bill, showed me the danger of delay. "Ah, Geordie, a miss is as gude as a mile; gude bye, tak tent o' yoursel; tell our folk where I'm sitting, when it's ower," cried the hearty old fellow, who had come through the Peninsula and Waterloo, unhurt, to be wounded in this shabby affair, as I afterwards heard him express himself. It was not long before I reached the bottom of the hill.

On arriving there, both men and officers paused, but only for a few seconds, to recover breath. Here, feeling my havresac, containing biscuit and other articles, an incumbrance, I took it off and threw it down at the foot of a large rock, intending to call again for it if I could find an opportunity after the action. We then began to climb the hill, which was very steep, but being rocky, and covered with brushwood for about two-thirds of the way, the enemy's musket balls passed quite harmlessly over us until near the top. When we arrived at the summit, a hundred or two of the Mexican infantry posted behind a breastwork of large stones, checked our advance for three or four minutes, until seeing us reinforced by a number of infantry coming up the hill cheering, they threw their muskets down, and scampered in the utmost confusion down the opposite side of the hill. Several of the enemy's guns were now manned, and fired on the retreating enemy, a disordered mass, running with panic speed down the hill, and along the road to Jalapa. The battle was now won; the other two forts, that a short time before had repulsed the volunteers, seeing the fate of Cerro Gordo, immediately pulled down their flag and hoisted a white one. They made an unconditional surrender, and the garrisons were marched out of the batteries to the road, without arms, to the amount of about 8000; they were employed to dig pits for the interment of the dead, and were afterwards permitted to go to their homes, on promising not to take up arms against the United States during the existing war.

CHAPTER XVII.

After the battle—The wounded—Mexican surgeons—The litter of dead—An unexpected regale.

GENERAL SCOTT was much censured by the men for releasing the prisoners taken at Cerro Gordo on the terms he did. It was argued that though he had no provisions, yet the road being open to Vera Cruz, a few hundred dragoons might have marched them back to that garrison, where supplies were plentiful, while the garrison left there would have been quite adequate to take charge of the prisoners. It certainly did seem rather questionable policy, as whatever were the faults of the Mexicans as soldiers, they were tolerable artillerists, and when inside of one of their formidable batteries, the only position seemingly in which they would fight, they did us a good deal of damage before we succeeded in dislodging them. Now if he had kept these prisoners, it was evident that they would either have had to man their batteries with inferior men, in which case our army would have suffered less in the subsequent engagements; or wanting the assistance of those prisoners they might have been more inclined to come to terms. The letting them go, however, was not disapproved of by the Government, though among the soldiers of our regiment it was generally condemned when talking over the policy of the campaign.

We had now leisure to reflect upon our good fortune in having succeeded so much more easily than we anticipated in our hazardous assault, and I thought I perceived a moisture glistening in the eyes, and an unusual tremor affecting the voice of many brave soldiers, as they shook hands and congratulated each other on their mutual safety. Shortly afterwards General Scott with a few of his staff came riding up, and shaking hands with all who approached, congratulated them warmly on the victory. A number of the men and officers having crowded round him, he made a short and affecting speech, as near as I can recollect in the following words: —" Brother soldiers, I am proud to call you brothers, and your country will be proud to hear of your conduct this day. Our victory has cost us the lives of a number of brave men, but they died fighting for the honour of their country. Soldiers, you have a claim on my gratitude for your conduct this day, which I will never forget." During the delivery of this short address he was on horseback, and held his hat in his hand. He was very much affected, and tears rolled over the furrowed cheeks of the majestic old hero, the sight of which caused sympathetic drops to start to the eyes of many a rough and weather-beaten countenance, " albeit unused to the melting mood." At the conclusion, he was enthusiastically cheered, when he slowly rode off, bowing, and waving his hat.

Parties of the men were now despatched in all directions, to search for and bring in the wounded. A number of the men also set out in small parties to explore for water; as the morning being very hot, most of the men were suffering exceedingly from thirst. The wounded as they were brought in were attended to as well as under the circumstances could be expected, amputations being performed, and the most urgent and dangerous cases attended to first. One or two Mexican surgeons also made their appearance, and proceeded with much apparent skill to dress and bandage the wounds of their unfortunate countrymen, in which they were assisted by our surgeons, after they had dressed all their own wounded. These Mexican surgeons are reputed to be very skilful in the treatment of wounds, which seems likely enough; as there is probably no country in the world, if we except Texas, or California, where so large an amount of practice may be found in curing wounds of all the shooting and stabbing varieties. Be that as it may, however, it was currently reported that General Shields owed his life to the skill and care of a Mexican surgeon, who undertook and completed his cure after his wound had been pronounced mortal by those of our surgeons who examined it. Our wounded being supplied with blankets, and a sufficient number of men being appointed to attend on them, they were placed under a temporary shed which at least screened them from the scorching rays of the sun. Next day they were removed to Jalapa, where a large convent near the Plaza was appropriated to their use as a hospital.

In this engagement the American loss was between 500 and 600 in killed and wounded, and the Mexicans lost probably fully as many. Between 200 and 300 bodies of dead Mexicans were collected on the field, principally on the hill of Cerro Gordo, and a great many were killed by our dragoons and light artillery, who pursued them on the Jalapa road. Some of our men obtained considerable sums of money after the battle was over, by searching the clothes of the dead; but though the practice may be in accordance with the usages of war, there always seemed something so revolting to the feelings in it, that I could never think of trying that mode of recruiting my finances, though suffering a little sometimes from a deficiency of the exchequer. Neither was I the least singular in this respect, as I learned afterwards; the feeling being quite general amongst the men, more especially amongst the Irish, who had a superstitious horror at the idea of rifling a dead body, believing that it would be sure to call down a judgment on those who would do it, in a future engagement.

Several bodies of Mexican officers who had been killed while defending the hill, lay here, one of which was said to be that of a General who had been allowed to go on parole with the rest of the garrison from Vera Cruz when it capitulated. He was near the stockades, as if he had fallen while in advanced position, encouraging the soldiers by his example. One of our men had taken off his boots; the scoundrel, I am sure, would not be able to wear them, as the officer's feet, on which he had fine white stockings, were remarkably small. His hands too were very small and delicately formed, so much so as to cause remark by almost all who looked at the body. He was an old grey-headed man, seemingly about sixty years of age, of a rather slight though active make; and there was something noble in the expression of his countenance, which was calm and placid, as if he had died without pain. He was wounded with musket balls in two or three places of the body, and as he lay "with his face to the sky, and his feet to the foe," I could not help feeling a mingled thrill of admiration and pity at the fate of the brave old hero.

There was another Mexican officer breathing his last, near a small stone building which the Mexicans had used for a magazine, and on which they had a flag when we carried the hill. He was wounded in the breast with a musket-shot, and blood was oozing from his mouth. He was a large, stout-bodied man, and from the indications of Indian blood in his colour was evidently a Mexican, and not a pure Castilian like the other. A letter taken from his pocket contained his commission, dated only a few weeks before, and signed by Santa-Anna, by which it appeared that he was Diego

Martinez, *Capitan de Infanteria.* He wore a gold chain about his neck, to which was attached a miniature picture of a very fine-looking child; we could trace no resemblance in the child's countenance to his, but then his features were distorted by pain. Poor fellow, if many of the Mexican officers had imitated his example, I believe we should not have won the battle of Cerro Gordo so easily.

We now began to suffer from the cravings of hunger and thirst; few of the men had eaten anything that morning, in fact many of them had nothing to eat, and water could not be obtained even for the wounded, who felt a perpetual craving for it. I was therefore very glad when the adjutant coming up to where a group of us were standing, asked me if I thought I could find my way to where we had bivouacked on the previous night. It occurred to me that this would be a good chance to find some water; on my way I should also pass where I had left my havresac at the foot of the hill, and where Bill Crawford was wounded, and I should see whether he had been taken care of. I therefore told him I could find my way there easily. He then gave me a message to his servant, whom he had left behind with two horses in charge, his own and the colonel's, directing him to bring them round by the village, and wait with them at the bottom of the hill, as the regiment would march down in a short time. I started on my mission, and had little difficulty in finding my havresac; it lay in the position in which I had left it, nearly covered up with the long grass. I was very glad to see it, and picking it up I threw it over my shoulders, and pursued my journey. I soon came to the place where Crawford was wounded, but he was not there, so I was satisfied that he had been taken care of. I passed the dead bodies of a great many who had been killed the day before, both Americans and Mexicans, though principally the latter. They presented a shocking spectacle; these ghastly corpses but yesterday were as full of life and animation as I was at that moment, and now there they lay with their features distorted and blackening in the sun. I felt a sickening loathing at the idea of these human sacrifices, these offerings to Mars, which the poet and the historian dignify with the titles of glorious victories, and I cursed in my heart the infatuation which had linked me to the inhuman profession of a soldier.

I soon found the groom of the horses; he was an old grey-headed man, a countryman of mine, named David Gourley, and one of the finest old fellows in the regiment. After communicating my message, I got an invitation from him to take a little breakfast before starting, and I could have the adjutant's horse, he said, to ride to the bottom of the hill. I very gladly accepted both of these offers, feeling tired and faint; the excitement of the previous afternoon and that morning, with hunger and thirst, made me feel a strong inclination to lie down under a tree and enjoy a sound sleep. Observing my appearance of weariness, Gourley pulled out a flask from his havresac, which, having tasted, he handed to me, recommending it as a sovereign cure for lowness of spirits. I took a mouthful or two from the flask, which I found contained some excellent brandy, and felt immediate benefit from the invigorating cordial. "Ay, ay," said Gourley, as I handed it back to him, "ye'll come roun' bye and bye; Lord, man, ye glowred as if ye had seen a warlock a wee sin'; faith a mouthfu' o' that might be excused to a teetotaller on a morning like this. An' hoo did ye like ye'r race up the hill this morning, Geordie?" he continued; "faith, there's mony a braw fallow that'll never turn up a wee finger again, that got up this morning as well as you or I." I told him of several men who were killed and wounded whom he knew, and mentioned Billy Crawford. He said he had seen him; that he had got his leg dressed, and had been conveyed along with some others of the wounded to Plan del Rio. Having displayed his provisions, which consisted of some biscuit, and a few slices of fried beef, to which was added the luxury of a canteen of good water, I assisted my honest old friend to dispatch a most excellent breakfast, and having taken another mouthful of brandy, I felt like a new being.

CHAPTER XVIII.

Santa Anna's leg—Distribution of spirits—Colonel Childs—Interring the dead—March to Jalapa.

MOUNTING the horses, we proceeded down the ravine to a small village on the road to Jalapa, and about a mile from Cerro Gordo. This was the place where Santa Anna had his head-quarters for several days previous to the action. The Mexicans say he was the cause of their disgraceful conduct on that occasion; as he left precipitately an hour before the storming of Cerro Gordo, by his example so discouraging the officers and men—that they soon after broke and ran, believing the battle lost—when they heard that he had gone. It was commonly said and believed by our men, that in his hurry to be off he had left his wooden leg behind, and that it was preserved and sent home to the States as a trophy. As Santa Anna wears a *cork* leg, I think it is probable that the wooden leg found there must have belonged to some less illustrious personage. But the story was turned to good account by several enterprising Yankees, who for some months after continued to exhibit veritable wooden legs of " Santa Anna" through the towns and cities of the States, with great success, making a pretty considerable speculation of it. A more important prize consisted of several chests, or boxes, containing upwards of a hundred thousand silver dollars. One of the soldiers who first discovered it, had succeeded in breaking open one of the chests, and a few of the first comers had helped themselves to a pocketful, when an officer hap pened to arrive, who put a stop to further proceedings, by placing it under a secure guard, and reporting the seizure to General Scott.

On arriving at the village, we found it full of our infantry, our whole army nearly being drawn up in column, waiting the order to march. The Mexican troops having left their provisions behind, most of our men got some refreshment here, of which the poor fellows stood much in need. But a number of the small shops in the village having been supplied with aquadiente, for the purpose of retailing it to the soldiers of the Mexican army, there was a danger of our men getting drunk. To prevent this, the aquadiente was very properly ordered to be spilt, and I saw several barrels of it emptied upon the road, an officer standing by to see it effectually done. We also passed some companies where the officers were superintending the distribution of a portion of it, by seeing the sergeant serve the men with a glass of it in succession; this was a most judicious proceeding, which I am sure the men would appreciate. If officers were more generally aware what a large return of popularity they might secure among their men by ministering to the wants and comfort of those under their charge, I believe it would do much towards improving the condition of the army.

But in spite of every precaution, a number of the men I could see had got their canteens filled with the liquor, which had cost them nothing; all the houses in the village being robbed of their supplies of provisions and liquor in a very short time. A jolly fellow, belonging to an infantry regiment, came up to Gourley and me, and asked if we would drink the health of General Scott, handing us his canteen, which was full of aquadiente. We tasted his liquor, which was very fiery and unpalatable, when he very generously gave us a few *tortillas*, thin cakes made of Indian corn meal, and a piece of cheese, of which commodities he had a havresac nearly full. He advised us to dismount and have our canteens filled with the aquadiente, offering to show us where we could get it; but not wishing to quit our horses, for fear of losing them in the crowd, and the liquor, to judge from the specimen we had just tasted, not being very palatable, we declined his invitation.

After leaving the village, and as we passed on to the bottom of the hill of Cerro Gordo, we found the road strewed with the muskets and bayonets which the Mexicans had thrown away in their hasty retreat. These muskets were all of British manufacture, and had the *Tower* mark on their locks; but they were old and worn out, having evidently been condemned as unserviceable in the British army, and then sold to the Mexicans at a low price. Undoubtedly they were good enough for soldiers like the Mexicans, who generally throw them away on their retreat, but after examining a few of them I came to the conclusion that for efficient service one of our muskets was equal to at least three of them. Some thousands of these muskets were collected and destroyed, and the guns taken at the different forts were also burst and rendered unfit for use, by the men left behind for that purpose under the direction of an engineer officer. A great number of dead Mexicans, whose bodies had been collected for the purpose of interment, lay at the bottom of the hill. Among these we observed the body of a young and handsome though coarsely attired female, apparently not more than eighteen years of age. She had been the wife of one of the soldiers, and had stayed with him during the action. Perhaps they were newly married, and had been spending their honeymoon amid the horrid din of war. One could scarcely help wondering which among that group of ghastly corpses had been her husband. For among them he must be; it were impossible to picture him flying on the road to Jalapa, and leaving behind the bleeding corpse of his young and beautiful bride. The wives of the Mexican soldiers are in the habit of following the army, and sharing in the fatigues and dangers of a campaign, and there were several of them among the killed and wounded, both at this and at subsequent engagements. I was told of one woman who was wounded in the leg at this battle, who displayed a great deal of reluctance in allowing our surgeon to examine and dress the wound, though such extreme feelings of modesty, I am bound to acknowledge, are exceedingly rare among the women of the lower classes in Mexico.

Leaving Gourley at the bottom of the hill with the horses, I now proceeded to inform the adjutant that I had performed my mission. I found him seated on the ground, with Colonel Childs and several of the officers, and was proceeding to make my statement, when the colonel, interrupting me, exclaimed, "But where are the horses?" I told him I had got instructions from the adjutant to leave them at the bottom of the hill. The adjutant confirmed my statement, and appeared to think I had done very well; but still the colonel continued to mutter his dissatisfaction at my having obeyed the instructions too literally. I inwardly smiled at the unreasonable humour of the colonel, but at times like the present, when human life seems of about as much value as an old shoe, the humours of your big men seem mere trivialities; and luckily for my equanimity, just at that time, I felt a most sovereign contempt for the good or bad opinion of breathing mortal, myself excepted. Besides having satisfactorily obeyed my instructions, I had made an excellent breakfast, and found my havresac. With these results I felt very well satisfied; and if the colonel was not pleased, why, he might whistle on his thumb.

About two or three o'clock our regiment was directed to join the main body of the army, which had received orders to proceed towards Jalapa. According to instructions, one company of our regiment was left to assist in the interment of the dead, and the destruction of the guns and ammunition not considered requisite for the use of our own army. The regiment then descended the hill of Cerro Gordo, and having taken its place in the column, we were soon marching along the highway to Jalapa. A great quantity of clothing abandoned by the Mexicans strewed the road, and as many of our men had neither great-coat nor blanket, having left them in the baggage waggons at Plan del Rio, they eagerly appropriated those which the Mexicans had thrown away. But they soon discovered that they had made a most miserable prize, few or none of these clothes being wholly free from a tormenting and disgusting species of vermin to which the Mexicans seem universally accustomed and reconciled. Most of the men, on discovering the condition of these clothes, threw them away, but a number retained possession of some of them; and from that period until after we entered the city of Mexico, even those most scrupulously attentive to personal cleanliness could not wholly divest themselves from that most annoying and detestable of the plagues of Egypt. After entering the city, we were supplied with new clothing, and being in tolerable quarters, and furnished with a plentiful supply of soap and clean water, we succeeded after a time in eradicating the abominable pest. We only marched about eight miles that evening, bivouacking on the grass plats that stretched along on each side of the road. A small stream of clear water which the Mexicans had conducted a distance of ten miles, by cutting a channel for it along the edge of the road, to supply the garrison at Cerro

9*

Gordo, supplied our evening beverage, and as we were tired with the excitement and fatigues of the day, we were soon folded in the arms of Morpheus.

CHAPTER XIX.

Santa Anna's house—Aspect of the country—The ladies of Jalapa—
A Mexican funeral—Description of the city—The priesthood—
Procession of the Host—Paying the troops.

ROUSED from our sound slumbers by the bugle at daybreak next morning, we were soon on our march again for Jalapa. After marching a few miles we came to Encerro, the favourite residence of Santa Anna, who owns a large and fertile tract in that neighbourhood. The house in which he had formerly lived—called by our men *Santa Anna's House*— is a large plain building on the side of a hill, about a mile from the road, and on the left hand going to Jalapa. Its situation is admirable, the view of the surrounding country being of the most delightful character, wooded mountains and grassy plain stretching away as far as the eye can reach. But water, that principal auxiliary to fine landscape scenery, it lacks in common with most Mexican scenery. True, a rivulet crosses the highway at Encerro about the size of a Scotch burn, which leaps and tumbles in a series of sparkling cascades down a romantic and deep rocky glen on the right hand ; but any rivulet or sheet of water large enough to give a tone to the extended landscape, one may look for in vain in that portion of the country that lies between Vera Cruz and the city of Mexico.

We experienced no interruption from the Mexicans on our march ; indeed it would have been strange if we had, considering their contemptible defence of Cerro Gordo. The appearance of the country as we approached within a few miles of Jalapa, seemed one continuous garden, teeming with the richest luxuriance of tropical vegetation. The mountain of Orizaba, with its dazzling white and clear cold summit piercing the blue cerulean, seemed within a few miles of us, though in reality we were about twenty-five miles distant. This effect was produced by the remarkable purity and clearness of the atmosphere, and the sun shining upon the snow with which it is always covered. The town of Jalapa is four thousand feet above the level of the sea, and is situated on the side of a hill. It is embraced by an amphitheatre of wooded mountains, which rise immediately behind it to the height of several thousand feet; but in front, looking towards Vera Cruz, there is an open view of the sea coast, and in fine clear weather the ships may be seen in the harbour at Vera Cruz with an ordinary spy-glass.

As we entered Jalapa, the windows and balconies were crowded with females, white, yellow, and brown; the youthful and fair portion of whom, we were quite willing to imagine, surveyed our appearance with sparkling glances of admiration and applause. As for the spiteful and vindictive looks of the old and the ugly, why that was perfectly natural. Old age and ugliness in Mexico are the firm allies of bigotry and superstition, and we were no favourites with holy mother church, who would willingly have consigned the whole tribe of heretico-Americanos to a far hotter climate than Mexico.

We marched through some of the principal streets by a circuitous route to the barracks which the Mexican soldiers had formerly occupied, a large substantial building, the apartments of which were excessively dirty. Several regiments of infantry, with the Rifles and 1st Artillery, were crowded into these quarters, which were too small to contain one half of them with anything like comfort: and at night many of the men brought out their blankets, and lay down on the cold paving stones in the open square, in preference to sleeping inside. Indeed, it was exceedingly disagreeable to sleep in these rooms, as they were utterly dark, and the floor being completely covered with men lying rolled up in their blankets, if one got up in the night time and tried to reach the door, he was sure to stumble over and awake some of his sleeping comrades. A number of the men who lay there had also received slight wounds, and when any person happened to touch one of them the cursing and swearing that usually ensued, awoke all in the room. But as we were now four thousand feet above the level of the sea, having left the *tierra caliente* at least a day's march behind us, this exposure to the cold and damp night air gave colds and other diseases to many of those who slept in the square, some of which terminated fatally. The volunteers were marched to a camp-ground about three miles from town, where in consequence of the heavy rains at night, which had then set in, and having no tents along with them, their condition was most deplorable. A great deal of sickness and mortality immediately ensued among the volunteers—the natural and inevitable consequence of this unfortunate predicament, which severely shook the hardiest of the half horse and half alligator breed, and made short work with those whose constitutions were of merely human organization. The desire of General Scott to conciliate the inhabitants of Jalapa, who, though friendly to the Americans, yet dreaded the presence of a large body of volunteers in the town, was the cause commonly assigned for the arrangement by which the volunteers were sent out to the camp. But I think a sufficiently obvious cause was the absence of buildings in the town capable of containing both them and us; seeing which, I suspect, there could be little hesitation about which of the two parties it was proper to send away, and which to retain as a garrison. A few days after our arrival, there was a proper arrangement of the troops, and they were distributed to different parts of the town. Our regiment found quarters in a large building at the corner of the *Plaza Nacional.*

About a week after our arrival I was sent, with a party of men, to dig graves for six of our own deceased comrades, who had died in consequence of wounds received in the late action at Cerro Gordo. In digging these graves we remarked, though we dug up a number of skulls and bones of the human skeleton, that there was not a fragment of a coffin visible. From this circumstance we inferred that the poorer classes, in this part of Mexico, dispense with coffins in burying their dead. This, I have since heard, is the case, and the funeral of a Mexican child which we met shortly after we left the burying-ground, tends to confirm the opinion. The corpse of the child was laid upon a board which a Mexican peasant carried in his hand. Its feet and hands were tied with ribbons, the hands joined over the breast, and pointing upwards in the attitude of prayer. Its hair was interwoven with flowers, with which also the body was profusely decorated. The whole of the funeral party consisted of the bearer and two women who accompanied him.

Soon after our arrival in Jalapa the mortality among the troops increased to a frightful extent, and the obvious fact that all was not done, that under the circumstance could have been done, for the comfort and alleviation of the sufferings of the sick, rendered the condition of the hospital a painful subject of reflection to those whose constitutions had yet resisted the approach of disease. Some allowance must be made for the imperfect state of order inseparable from a campaign, but after every liberal deduction that charity can suggest, there will still remain a large amount of blame to be awarded somewhere for the state of things then existing in the hospital at Jalapa. I passed through it several times, having been sent there on various duties, and the scenes which I saw there gave me the most painful and shocking impressions of any which I observed during the whole campaign. Sick men, some of whom were wounded, and others wasted to skeletons with diarrhœa, and in the last stage of illness, lay on a thin piece of matting or a dirty doubled-up blanket, on the cold and hard brick floor. Many of them had on shirts which they had evidently worn for weeks, and I was told by some of the patients that nearly all of them were infested with vermin. Their diet was bread and coffee, which few of them could eat; indeed a more unsuitable diet could scarcely have been chosen. I should be sorry to attach blame to any person in particular for this notoriously bad management, but I can scarce help thinking, that as a considerable sum of money had been seized at Cerro Gordo, a large portion of it might have been very beneficially employed in remedying these evils. At least clean and comfortable bedding might have been furnished to the patients, who might also have had their linen washed. There was abundance of soap and water in Jalapa, and hundreds of poor women who would have been very glad of the employment. It seems strange that such an idea never suggested itself to any person competent to have it carried into effect. I know that among the soldiers of our company, who discussed the matter frequently, the remedy always appeared as simple and easy of execution as desirable.

The town of Jalapa, from which (by the by) the medicinal plant *jalapa*, which grows extensively in that district, takes its name, is an exceedingly pleasing specimen of a Mexican town. Besides the natural advantages of the rich soil and fine climate of the neighbourhood, and its admirably pictu resque situation, there is an air of cleanliness, industry, and comfort about the poorer classes of the inhabitants, both in their personal appearance and in that of their houses, rather unusual to see in Mexico. The houses are mostly one story, and at most two stories high, and their thick walls, built of stone, are nicely white-washed, contrasting beautifully with the deep verdure of the luxuriant vegetation everywhere seen. Orchards, gardens, and green and shady lanes, where creeping vines trail their tendrils, blossoms, and flowers in wild and graceful profusion over the walls and fences, intersect all parts of the town, except a few streets in the centre. It is well supplied with good water, conducted from the neighbouring hills, and in every quarter of the town are commodious washing-sheds for the use of the public. These sheds are supported on stone pillars, and have rather an ornamental appearance. Tubs are dispensed with in them entirely; a range of separate washing places, made of smooth tiles, and running the whole length of the building, supplying their place. All the linen of the town is washed at these places, no one ever thinking of washing at home, and there a number of women and girls may be seen washing from morning till night, singing, chatting, and laughing the while, as only cheerful health and industry can make people. Any person who thinks the Mexicans cannot be industrious should see these girls washing in Jalapa.

A great many wealthy old Spanish families reside in Jalapa, and the beauty of the *senoritas* (young ladies) of that pleasant little town was generally admitted by the young Americans to equal at least, if not to surpass, the beauties of the States. Groups of these senoritas, from sixteen years of age and upwards, might be seen standing in the balconies that front their windows in the cool evenings, chatting, laughing, and smoking the cigarito. The long, lustrous black hair and clear rich brown of her complexion, the roguish twinkle of her dark eyes, and in spite of her indulging in an occasional cigarito, the pearly hue of her admirable teeth, seen to excellent advantage as you listen to the silver tones of her delightful laugh, render the senorita of Mexico rather interesting. In fact, I believe the Mexican girl, or senorita, has the most musical laugh of any in the world. There is an absolute magic in it, and I would defy an anchorite to hear it without feeling a sympathetic twitch of his risible organs, its pure heart-easing mirth, and ringing melody, carrying all before it as triumphantly and irresistibly as the notes of the famous world-enchantress Jenny Lind. If we add to these, that peculiar Nora Creina-like ease and natural grace of motion and gesture which distinguish the Mexican females, probably the result of their emancipation from those ingenious instruments of female torture still in use among half-civilized nations, called corsets, it will be at once conceded that their claims to several of the attributes of beauty are by no means contemptible.

The principal church stands at the corner of the *Grande Plaza*, and is a strange, quaint-looking, but massive and strong old building. It is a large church, and the interior is very richly and gaudily decorated, with the usual paraphernalia of these churches, of which there are three or four more in the town. Mass is performed in this principal one, and in one or two of the others every day. But it seems to be almost wholly for the benefit of females on working days, as I have frequently observed, when the congregation was coming out, that there was scarcely a single man to be seen, and certainly not one in ten were of the male sex.

The market is held in the Plaza, a large open paved square in the centre of the town, every morning; Sunday, as in all Mexican towns, being the principal market. It commences about six in the morning, and is usually over about three or four in the afternoon. Fruit and vegetables are the principal articles sold, and these are very cheap. Fowls and eggs were also tolerably cheap when we arrived; a good fowl being sold for two reals, or a shilling, and a dozen of eggs for one real; but a rapid rise in prices took place soon after the troops entered the town. The *alcalde*, an honest old fellow, who, I dare say, never had heard of political economy, and the law of supply and demand, was perfectly shocked at the extortion practised on the soldiers by the vendors of commodities. He endeavoured to bring back the prices to what they were before our arrival, by publishing an edict fixing the price of articles; but it was of no practical effect, as they easily found means to evade it.

The number of priests one sees in the streets of this small town is astonishing. Many of them are Mexicans of the lower class, that is half Indian caste, and these are generally of most forbidding aspect, having the oblique, sinister eye, and " forehead villanous low," of the Indian, and a complexion tallowish and singularly disagreeable. I could scarcely help fancying sometimes, when I have suddenly met one of these hooded monks, that there lurked a twinkle of the unholy fire from that "light of other days," the *auto da fé*, in the scowl which he threw from under his beetle brow on the *heretico Americano*. Indeed I believe the majority of them would have considered a little religious roasting only a fair *quid pro quo* for the sound basting the Americans were giving their countrymen, and which threatened serious damage to the monopoly of religion which the Virgin and her cowled and hooded ministry enjoyed in Mexico.

Shortly after our arrival in Jalapa, General Scott, who was anxious to place his army in winter quarters, as the rainy season was commencing, proceeded with the main body of the army to Puebla, leaving Colonel Childs, of our regiment, governor of Jalapa, with a garrison of about a thousand effective men, of which our regiment formed a part. The garrison and sick left behind at Vera Cruz, the discharge of a regiment of volunteers whose term of service had expired, and the great number of sick in hospital, with the killed and wounded in the late action, had reduced our effective strength more than half, and we were now a very insignificant force for active operations. But as the rainy season continues for two or three months at this period of the year, during which it would be folly to bring an army into the field, we should have time to wait for reinforcements.

Shortly after our arrival at Jalapa, the secretary of war, under the direction of the President, I suppose, sent instructions to General Scott, to commence taking provisions and forage for the subsistence of his troops wherever he could find them, without paying for the same. This they called making the war support itself, and said it was the only way to make the Mexican people anxious to end it, by making them feel its burden. With these most stupid and atrocious instructions, acting with sound policy, as well as from motives of justice and humanity, General Scott in the most explicit and decided terms refused to comply. He declared in his reply to the Secretary, that he would pay, or pledge the credit of the American Government for every cent's worth of produce which the Mexicans should furnish the army while under his command. The good consequences of this just and honourable conduct were felt throughout the subsequent part of the campaign in the comparative ease with which we found supplies of all descriptions; and to the mild and mitigated form which the war assumed under this system, as compared with that to which another course would have led, the speedy and favourable conclusion of the war may be partly attributed.

Colonel Childs, the governor of the town, with a view, I suppose, to conciliate the priests and inhabitants of Jalapa, had consented to take a part in a procession of the host. This caused a good deal of grumbling among a regiment of Pennsylvania volunteers, who lay here at the time, and who were loud in their denunciations of his conduct, considering it a complete compromise of the national honour. One evening a procession of the host going to the house of a sick grandee, a number of chanting friars and priests, drawling Latin hymns, and ringing bells, each with a thick wax candle, lighted, in his hand, and all bareheaded, and in black or white gowns, were seen issuing from the church door into the street. There were about a hundred priests, and a number of boys in surplices, carrying pots of incense. In the midst of this procession, Colonel Childs, Captain Burke, and Lieutenants Brannan and Hoffman, of the first artillery, made their appearance, dressed in full uniforms, each carrying a lighted wax taper in one hand and his cap in the other. The whole affair, as a matter of taste, was simply absurd; as a matter of policy, questionable. One can hardly imagine that the Mexicans would be so easily gulled as to believe that the officers cared a farthing for the ceremonies they were engaged in. It was more probable that the parties most inimical to us would construe the desire to conciliate them into a distrust of our own resources, which might strengthen their presumption and resistance to the just demands of America. However, had the display been limited to an exhibition of himself, and the subordinates who attended him on the occasion, I believe no one would have thought it worth more than a passing laugh; but unfortunately this was not the case. The officer commanding the main guard, had received orders to have the guard under arms, and on the approach of the procession to cause them to present arms, and then kneel with their muskets in the left hands, and their caps in the right, until the procession had passed. To the credit of the volunteers who formed about two thirds of the guard, they refused to obey this absurd order, which was luckily not insisted on, or the consequences might have been serious. As for the portion of the regular soldiers who were upon guard, they performed their part of the ceremony without hesitation, evidently considering it a piece of foolish enough drill, and nothing more. The officer of the guard was a sensible fellow, and deserves credit for not rigidly enforcing the obedience of the volunteers, and indeed it is probable that he saw the absurdity and unconstitutional nature of the proceeding. But it was a great blunder for Colonel Childs to issue an order of such a nature, and had it led to serious consequences, as with a blundering headstrong officer on guard, it most likely would have done, he would have incurred a heavy responsibility.

About the latter end of May, we received four months' pay. This had been very much wanted for some time; and for the last month especially, the men had grumbled loudly at the long delay of the paymaster. The long periods that elapsed between the payments of the army while in Mexico was a serious grievance, causing much suffering and dissatisfaction. Soldiers are exceedingly improvident, and many of them, indeed the far greatest number of them—squander their pay, of which they receive two months at once, in a few days, or weeks at farthest. Sometimes they are not paid for a period of four months, as in the present instance, when a private receives twenty-four dollars, about five pounds. This produces a short saturnalia succeeded by months of destitution, during which a soldier feels the want of a number of those little comforts and luxuries, which habit has converted into necessaries, most acutely. Tobacco to those who are habitual users of it, as nine tenths of the soldiers are, or a glass of spirits when cold or wet in camp, or on a march, and without the means of getting dried or warmed, these are not only harmless luxuries, but necessary restoratives in many cases. Such apparent trifles as these are essential to the comfort of most soldiers, and render endurable the thousand petty annoyances and discomforts of a life full of hardships; and for want of these, or the means of obtaining them, I have seen soldiers become gloomy, irritable, and even disobedient and mutinous. As a means of preventing these results, consequent on the payment of two or four months' pay at a time, an excellent remedy might be found in giving each soldier a small sum weekly through the medium of his captain, which might be charged on the monthly pay roll.

CHAPTER XX.

Departure from Jalapa—Deserters—On the march—Captain Walker—Perote—Tepe Agualco—Puebla.

ABOUT the middle of June, a large reinforcement under the command of General Cadwallader having arrived at Jalapa, according to the instructions which Colonel Childs had received, we had orders to prepare for a march to join the main body, then quartered in Puebla. The lieutenant who commanded the company to which I belonged, had, shortly before this, been promoted to a captaincy in another company. We had got as our captain, when he left, a dashing sort of fellow called Captain Magruder, who being particularly distinguished for his skill in light artillery manœuvres, got charge of two twelve-pounder guns; our company was thus converted into horse artillery, and had charge of a battery. We therefore gave our muskets into the charge of the ordnance department, and received in exchange about forty of the quartermaster's best horses, for which a number of Mexican saddlers were immediately employed in altering and fitting harness, and in a few days we were fully equipped as mounted artillery. Our battery, which was principally got up for the purpose of being used on the march, as it was expected that the enemy would oppose us at some of the mountain passes between Jalapa and Puebla, consisted of two twelve-pounder brass guns, and a small brass howitzer. It having been General Scott's instructions to evacuate Jalapa and join head-quarters at Puebla, with the next reinforcement, all the sick who were able to bear the journey were to be conveyed in waggons to the castle of Perote. The authorities of Jalapa had humanely undertaken the care of those too ill to be removed, a charge which we afterwards learned they most faithfully and honourably fulfilled.

On the 25th of June we commenced our march, but only proceeded to a plain called the Camp ground, where the volunteers lay before leaving for Puebla. It is about three miles out of the town on the road to Perote; there we pitched our tents and encamped for the night. The train which arrived with Cadwallader had brought our tents from Vera Cruz; as it would have been impossible for an army to encamp on the table lands without tents, owing to the coldness of the nights. For some time before we left Jalapa the emissaries of the Mexican Government had been busy tampering with the soldiers of our army, holding out large promises of preferment and distinction to any of our men who would join their army, and giving them money and liquor as earnest of a future higher reward. Unfortunately for their dupes, they were only too successful, and a great many of our men stayed behind. This result was also partly occasioned by the foolish and tyrannical conduct of a number of the young officers of the American service, who abused their authority greatly, and who were not sufficiently checked by the senior officers of the service. Out of the company to which I belonged ten deserted, more than an eighth of our entire company, which was not eighty strong at the time. I cannot say for its correctness, but it was currently rumoured, and I think it highly probable, that there were between two and three hundred desertions from our army while we lay at Jalapa.

The ground where we encamped was a fine grassy plain, and near it ran a stream of pure water; it was capable of affording accommodation for an army, being several miles in extent. Our guns were placed in front of our tents at a convenient distance, and the picket rope having been stretched between the caissons extended for the purpose, our horses were fastened to it for the night. It rained a good deal during the night as usual; for during the rainy season in this part of Mexico a heavy fall of rain, often accompanied by thunder and lightning, usually takes place every afternoon or evening, and continues during the greater part of the night, the mornings and fore part of the day being invariably bright and clear.

We were roused by the bugle sounding the stable call in front of our tents at half-past three o'clock in the morning; I mean our company, for the remainder of the division did not get up for an hour and a half after that. One of the evils of having horses on a march, is that you have to get up considerably earlier than the rest of the division, as you have to rub down your horses, take them to water, and harness and feed them. But still there are advantages to be derived from them which more than counterbalance any slight trouble they may occasion. Just imagine the difference of getting yourself carried, in place of carrying a musket and knapsack, and limping along tired and foot-sore, after a long day's march, as an infantry soldier. In the evening, after a long day's march, while the infantry soldier feels every joint aching and can hardly drag his tired limbs round the camp, the soldier who has been riding all the day finds it a pleasant and relaxing exercise to rub down and curry his horse, ride him to water, and carry him his forage. Indeed, I believe it would take a great deal to tempt a man who knows the difference of campaigning as a dragoon or light artillery-man, to change situation with a soldier belonging to an infantry regiment. But very few of our men thought so then I dare say, and as many of them knew nothing about the management of horses, they thought it a great bore to have anything to do with them. For my own part, I must confess that this was the case with myself at the time. I had only been on a horse's back two or three times in my life, and that more than twenty years before; the plain fact being, that I knew as much about a horse as a horse knew about me. But one of our sergeants was sick, and I being the senior corporal, was furnished with a tall grey charger, and compelled to take his place. However, my gallant grey was a very quiet sort of animal, and too generous to take advantage of my ignorance in the noble art of horsemanship, which I have not the least doubt his sagacious penetration was not long in discovering. In fact, I could almost imagine sometimes, from the peculiarly sly and humorous expression of his eye as he observed my want of tact in the arrangement of his furniture, that he was indulging in an inward chuckle at my awkwardness, though too well mannered to break out into a loud horse-laugh to my face. Still we got along very well together, and before the end of the march I felt quite satisfied that I performed the various duties of a groom very much to his satisfaction.

Our second day's march was nearly all up hill, and to drag our heavy guns and caissons was killing work for the poor horses. About two o'clock we reached a stream of water and a convenient camp ground, where we pitched our tents for the night; strong pickets being sent out to guard against night surprise by the enemy. We had scarcely pitched our tents when the rain began to fall in torrents, and as we had to unharness and water our horses, and afterwards go to a barley field and cut a supply of forage for them, we were thoroughly drenched. A most providential discovery having been made of a large quantity of aquadiente in a distillery which stood in the immediate vicinity of the camp, General Cadwallader immediately ordered its distribution among the men, and each man received a gill of it. This was an excellent preventive to the bad effects of the cold and wet, and General Cadwallader was unanimously voted a Christian. The distillery also contained a large quantity of brown lump sugar, and several tons of it were carried off in our waggons. About two hundred pounds of it were put into a barrel by a man belonging to our company, and thrown into one of our waggons; our men were allowed to use as much of it as they pleased, and I believe many of them hurt themselves by using it immoderately. It continued to rain all night, but was dry before we got up to attend to our horses. The morning turned out very fine, and we had breakfast and were all ready for marching at six o'clock.

We began our march between six and seven o'clock, and as an attack was threatened at the pass La Hoya which we were approaching, we moved slowly, halting half an hour or an hour occasionally, while a party of dragoons were sent forward to reconnoitre. On these occasions we had leisure to admire some very fine scenery, one of these views I think the finest I have seen in Mexico. From the right of the road there is a deep green valley, which descends abruptly, stretching away a long distance, until bounded by a lofty and perpendicular wall of bare rock. From the edge of this rock and along its summit a large plain extends, cultivated in wheat and barley, and dotted with *haciendas*. On the plain and near the precipitous wall, we could see the spires and white buildings of a good-sized town. A river which flowed along the plain at the summit, passed near the town, and then fell dashing and sparkling over the sheer precipice into the deep green valley beneath. The whole was seen distinctly, and yet sufficiently distant to be taken in by the eye at one view. It was truly a glorious sight, and though not so magnificent as the views in the neighbourhood of Puebla and Mexico, yet it was more pleasingly romantic, and just the sort of smiling scene calculated to make one wish he could pass the remainder of his days near it.

We halted near evening at a camp ground, surrounded by a complete amphitheatre of hills. It was a fine level grassy bottom, with a clear stream at one end of it, and a large wooden trough in the centre, which had probably been erected by the Government for the use of cavalry on the march. It rained this evening as usual; and as the enemy, several thousand strong, were known to be in the neighbourhood, pickets had to cover all the adjacent heights to guard against a night surprise. These poor fellows, after marching all day, and so tired that they were incapable of keeping up the circulation of the blood by motion and exercise, had to be out all night in the cold and wet. We were now at an elevation of about 7000 feet above the level of the sea, nearly twice the height of Ben Lomond, the highest hill in Scotland, and the nights were very cold. After all, it is no wonder that the mortality is so great in an army during a campaign, when one considers the constant exposure to extremes of heat, cold, and fatigue, to which the soldier is subjected, and the hunger and thirst he has frequently to endure, or the bad quality of the food or water he is sometimes glad to use. It cleared up about the middle of the night, and when we rose in the morning there was hoar frost on the ground.

We had the most dangerous part of the pass to go through, and we had orders to keep our slow matches burning in the linstocks, and be ready for instant action. Our road for the first few miles was over an ascending tract of broken lava, presenting the most singularly irregular surface of a country imaginable. On each side of the road huge masses of lava stood at intervals like gigantic pillars. Between these, and covering the whole surface of the ground, broken lava was strewn, with a crumbled sort of appearance, as if it had covered the ground in one vast sheet, and cracked into fragments by the process of cooling. If lava is contractile and expansive, like the metals, perhaps the intense heat of the sun by day and the cold frosts at night might partly account for the appearance of the crumbled portions. A great variety of cactuses, which, like the eccentric and jolly Mark Tapley, of the Blue Dragon, never seem to come out so strong and vigorously as when struggling with difficulties of situation, sprang up between the crevices of the rocks, and a few dwarf aloes and stunted pines endeavoured to gain a footing here and there. A wild and rugged range of hills covered with pine trees, bounded the road on the left; and in the hollows and ravines of these the enemy were supposed to be concealed, waiting a favourable moment for an attack. When we had travelled about four or five miles, a small body of the enemy were discovered about half a mile off, on the side of the hill. The division was halted, and our guns being unlimbered, and brought to bear on them, we fired several shots, when we could see their white dresses gliding among the green trees and bushes, in all directions, reminding us of a flock of scared wild fowl. At some of the points which had the most suspicious appearance, and presented a good point of attack for an enemy bold enough to avail himself of the advantage, companies were sent out as skirmishers, but the enemy kept cautiously out of sight.

About ten o'clock we met Captain Walker and his dragoons. He had received information that a force had been collected with the design of attacking us, and had come out from Perote to our assistance. He left Perote on the preceding evening, and being conducted by a Mexican spy to a place where a large body of the enemy were assembled, he routed them in the utmost confusion, his dragoons cutting down a great many with their sabres. We arrived at a village a little beyond the pass, about seven miles from Perote, which was said to belong to Canales, a Mexican general, known to be a most bitter enemy of the Americans. The village was completely deserted by its inhabitants, and as they were considered to form part of the guerilla force assembled to oppose us, it was set on fire and burned to the ground.

Captain Walker and his dragoons were much feared and hated by the Mexicans in the neighbourhood of Perote. They had the duty assigned them of hunting out and routing the bands of guerillas who infested that neighbourhood, and as might be expected from troops on a service of that nature, were said to commit actions at times that would scarcely bear a strict examination. It is reported that Captain Walker frequently told his men that he wished them to bring in no prisoners; the inference which his men were certain to draw from this hint may be easily conceived. But one of the great evils of guerilla warfare is, that it necessarily, by the process of retaliation which it induces, ends in a dishonourable and savage system of inhuman butchery and fiendish assassination. Captain Walker, a Texan, with his father and two brothers, had been taken prisoners by the Mexicans in some foray which they had made on the Mexican frontiers, a few years before the breaking out of the present war. With a large body of American prisoners taken at the same time, they were confined in the dungeons of the castle of Perote, where a number of them soon died of the bad treatment they received. A proportion of their number were ordered by the Mexican Government to be shot, the victims being indicated by drawing lots. Captain Walker's father and brother were among those shot on the occasion, and it is said that he then resolved to pursue the Mexicans with relentless revenge on every practicable opportunity. He obtained his release some time after, with the remaining prisoners, and on the breaking out of the present war, having obtained the command of a body of volunteer dragoons, raised in Texas, and called Texan Rangers, he returned to fulfil his resolution, and pour out the vials of his wrath on the wretched peasantry. He was killed at a battle fought at a place called Huamantla, near Puebla, about four or five months after this.

From the pass Los Vigas, the country begins to exhibit signs of cultivation, and we soon reached an extensive plain where we had a view of the town and castle of Perote. Large fields of barley and wheat, then ripe and yellow, extended for miles over the plain, with not a sign of an enclosure or a division, and the rugged hills on the left were cultivated, in some parts, half way up their sloping sides. The insulated mountain of Pizarro, a vast mass of rock, terminating in a lofty cone, rises in the plain, about a distance of eight miles behind Perote; on the left, in the distance, stand the volcanoes covered with snow, and in front of them a long line of craggy mountains. We passed on the side of the road a few miserable villages of mud hovels, the abodes of the wretched peons who cultivated the rich fields we were passing through; also several haciendas, the residences of the proprietor or manager of the estate, and were soon in the suburbs of Perote. The maguey makes its first appearance here, where it is used for fences, and from Perote to the city of Mexico, it constitutes a prominent feature in the landscape. This is the gigantic American aloe, from which the beverage called pulque is extracted, of which all Mexicans are so fond.

We encamped on the plains in front of the castle, which

is situated about a mile from the town of Perote: This strong garrison was taken possession of by General North, who followed the Mexicans in their retreat after the battle of Cerro Gordo, affording them no time to garrison or provision it for resistance. The town of Perote, one would naturally imagine, should have exhibited some symptoms of the prosperity which reigned so delightfully in the fruitful abundance of the surrounding landscape. But I believe I never saw a more melancholy and decayed town in any part of the country, which is saying a great deal. Nearly a third of the houses, which are nearly all built of mud, were roofless and in ruins, and the miserable inhabitants seemed to have in extreme degree the shivering, starved, and apathetic look of cheerless, indolent misery that characterises the Indian peasantry between Vera Cruz and the capital. The men haunted the silent and ruinous streets with their melancholy visages, and wrapped in their dingy blankets, looking like spectres of famine; no employment, or any appearance of it, nothing but dirt, indolence, hunger, and utter Mexican wretchedness, in the midst of scenes of smiling plenty.

We stayed in Perote two days, during which we had a number of our horses shod, and on the 29th we resumed our march. For some distance after leaving the town of Perote, our road lay through fields of wheat and barley, and occasionally a large field of beans, a great article of food in Mexico. But the same wretchedness of appearance distinguished the huts of the peasantry, and the men, women, and children whom we saw in their vicinity, that we had remarked in the same objects for the few previous days. As we neared the mountain of Pizarro we left the cultivated part of the plain. The road winds round the base of this volcanic mountain for a considerable distance, and on a near view on the highest peak of the rock a large wooden cross is visible. By the by, it travelling between Vera Cruz and the capital, one every now and then observes a small wooden cross erected by the road side, wreaths of withered flowers hanging on some of them. These, we were told, had been erected to indicate the spot where the dead body or bodies of murdered travellers had been recently found, and buried, and the frequency of their appearance said volumes on the insecurity of human life while travelling on that route. A peasant, on passing these crosses, if a man, takes off his hat, and if a woman, she drops a curtsey; I have frequently seen them kneeling and saying prayers in front of them. As we circled round the base of the mountain, we saw the *mirage*—that singular natural phenomenon which one reads of in books of travel, and which I had somehow always supposed was confined to the sandy plains of Africa. I was prepared to look for it here, however, having been told by one of my comrades, as we came along, who had been reading in a book of Mexican travels an account of its being always seen in the plain beyond the Pizarro on a clear day. But so perfect was the optical illusion, that reason could scarcely prevail against the seeming evidence of sense. It appeared, at the distance of three or four miles, to be an extensive lake distinctly set in the plain, and reaching to the base of a range of hills, whose dark masses were distinctly seen inverted in the clear mirror. As we approached, however, the lake was gradually converted into a large sandy plain, over which the rays of light trembled with undulous motion through the highly rarified atmosphere. At length we reached *Tepe Agualco*, a town of mud houses, near a range of dismal, dark, and rugged mountains, bare to their summits, half way up one of which was seen a quaint-looking old church. A few straggling fences of the maguey were the only ornament in the village, which contained three large mesons, or inns.

10*

These mesons are so nearly alike in their accommodations for travellers in all the towns and villages on the road from Vera Cruz to the city of Mexico, with the exceptions of Jalapa and Puebla, that one description may suffice for all. They are usually built in the form of a large square, the buildings being one story high. The front of the square, through the centre of which there is a wide entrance, carefully closed at night by a large gate, contains the domestic establishment of the proprietor, with his offices and kitchens. The furthest end of the square is a range of sheds furnished with stalls and feeding troughs for an unlimited number of quadrupeds, and the sides of the square are ranges of small unventilated apartments, about six feet by ten, with a door in the centre, but no windows. Into one of these cells the traveller and his luggage are stowed; he makes his bed, if he is so fortunate as to possess the means of doing so, on the floor, never very clean, but which he may sweep if he can find a broom on the premises. An air of the most perfect contempt for the virtue of cleanliness pervades every corner of the establishment, and the bill of fare is usually limited to a very few simple dishes, among which *tortillas* and *frijoles*, maize cakes, and beans stewed in lard, form prominent items. In short, the person purposing to visit Mexico who is not prepared for being robbed on the highway by banditti, or is nice in the article of diet, or not impervious to the attacks of fleas and other unmentionable vermin, would be wise either to lay up a considerable share of stoical endurance, and resolve to submit heroically to the force of circumstances, or altogether abandon the rash purpose.

We remained in Tepe Agualco two days, as General Cadwallader wished to allow a reinforcement of troops under General Pierce, who were only two or three days' march in rear of us, to come up with our division. Pulque is one of the principal products of Tepe Agualco, and three or four old women were seated in front of one of the mesons, each with a pitcher of that liquor and an earthen jug, which held nearly a pint, and which they sold for *dos clacos*, about three cents. I drank a jug full of it, and although the first time I had tasted it, relished it very much. It produced the same sort of exhilarating effect as an equal quantity of moderately strong ale.

On the 1st of July we commenced our march over an extensive plain, uncultivated, except an occasional patch of beans or barley along the edge, at the bottom of mountains which bound it. The plains here are covered with short grass, and a variety of flowering and sweet-scented herbs, and in the morning when we began our march the air was deliciously perfumed with the odour they diffused as we trod on them. In the neighbourhood of Tepe Agualco the plain is covered with pumice stones. These some inventive genius conceived the idea of converting into tobacco pipes, by cutting the soft stone into the shape of a bowl, and sticking a reed or hollow tube into it. Our supply of pipes had become quite exhausted, and none could be procured, as the Mexicans never use anything but the *cigarito* or *puro* in smoking. Necessity suggested the pumice stone, which answered the purpose so well that one-half of the men might be seen smoking them in the course of a day or two after the first one had been seen. I may remark for the benefit of the reader that a *puro* means a cigar, and a *cigarito* is only a small quantity of finely-cut tobacco rolled up in a paper about a couple of inches long, and the thickness of a very fine quill. One puro or cigar contains as much tobacco and will cost as much money as twenty cigaritos. You may have a bundle of cigaritos containing from fifty to a hundred for *une medio* (six cents), but you can only purchase two or three puros for the sa.ne sum.

The plains, or table lands, *tierra templada*, commence a few miles from Perote, and this *plateau* continues to a considerable distance beyond Puebla, where a high range of mountains divides it from the valley of Mexico. These plains, which are perfectly level, and on which there is not a single tree, ditch, fence, or habitation, or a shrub higher than a man's knee, present a desolate and deserted appearance. They are everywhere bounded by mountains, and vary in width from thirty or forty to eight or ten miles, where they are narrowed by the spurs of opposite mountain ranges. The villages or haciendas are built in retired nooks behind the skirt of the hills which bound them, and any partial cultivation visible from Perote to Nopaluco, a distance of between forty and fifty miles, is a slight patch at the foot of the mountains. There are a few exceptions to this general description, and round Perote, Nopaluco, Amazook, Puebla, and San Martin, there are portions of the soil tolerably well cultivated. But these cover a small portion of the *tierra templada*, and I think there is not a twentieth part of the available surface of the country under cultivation between Vera Cruz and the city of Mexico that would be in a short period if the country was possessed by a more active and vigorous race. After a march of about fifteen miles we arrived and encamped at a place called *Ojo de Agua* (the Eye of Water); a spring which gushes out from a rock in the side of a hill here gives the name to the place. It is a shallow, insignificant stream at its source, but it gradually widens, and about a quarter of a mile from the spring my comrade Nutt and I found it wide enough to bathe in.

On the fifth and sixth we remained in the vicinity of *Ojo*

de Agua to enable General Pierce's division to overtake ours before we undertook to pass the Pinol, a dangerous pass, about eighteen or twenty miles further on. On the morning of the seventh we again resumed our march, and about ten o'clock we arrived at Nopaluco, where we halted to procure water and such refreshments as the place afforded. A quantity of fruit and other edibles speedily made their appearance in the market, and I breakfasted luxuriously on fresh bread, delicious ripe bananas, and chocolate; for *une real*, (twelve and a half cents.) Nopaluco is built of adobe or unburnt brick, and is finely situated on a gentle rise. The land for several miles round is tolerably well cultivated in wheat, barley, Indian corn, and the agave. About three o'clock we reached the edge of the pass, where we encamped for the night.

On the morning of the eighth, General Pierce's division joined, having been encamped a short distance behind ours on the previous night. A strong body of skirmishers were sent up to explore the woods, crowning the precipitous cliffs which overhung our road for several miles, and on the edge of which cliffs the enemy had poised huge masses of rock ready to tumble on our approach, but no trace of an enemy could be discovered. After all their preparations they had very prudently given up the attempt, and we passed the Pinol without hearing a shot fired. After leaving this pass, our road for a few miles passed over what seemed the bed of a mountain torrent, it was so torn up and furrowed by the heavy rains; a considerable tract of loose sand, interspersed with large masses of porphyry, succeeded, until we arrived near Amazook, where the country is very well cultivated. Like all the small Mexican towns on this road, Amazook consists of a collection of adobe and mud buildings, with the exception of a few of the principal houses in the Plaza, where there is also a very handsome church. The principal feature in every little town and village in Mexico is the church. It is always quaint-looking and picturesque, and invariably beside the Plaza. It is not customary to have the burial-grounds adjacent to the churches in Mexico. In spite of the dirt, slovenliness, and misery which seem to envelope the population and their wretched-looking habitations, the towns and villages of Mexico have always a remarkably picturesque appearance. I believe a good deal of this effect is produced by the remarkable purity of the atmosphere, and their quaint old churches, with their exterior carved and painted decorations. The Plaza, being the market-place, is usually a large open space, giving effect to the view of the church, and it mostly contains a fountain of water in its centre, and has a row of trees around it, which also adds to the general effect.

On the ninth we marched through a tolerably well-cultivated tract of country to Puebla. As we approached within five or six miles of the city we enjoyed one of the finest views of a city at a distance that I have ever seen. The lofty snow mountains of Popocatepetl and Iztaccihuatl, with their broad and heavy-looking dark bases, and their dazzlingly bright pyramidal summits, rose in the background. In front, on the side of a gently rising and delightfully wooded hill, sat Puebla, every outline of its numerous spires and churches seen through the highly-rarified and transparent atmosphere as distinctly as the lines of a highly-finished engraving. On arriving at Puebla our company, on account of requiring accommodation for the horses, were comfortably quartered in a large *meson*, where we remained until the army marched on the capital.

CHAPTER XXI.

Puebla—Convents and public buildings—Newspaper generals—An Indian city—San Martin—Valley of Mexico.

PUEBLA is distant from the city of Mexico 93 miles, and from Vera Cruz 186 miles; the distance from Vera Cruz to the city of Mexico by the road being 279 miles, though in a direct line, I believe, it is not more than 150. The Spaniards have a proverb, "Puebla the first heaven, Mexico the second," and I believe there can be no question as to the superiority of the site on which Puebla is built as regards its salubrity and healthiness. The situation of Puebla does credit to the taste and judgment of the Spaniards; this being one of the few cities founded by them in Mexico, the others being principally on the foundations of Indian towns and cities. It is built on the side of a beautifully wooded hill, and its streets, though not very wide, are well paved, and have good side walks of flagstone. The houses are mostly two stories high, some of them being gaudily, some fantastically, and others tastefully, ornamented with painting and carving. Many of them have the entire front inlaid with painted and glazed tiles, and the whole produces a sort of bizarre, yet rich and pleasing effect. One of the suburbs contains a fine public garden called the *Alameda*; it is more than a mile in circumference, adorned with fountains, *jets d'eau*, and statues, and is very neatly kept in order, and tastefully ornamented with flowering shrubs and trees. The houses are all built of stone, and large and commodious, and but a small portion of their number would seem to denote poverty; yet the city swarms with squalid beggars, clothed in rags and exposing their diseases and deformities. There are several cotton factories in operation in Puebla when things are in a peaceable state, and a number of Englishmen are employed in them at high wages, superintending and instructing the natives there employed. But the war had stopped all the machinery, and some thousands of the inhabitants of Puebla, thrown out of employment, were suffering great privation, both from that circumstance and the rise in the price of commodities, caused by the presence of such a large body of our army. The goods made in Puebla are very dear, and of coarse qualities, and only for the enormous duties levied on foreign goods, these cotton factories could not be carried on at all. The new tariff by which American goods were admitted at an almost nominal duty, had caused the stoppage of all the manufacturing machinery in Mexico.

There are said to be more than a hundred domes and spires in this city, which has a population of 80,000. It abounds in convents, and each of these distributes daily an allowance of provisions at the convent door, without money and without price, or even the formality of a ticket from a member of the mendicity society; a discriminating charity being no part of the policy of the Church of Rome, one of whose deliberate aims seems to be the fostering of ignorance and poverty. To endeavour to unfetter agricultural, manufacturing, and commercial industry, and to have the accursed laws of peonage abolished, so that the people might gradually emerge from this miserable serfdom to a more elevated and self-dependent state, would scarcely suit the views of that Church. I believe the jealous system of Spain in discouraging commerce and free intercourse between her possessions and those of other countries, was dictated by the Church of Rome, afraid of the dangerous activity of mind which commerce and manufactures must inevitably produce. Every stranger who visits Mexico, and does not wilfully shut his eyes to the fact, must perceive the culpability of the clergy in causing and perpetuating the present condition of affairs. They seem to have cared about nothing but the endowment of churches, ornamenting of shrines, and all the childish mummery of their pageantry. Under the present system of religious intolerance which prevails in Mexico, it cannot be expected that the country will become progressive or prosperous. And if anything can reconcile one to the injustice of carrying the war into the interior of Mexico, it would be the benefit that might possibly result, by showing the Mexicans the grievous inferiority of vigorous action which the deadening influence of this system has produced.

The convents and public buildings in Puebla afforded ample accommodation to our army, but few of our men seemed to enjoy robust health. The sick list and the hospitals were full to overcrowding, and one-half of those doing duty, wasted with diarrhœa, looked like skeletons or mummies; the hardships and privations of the previous part of the campaign, telling more or less severely on nearly all, and one could not walk far through the streets of Puebla without hearing the mournful strains of the soldier's funeral procession. At Perote too, where a large number of sick had been left, the castle having been converted into a depôt, the sick died at the average rate of twelve a-day for a series of months. These were interred without any military formalities, or even the usual burial service; being wrapped in the blankets in which they died, they were carted out and thrown into pits dug for the purpose daily outside of the garrison. I suffered a good deal for several months with the prevalent complaint, but like a great many others continued to do duty when not very able, being determined not to give in if possible. I derived considerable benefit from the use of pulque and aquadiente, and at other times from opium, a small piece of which I carried in a box in my pocket during the campaign, frequently taking a few grains of it before going to sleep at night.

The rainy season was now nearly over, and all attempts at negotiation with the enemy, who it was now known had fortified the approaches to the capital, having failed, General Scott being ready for the field about the beginning of August, decided on moving towards the city of Mexico. Accordingly on the 6th of August the first division marched under the command of General Worth, on the 8th, the second division under the command of General Twiggs, and the third under General Pillow on the 9th. The company to which I belonged had turned in the two 12-pounders which we brought up from Jalapa, and had got instead a light battery consisting of two 6-pounder field pieces, and two 12-pounder howitzers. We now belonged to General Pillow's division. The whole effective strength of our army, which was subdivided into three nearly equal divisions, consisted of about ten thousand men, including cavalry and artillery. Of cavalry, we had about a thousand, three troops of light artillery, one heavy field battery, and a siege train consisting of a few large mortars and guns.

On the morning of the 9th of August, on leaving Puebla, we passed through a partially cultivated tract for a considerable distance. About six miles from Puebla we passed, two or three miles off, on the left side of the road, the ruins of Cholula, an Indian city, which the Spaniards destroyed on taking possession of the country. A pyramid erected before the arrival of Cortez is still standing, and we could see it distinctly from the road. It was covered with shrubs, and presented the appearance of a natural hill, with a neat church on the top of it. Its height is said to be a hundred and sixty-two feet, and each side of its base 1300 feet. It is built of unburnt bricks and clay, and contains cavities intended for sepulchres. There are about 6000 inhabitants in Cholula, and they still manufacture a description of earthenware for which they were famous in the time of Cortez. We met some of these Indians carrying immense loads of this earthenware to Puebla for sale. It is surprising what heavy loads they carry on their backs for a long distance to market. I have frequently seen them bringing a load weighing at least a hundred pounds into the city of Mexico, which I was assured they had brought on their backs from the mountain eight or ten miles off. They support the burden behind by a strap which passes across their forehead, and carry a stick with which they prop it when they are tired.

We encamped about twelve miles from Puebla on a meadow by the roadside, where there was a pond of indifferent water. But San Martin was twelve miles further and there was no other place nearer, and as the next stage between San Martin and Rio Frio was twenty-four miles, and difficult for the horses, being mostly up hill, it was necessary they should be fresh for that day's march. San Martin, which we made our second day's stage, is a small town containing a church and convent, and surrounded by a tract of fertile and well-cultivated land. We left San Martin early on the morning of the third day's march, and after passing through a tract of country covered with loose stones of porphyry, and sprinkled with pines and cedars, began to ascend the hills that separate the valley of Puebla from that of Mexico. After marching about the half of our day's journey we arrived at a well-built stone bridge thrown over a deep precipitous gorge, with a stream of good water in a rocky channel at the bottom. A little way up the hill on the other side of the bridge, we halted at a *meson*, and here my comrade Bill Nutt and myself, with several other fortunate individuals, were in time to procure some fresh bread, sausages, and a drop of *aquadiente*. Our road for the remainder of the day's march was up hill, rough, and through a thick wood of pines. After travelling up hill for two or three hours, we began to descend into the valley of the *Rio Frio* (Cold River). The enemy we could see had made some preparations for defending the pass by forming breastworks of felled trees at various parts of it; but they had afterwards abandoned the idea, being resolved, we supposed, to concentrate their forces in defending the near approaches to the city. Descending into the valley we passed *Rio Frio*, an insignificant stream, which runs across the road, and which deserves its name, as it is nearly as cold as ice. It comes down from the snow mountains and is shaded from the hot rays of the sun by the fine woods through which it passes. We encamped on a fine grassy plain a little beyond it. We began our march early next morning, and kept winding round hills covered with thick woods of pines, and carpeted with a variety of wild flowers, until about eleven o'clock, when we reached a meson on the summit of the mountain, and obtained a view of the far-famed valley of Mexico.

Description is tame when one tries to convey the impression which this scene usually makes on all who see it for the first time. It is certainly the most magnificent view in Mexico; perhaps, of the peculiar description, the first in the world. At an elevation of about 3000 feet, the spectator sees, as if spread at his feet like a map, the whole of the valley of Mexico, its circumference, at the base of the mountains which form the sides of the mighty basin, being 120 miles, and at the crest of the mountains 200 miles. The whole of the plain, from the height on which the spectator stands, is distinctly taken in at one view, and the most minute details are distinctly defined and delineated, owing to the remarkable transparency and purity of the atmosphere. The towers and spires of the city of Mexico, twenty-five miles distant, are distinctly seen peering out from the foliage and trees; almost the only part of the valley where trees are to be seen, by the by, is that round the city. The remainder of the valley presents the uniform appearance of a large green plain, dotted with white churches, spires, and haciendas, and containing several large sheets of water, the remains of the lakes which are said to have once nearly covered the whole valley. Several small insulated mountains may also be distinctly discerned, the only large objects that rise on the surface of the vast unbroken green plain. The mountains of Pocopocatepetl, and Iztaccipuatl, its brother giant, rise about twenty miles to the left, and tower to a height of 7000 feet higher than where the spectator is standing, though owing to the bright atmosphere and the sun shining on the snow, it seems only two or three miles distant. The whole of this beautiful valley is hemmed in by a circle of stupendous, rugged and dark mountains, the rough but sublime setting of nature to one of her most inimitable pictures, and forming a most perfect combination of the sublime and beautiful.

Seen from that elevation, the valley of Mexico is a most glorious and magnificent sight, but "'tis distance lends enchantment to the view," and as we descend into it, its beauties vanish. The lakes become marshes, the fields are not cultivated, the villages are mud, and the inhabitants wretched-looking Indian peons, in rags and squalid misery. We encamped outside of a small town, called Chalco, on the lake of that name, and near the left edge of the valley

On descending the hill, where we lay two days, General Scott in the meantime having reconnoitred the enemy's fortifications at the *Penon*, decided on trying if another way could not be found to reach the city. Colonel Duncan having satisfied General Scott that a road for artillery could be cut from Chalco to Augustine, General North's division moved in that direction on the 15th, followed by Twiggs's and Pillow's. We marched by short day's stages over a terribly bad road, and on the 18th we arrived at Augustine, within a few miles of the enemy's position.

CHAPTER XXII.

San Augustine—Reconnoissance—Guard-house luxuries—A convivial party—An unexpected interruption.

ON arriving at San Augustine we encamped in the main *plaza*, stretching our picket ropes across the trees that surrounded it, to which we fastened our horses by the halters, but without taking off their harness until further orders. A large force of the enemy had left San Augustine shortly before we arrived; they had some intention of making a stand, and opposing our entrance to the village, it was said, but their courage had gradually oozed out as we approached over the adjacent plain. San Augustine is a neat little town, with a fine old church, and a large *plaza* well ornamented and shaded with trees. But it had a very deserted appearance, most of the inhabitants having left in consequence of the anticipated battle to be fought there, or in the vicinity. Only a few had stayed in charge of goods and such property as they had been unable to remove easily. This was the first place in which I had seen apples since I came to Mexico, several Indian women being here with baskets of them, ripe, mellow, and delicious. As these poor people eagerly exchanged them for biscuits, a rapid transfer of the contents of the soldiers' havresacs and their baskets speedily took place, to the mutual satisfaction of the parties. I ate a couple of them, and I do not think I ever relished an apple so much before or since, which is not much to be wondered at considering the heat and thirst of the few days' march preceding. These apples were very abundant in the neighbourhood of San Augustine, where I saw some of the finest orchards I have ever seen; our men suffering a good deal from heat and thirst, were sometimes tempted to indulge in them to an injurious excess. Indeed our surgeons generally blamed the excessive use of fruit as a principal cause of the mortality of the troops during the whole campaign.

After the return of a party who had been reconnoitring the enemy's position, and found them strongly entrenched on the side of a hill commanding the road to Mexico, we received orders to take up our quarters for the night but to hold ourselves in readiness for a sudden call, being cautioned against leaving the camp. General Scott wished to know as accurately as possible the strength of the enemy's position, before hazarding an engagement, a desire to gain a victory with the smallest possible sacrifice of life, being a decided characteristic of that excellent commander, who knew that however despicable an enemy may be in the field, he may become formidable if unwisely attacked while strongly entrenched and fortified, and occupying an advantageous position. Our infantry were quartered in the various empty buildings in the town which had been deserted by their owners, while our captain decided that our company should pitch their tents in the *plaza*, and remain there with our battery. Our horses were put up, however, in an empty range of stables at one end of the *plaza*, being still left in harness in case of a sudden call for their services. A guard of twelve men and a corporal having been ordered by the captain, I found that it was my turn to mount that evening. Having according to instructions posted four sentries, one on the officers' quarters, one on the horses, and two on the guns and ammunition in the *plaza*, I marched the remainder of the guard to the stable-yard, where, finding a butcher's shop and dwelling-house empty, but locked-up, we very deliberately forced the lock, and appropriated the building to the use of the guard. This proceeding of ours was strictly in order; but even if it had been rather irregular, the exigencies of the case might almost warrant our proceedings. It had begun to rain, and the nights at that season and in that high region are excessively cold, and unless we had secured a building of some sort for the use of our guard, we should have suffered from cold and wet during the whole night. During all that day until near evening we expected an immediate engagement, there being a constant cannonading interchanged between the enemy's entrenchments and our heavy field battery. This firing we learned was in consequence of a reconnoitring party, consisting of several engineer officers, having been observed by the enemy, who opened a fire on the party, killing Captain Thornton of the dragoons, and seriously injuring a guide. In the evening, the firing having ceased, strong out-lying piquets were stationed outside of the town of San Augustine, and we were told to be ready for an attack on the enemy's position next day.

In the meantime we made ourselves very comfortable in our guard-house, having kindled a large fire and procured an ample supply of wood to last during the night. The butcher had left a quantity of sheep skins, which were perfectly dry, and had the wool on; these being laid on benches, or even on the floor, formed a most luxurious couch; though certainly to a person of the most delicate olfactory nerves, I believe they would have seemed rather redolent of a peculiar odorous effluvium, exceedingly suggestive of dead mutton. But that was a trifle compared with the grateful softness and warmth derived from lying on them; we were, therefore, very well contented with our

11

quarters for the night. The fact of the matter is, that in our present circumstances small favours were generally very thankfully accepted; cold, hunger, thirst, mental anxiety, and bodily suffering, being admirable cures for fastidiousness. The rose leaf frets the Sybarite, while a bundle of straw is a luxury to a beggar, or a parcel of rank-smelling sheepskins to a poor, tired and half-starved soldier upon a campaign. Having found a large copper boiler on the premises, such as the Mexican butchers use to melt lard in, some one suggested that as we had a good fire we might have a supper cooked in it for the whole guard. This was a very good idea; and a few active foragers were immediately despatched on a secret expedition for the purpose of levying contributions wherever they could be most easily collected. These were successful beyond expectation, speedily returning with supplies which gave us anticipations of a feast such as we had not beheld, except in dreams, for a long time previously. After an inspection of the stock of provisions on hand, with the very handsome additions made by our active and highly-intelligent party of foragers, for which they received high commendations, the dish which seemed best adapted to our circumstances, and which we agreed to have cooked, was a sort of gipsy hodge-podge or Salmagundi; in fact a heterogeneous omnigatherum of all come-at-able comestibles. In the first place, we had a quantity of biscuit, the proceeds of the joint contributions of our havresacs, several pounds of bacon furnished by Government, having been procured without leave asked or obtained, from one of the wagons containing supplies for Uncle Sam's troops; and further by supplies obtained by our party of foragers, one turkey, two fowls, a piece of mutton, some potatoes, chili peppers, tomatoes, and onions. These **various ingredients** being first well cleaned, were cut into pieces, and the whole compound being seasoned with salt and pepper, was afterwards boiled in the huge cauldron, which was propped in the centre of the floor by three stones, for the purpose of admitting the fire under it. After our potage had been sufficiently boiled, we resolved on inviting a few of our comrades to the feast, as it was evident that there would be at least twice as much as we could consume, and it would be a pity that any of our delicious fare should be lost. Accordingly every one bringing a comrade, we soon had an addition of ten or twelve more to our party, forming, about ten o'clock on the same night, a snug little party of about twenty.

Everything went off admirably, as the phrase is. The dish or the mode of cooking it was not perhaps the most scientific, yet I am persuaded from the celerity with which it disappeared, and the apparent gusto that marked the process, that it was relished as highly and gave as much satisfaction as if it had been the most elaborate specimen of artistic cookery ever served up at the table of the most aristocratic of the clubs of London. The hilarity of the evening was wonderfully augmented by the addition to our company of those comrades who had been invited; for several of them, having found their way into a liquor store in the evening, had filled their canteens with *mezcal*, a coarse and not very palatable spirituous liquor, but highly stimulating and intoxicating, and therefore nectar to a soldier on occasions like the present. This liquor which they had brought with them, they now produced as their quota to the feast. To drink ardent spirits when upon guard is strictly forbidden by the rules of the service, but the absurd strictness of the prohibition renders it completely null. I must say that in the whole course of my experience I never knew or heard of a soldier refusing a glass of spirits while on guard, on the ground of its being an infringement of military discipline. Paradoxical as it may seem, I believe that the utmost latitude permitted to the soldier in some of these matters, would, by producing habits of self-control, act as a far better preventive to the crime of drunkenness than the present system. Unless a soldier acquires the habit of self-control as regards the use or abuse of ardent spirits, (and no person has greater need to do so), prohibitions and threats of punishment are rather worse than useless—they are mischievous: but if he has acquired these habits, these prohibitions are not needed.

On the present occasion, however, I felt that there was no danger of any of the present company rendering themselves unfit for duty, as we were all well aware that we had work before us next day for which a night's debauch would be a sorry preparation. I have observed that men, careless of consequences on other occasions, are cautious of allowing themselves to become intoxicated before an expected engagement. This caution on the part of the soldier probably arises from a dread of the imputation of cowardice, and a fear of losing caste among his comrades, by making it seem as if he was seeking to supply a deficiency of native stamina and nerve, through the medium of a foreign and artificial stimulus and excitement. In some cases also it may be the result of a knowledge of the dangers of too free indulgence at a time when all require the perfect use of their faculties for the performance of their duties. Soldiers are mostly keenly sensitive to the ridicule of their companions, whose good opinion they generally esteem more highly than that of their officers. To stand well in the estimation of his special comrades, and of the company to which he belongs, is the most powerful incentive to the soldier's good conduct in the field of action; and in the absence of a brave officer to lead them to the attack, the love of Bill, Tom, or Harry's approbation, or the dread of being called a coward, has often been the means of gaining the battle.

The following characteristic anecdote, which is highly illustrative of that fear of an imputation of cowardice by his comrades, which is such a marked trait in the soldier's character, and which seems to have been turned to excellent account in the present instance, I heard related by one of ours who had served in the British Legion during the late Spanish war. A regiment of the British Legion, who were notorious for their too ardent devotion to Bacchus, unluckily for their health and discipline, happened to be quartered in a vicinity where brandy was too plentiful and easily procured. The colonel, being made aware of the case, tried several remedies without effect, and finally, he saw that, unless the men were convinced of the necessity of voluntary abstinence, no precaution that he could adopt would prevent his regiment from getting into a state of utter inefficiency. To add to his difficulties, he expected every day that they would have to join in an attack on the enemy's position, close to which the army lay, and he was afraid that if things continued to go on in the way they were doing, both he and his regiment would reap nothing but disgrace. In this emergency he issued an order to his men, stating that he expected an engagement with the enemy shortly, and that he trusted the men would see the propriety of keeping themselves sober until after the battle. For his own part he had come to the resolution, that any person of his regiment who should be reported drunk to him in the interval between the issuing of the order and the expected engagement, should be left tied in the camp along with the baggage until after it should be over. The fear of this dreaded disgrace operated like a charm; and though the action did not take place for near a fortnight after, there was not a single case of drunkenness during the interval, and his regiment was highly praised for its share in the action, in which the enemy were completely routed.

To return to our convivial party in the guard-house, songs and toasts began to circulate with the aquadiente, while the expected battle of next day engrossed a considerable share of the conversation. " Come, my lads," said Corporal Bell, a north of Ireland man, who spoke in a broad Scotch dialect, "here's a toast—May the balls be divided to-morrow, the same as the pay and the honour." " Bravo! Corporal Bell's song—a song from Corporal Bell, 'Bucking and Gagging,'"* shouted a dozen voices at once. "I say, boys," expostulated a sentry, looking in, " you had better not make just so much noise if you don't want the officer of the day here." " Ay, faith, freen, ye're no far wrong," said Corporal Bell, while handing him the canteen; "here, man, take a drap o' that to keep the could frae ye'r stomach. I say, lads," he continued, addressing the party, " we had better ca' canny, or faith, we'll maybe hae some bucking and gagging instead o' singing aboot it." "Is it the night before a fight," cries Mike Ryan; "by the holy fist of the blessed Saint Patrick, the mean schaming villians, that are so ready to ill use a poor devil at other times, are mighty kind an' civil them days. The devil a taste o' fear of any bucking an' gagging for this night any way; so, if you plase, Corporal Bell, just favour the present company with a few verses." " Weel, lads, I'll just sing you a verse or twa aboot bucking an' gagging, an' then we maun toddle awa' an' tak' a bit sleep, an' be ready for our work in the morning." So saying he

* A favourite mode of punishment in the American service.—See Chapter XXV.

commenced, in a good sonorous but subdued voice, to sing the following verses :—

> Come, all Yankee soldiers, give ear to my song,
> It is a short ditty, 'twill not keep you long ;
> It's of no use to fret on account of our luck,
> We can laugh, drink, and sing yet in spite of the buck.
> Derry down, &c.
>
> "Sergeant, buck him, and gag him," our officers cry,
> For each trifling offence which they happen to spy ;
> Till with bucking and gagging of Dick, Tom, and Bill,
> Faith, the Mexican ranks they have helped to fill.
> Derry down, &c.
>
> The treatment they give us, as all of us know,
> Is bucking and gagging for whipping the foe ;
> They buck us and gag us for malice or spite,
> But they're glad to release us when going to fight.
> Derry down, &c.
>
> A poor soldier's tied up in the sun or the rain,
> With a gag in his mouth till he's tortured with pain ;
> Why I'm bless'd, if the eagle we wear on our flag,
> In its claws shouldn't carry a buck and a gag.
> Derry down, &c.

"What the devil is that?" cried several voices at once, as a loud rumbling noise resembling thunder, was heard. On opening the guard-room door the cause was soon apparent. The place where we had stabled our horses was an old rickety shed, with a shingle roof supported by three rows of wooden posts, one on each side of the shed and one in the centre. Running along the centre of the shed, there was a long wooden trough to which our horses were fastened by the halters; several of the horses had been fastened to the posts also, which being rotten had given way, and a large portion of the roof having fallen in on the top of the horses, they were kicking up a complete rumpus. A sentry, who was over the horses, was also jammed in among them, and we were afraid he would be injured. Cautioning him to remain quiet a little until we got a light, we speedily procured a lanthorn, and succeeded in extricating him safely, and also in unfastening and leading out the most entangled among the horses. Still as it was necessary to remove all the horses to some other place, it being evident that the remainder of the shed would be pulled down if it were not speedily done, I thought best to acquaint the officer of the day. I, therefore, sent one of the guard to his quarters to tell him the condition of the shed, and to ask for instructions as to where the horses should be taken to. The officer sent word back to have the whole company roused and turned out, and that he would be over presently himself. Accordingly in a few minutes he arrived, and having given directions to stretch the picket rope in the *plaza*, and lead the horses out and fasten them to it, in less than half-an-hour everything was right again. On examining the horses, several of them were found to have received slight injuries, but nothing to render them unfit for duty next day. Our party having been thus suddenly dissolved did not assemble again, and desirous of recruiting my strength for the next day, I lay down to sleep.

CHAPTER XXIII

The field of battle—King's Mill—The Execution—The pursuit.

NEXT morning about 5 o'clock we were roused by the reveille bugle, and having fed our horses and taken breakfast, we were ordered to harness the horses, and hitch them in the carriages. Regiments of infantry continued to arrive and form in the Plaza until it and the adjacent streets were crowded, and between 7 and 8 o'clock our force consisting of about five thousand infantry, two light batteries, and a squadron of dragoons, began the march for Contreras. The ground occupied by the enemy had been well reconnoitred on the previous day; they were entrenched on the side of a hill on the left hand side of the road leading to the city where they had thrown up embankments of earth, and had a strong battery of very heavy guns. As it was evident that to go by the main road would expose us to the fire of this battery, which we had no means of returning with effect, General Scott had decided on approaching their position by a circuitous route. We therefore commenced our march down a country road, leading through orchards and cornfields, while a great deal of caution was used in advancing, the division being halted every few minutes and skirmishers sent out in front and on the flanks. At last after ascending a steep hill where we had some difficulty with our battery, having to get a regiment of infantry with drag ropes to assist us in bringing up our guns and caissons, we came in sight of the enemy. We halted within two or three miles of them, while General Scott and his staff ascended a hill on our right for the purpose of obtaining a good view of their position. After resting about ten minutes we received the order to move on to the attack. The Rifles and another infantry regiment, were directed to drive in a body of skirmishers occupying a cornfield about a mile and a half in front of the enemy's position, and between us and them. Our battery was to go on at the same time, and take up a position where it could annoy the enemy. When we came to the edge of the cornfield, to admit our battery we had to pull down a piece of wall built of large pieces of lava piled on one another in the manner in which they build dry stone walls, or what are called in Scotland *dry stane dykes.* While we were busily engaged in pulling down the wall, which took us a few minutes, as the heavy masses of lava required several men to roll them one by one out of the way, the enemy commenced throwing large shells, a few of which dropped very near, but fortunately without doing us any injury. In the mean time General Twiggs, who, being in rear a little, did not perceive the cause of this delay, rode up, calling out, "Captain Magruder, why don't you go forward with the battery?" "So I will, general, as soon as my men can remove a piece of the wall which our battery is surely not expected to clear at a flying leap," was the reply of the captain. "Well, where are the rifles?" the general asked, "why dont they drive in those Mexican vagabonds; forward with the rifles; forward with the rifles; we must either make a spoon or spoil a horn this day." "Faith I doot some 'o us 'll no hae muckle mair use for a spoon after this day's wark's ower," drily remarked a Scotchman belonging to the rifles, who was helping to clear the way for our battery. The rifles, and the other infantry regiment, scrambled over the wall as our battery began to move, and were soon busily engaged with the enemy, whose balls came whistling among us, wounding two of our riders, who had to fall to the rear.

The field or plain over which we were advancing is strewed with large masses of lava. Between these we had to thread our way with the guns and caissons, sometimes brought to an abrupt halt by a mass of stubborn rock, over which we had to lift the carriages as if over a wall, the men lifting at the wheels and the horses whipped to their utmost exertions at the same time. At last after a great deal of exhausting fatigue we succeeded in planting our battery in front of the enemy, in a place where we could produce no impression on them unless they came out of their entrenchments, which they showed no disposition to do. Our guns were planted on a slight rise in front of the enemy, who were on the fuse of a rugged hill on the other side of the highway to Mexico, which passed nearly close to their breastworks. Our troops occupied a plain covered with large masses of lava, that afforded excellent cover to infantry in skirmishing, and a deep ravine crossed the bottom of the plain close to the road to Mexico. We fired twenty or thirty rounds at bodies of the enemy whom we could see drawn up as if they expected us to assault them immediately in front, but I think we must have been about a mile from them, as all our shots seemed to fall short. A division of the infantry under General Smith and Colonel Riley engaged with a body of the enemy; they kept up a brisk fire of musketry all afternoon, but without coming to close quarters; the enemy would not leave their entrenchments, and General Scott, it was evident, had not decided on the best mode of making the attack. The heavy guns of the enemy, among which were several long eighteens and twenty-four pounders, kept up an incessant fire during the whole afternoon. After the first half hour or so, the captain perceiving that our guns were useless at the distance we were from the enemy, ordered us to cease firing, bring our guns down off the elevation they were placed on, and lie down on the ground. By this time one of our officers, Lieutenant Johnstone, was mortally wounded by a cannon ball, and another poor fellow called Flentitz, a German, had his leg shot off. Another cannon ball smashed the axle of one of our pieces, dismounting it and rendering it useless for the time, while two of our horses were killed, and a number of our men and horses injured by grape. They were now beginning to get our range, and nothing but their excessively bad firing had saved our battery from being totally annihilated during the half hour in which we had served as a target, while it was evident that our six-pounders were useless. We lay therefore completely inactive during the remainder of the afternoon, under cover of the rising ground on which our battery had been placed. Indeed only a small portion of our troops were engaged, and I suspect the whole affair of the afternoon was only a feint for the purpose of discovering the easiest plan of assault.

At the commencement of the engagement, and as we were all busily employed in the loading and firing our guns, an infantry sergeant passing within a short distance of our battery, was observed to drop suddenly as if he had been struck by a shot. After the firing was over some of the men went to see if he was dead, or if any assistance could be rendered him. He appeared to have been dead for some time, but there was no mark of a wound on any part of his body. A small quantity of blood came from his mouth, nostrils, and even from his ears, and it was supposed that a large ball passing close to his head had caused his death.

At sunset the firing ceased and a heavy cold rain succeeded, lasting the whole of that night, and making it a most wretched night for a bivouac. To add to our misfortunes we were all suffering grievously from thirst, and there was no water within a mile whereof we were. About nine o'clock our captain received an order to retire on the division by the same way in which we had come. This was very foolish, as the night was so dark that it was impossible to see a yard in front. But orders whether foolish or not must be obeyed, though it is hard to hinder soldiers from grumbling, and there was plenty of it at this order, of which every one saw the absurdity. At last our men having been collected from various nooks and corners, and our guns limbered up, we commenced our singular march to the rear. After toiling for about six hours, and breaking and damaging the wheels and carriages, and utterly exhausting both men and horses in trying to force the wheels over impracticable masses of lava, we were compelled to desist after moving about four or five hundred yards. We then sat or lay down on the grass, our clothes clinging to us with wet, and the rain still pouring, yet so thoroughly were we tired with our fruitless toil that we slept soundly for two or three hours. We were roused at day-break and continued our march to the rear with comparative ease, as we now could distinguish objects for a few yards round us, and before sunrise we had gained the division.

The rain had now ceased, and about ten minutes after our arrival at the division several shots were heard from the enemy's battery followed by a brisk fire of musketry. On getting up on the top of our caisson boxes we could see a body of infantry approaching the flank nearest San Augustine of the enemy's position. They advanced at a quick pace loading and firing as they advanced, and receiving a fire of musketry from the Mexican infantry. But none of the guns of the battery could be brought to bear upon them; the

Mexicans had been completely taken by surprise, never having dreamed of an assault in that direction. As our infantry approached within a hundred or two hundred yards of their breastworks, we could see the Mexicans break and run in the utmost confusion, scrambling over the breastworks and out on the road to Mexico. Such was the battle of Contreras; and the time occupied in the assault, in which about two hundred volunteers and half disciplined soldiers, routed thrice their number of Mexican troops stationed behind formidable entrenchments, was about five minutes.

The brigade of General Smith, principally composed of volunteers, have the credit of this assault. These troops had been marched by a long and difficult route in the wet dark night to a position where they lay ready to flank and surprise the enemy as soon as it became sufficiently light for operations. Colonel Riley and General Smith led their men gallantly to the assault, which cost the assaulting party a merely trifling loss in killed and wounded compared with the enemy, who are said to have had upwards of 700 killed on the field. About 1800 prisoners were taken, and eighteen guns, besides an immense quantity of ammunition.

The whole of our troops were immediately put in motion to follow up the success by pursuing the flying enemy, towards the city of Mexico. As for our battery our captain considered it necessary to allow the horses a rest, as they were so weak from the exertions of the previous day and night, that they could scarcely stand. We remained therefore in the neighbourhood of Contreras until the afternoon, most of the men lying on the grass, and sleeping undisturbed by the ceaseless booming of the cannon and roll of musketry which told us of another engagement four or five miles in front.

About five miles from Contreras on the highway to the city, Santa Anna had strongly fortified a small village called

Churubusco. This, our division, which had followed up the flying enemy from Contreras, assisted General Worth's division in carrying after an obstinate resistance, which lasted five or six hours. The loss suffered by our army at this battle of Churubusco amounted to 500 in killed and wounded, of whom a more than usual proportion were officers. The regiment to which I belonged had five officers killed and several wounded in this engagement; among the killed were Captains Burke and Capron, the former of whom enlisted me, the latter had charge of the company to which I belonged until promoted a few months before to the captaincy of another company. Among the prisoners taken at this engagement were seventy deserters from the American army. They were tried by a general Court Martial shortly after the battle, and being found guilty of the crime of desertion were sentenced to be hung, which sentence was carried into execution in presence of a portion of the troops shortly before we entered the city. I sincerely pitied these poor fellows, many of whom I had reason to believe had been driven to the foolish step they had taken by harsh and cruel usage, operating on a sensitive and excitable temperament. The barbarous treatment which soldiers sometimes received from ignorant and brutal officers, and non-commissioned officers, on that campaign, were I to relate it in minute detail, would seem almost incredible. I have frequently seen foolish young officers violently strike and assault soldiers on the most slight provocation; while to tie them up by the wrist, as high as their hands would reach, with a gag in their mouths, was a common punishment for trivial offences. In fact such a bad state of feeling seemed to exist between men and officers throughout the service that I was not surprised that it should lead to numerous desertions. If our men had not known how utterly wretched was the condition of soldiers in the

Mexican service, deserting to which was literally jumping out of the frying-pan into the fire, I believe that numerous as these desertions were they would have been infinitely more so. These deserters were considered a principal cause of the obstinate resistance which our troops met at Churubusco, two or three attempts of the Mexicans to hoist a white' flag having been frustrated by some of them, who killed the Mexicans attempting to display it. The large number of officers killed in the affair was also ascribed to them, as for the gratification of their revenge they aimed at no other objects during the engagement.

In the evening our battery moved to Churubusco, and next day we were sent along with our division to a small village called Miscoac, about two miles from Churubusco, and about the same distance, four miles, from the city. There we were quartered in one end of a church, a regiment of infantry called Voltigeurs, occupying the other end. A few days after the battle, Santa Anna and General Scott agreed to an armistice, the former General pretending that he was inclined to come to terms and conclude the war on the basis of an honourable treaty of peace. For agreeing to this armistice General Scott was much blamed at the time by many of the men, as it was said that we could easily have taken the city if we had followed up our success after the battles of Contreras and Churubusco. I have no doubt that we could have done so, although I am inclined to think that the difficulty of restraining our troops from the commission of excess, would have been much greater if our success had been followed up at that time. A collision between the mass of the inhabitants and our troops in that case would most likely have ensued, which would have engendered a hostile spirit of opposition that might have embittered and prolonged the war, of which the Americans were now almost as tired as the Mexicans. By showing a desire for peace after these victories, he secured the good will of many of the influential inhabitants, and I believe it is chiefly owing to the spirit of conciliation and moderation displayed by General Scott throughout the whole of the campaign that America owes the speedy and honourable termination of the war.

The principal terms of the armistice were that neither army should erect any fortifications nor receive any reinforcements of troops without giving the other army forty-eight hours' notice. Our army was also to be furnished with supplies of provisions and forage from the city. But Santa Anna, who only wanted to gain time, had thousands of soldiers employed in digging ditches and making fortifications of earth at various points of the city, parties of them working day and night under his own direction. About the fourth or fifth of August a party of our waggons, in agreement with one of the conditions of the armistice, having been sent into the city for supplies of forage and provisions, the drivers were attacked by a crowd of people with stones, and a number of them severely injured. A party of Mexican soldiers were tardily sent to their rescue, who protected them out of the city. General Scott now declared the armistice to be at an end.

On the morning of the 9th August, General Worth's division, which was quartered at Tacubaya, according to orders, previously received, proceeded to make an attack on *Molino del Rey* (The King's mill). The enemy, it was believed, had a foundry for casting cannons there, besides a great quantity of military stores. It was also considered necessary to have it in possession before proceeding to the reduction of Chapultepec, to which it formed a strong outwork. The attack commenced a little before sunrise, but the enemy having been informed of this early visit, had drawn all their troops from the city during the night, who were posted in the most advantageous manner. Accordingly on the advance of our troops they received a most destructive fire, which compelled them to fall back, leaving the field covered with their killed and wounded. The Mexican lancers exhibited most characteristically both their cowardice and cruelty of disposition on this occasion, by riding out and killing the wounded who were lying on the field, while they never attempted to follow up the broken line of infantry who had been compelled to retire. But our troops though discouraged were not beaten, and after a fight of two hours, the Mexicans, who were at least four times their number, retreated, leaving them in possession of the field. The victory, though proving the immense superiority of our troops to those of the enemy, was a dear one, our loss in killed and wounded being between eight and nine hundred out of a force engaged numbering little more than three thousand.

About an hour after the commencement of the action our battery was ordered to be got ready and to hurry out to the ground. Miscoac, where we lay, is about four miles from *Molino del Rey*, and the road being rough and up hill a good part of the way, it took us nearly an hour to reach it. One of our men not holding on firmly while galloping over the rough road was thrown off the caisson box, and a wheel passing over his body broke two or three of his ribs and otherwise severely injured him. But our battery was short of men, and the captain could spare nobody to attend him, so he was left by the roadside in a seemingly dying state. He recovered, however, and was discharged in consequence of the internal injuries he had received. As we entered the battle ground we met a number of waggons returning with wounded, and a few wounded soldiers walking slowly, assisted by one or two comrades. There was an occasional gun fired from the castle of Chapultepec, and a party of our infantry kept up a skirmishing fire with a few of the enemy who were in the woods round the hill on which the castle is built, but the battle was evidently over. We unlimbered our guns and fired several shots at a large body of lancers who were hovering on our left flank, when they suddenly wheeled to the right-about. "I wish, captain, you would let them come a little nearer the next time; you scared them rather too soon," said General Cadwallader, who came up as the lancers rode off. A powder magazine belonging to the enemy, but in our possession at the time, blew up with a tremendous explosion, killing and wounding a great number of our men who were in its vicinity. We remained on the field, with several regiments of infantry and cavalry, until about noon, when we received orders to retire.

On the morning of the 12th of August our battery moved along with General Pillow's division to the field of *Molino del Rey;* our division being stationed there for the purpose of protecting a heavy battery advantageously planted in the vicinity for the bombardment of Chapultepec. This castle, a strong stone building, well furnished with artillery and ammunition, is built on the top of an insulated rocky hill, wooded from the base about half way up. As it commanded the entrance to the city on that side, it was considered essential that it should be taken. At daybreak on the morning of the 12th, our mortars opened on it and continued to throw heavy shells into it until night, by which time the havoc among the troop inside must have been very great, judging from the appearance of the building after the action. After the firing had ceased in the evening General Pillow addressed his men, telling them that they were to assault the castle early next morning, when he said he had no doubt they would easily carry it at the point of the bayonet in less than half an hour; which intimation the soldiers received with three cheers.

The duty assigned our battery was to approach the bottom of the hill of Chapultepec and throw in shells and round shot into the wood and up the face of the hill, for the purpose of driving in the enemy and affording a footing to our assaulting party. We accordingly placed our guns that evening in the position they were to occupy next morning, and shortly after sunrise we received orders to commence firing. An ill-directed fire of musketry from the enemy's outlying piquets stationed in the woods, reached us as we commenced firing, slightly wounding several of our men. But a few shells thrown in the right direction soon removed that source of annoyance, and where we were the guns of the castle could not be depressed sufficiently to bear on us. We continued to fire until we had thrown over a hundred shots into the grounds, when we were told to cease firing and allow the infantry to advance. Two or three regiments of infantry, among whom I recognised the regiment of Voltigeurs who had been stationed with us in the church since the battle of Contreras, now advanced, some of them carrying a ladder between two of them besides their guns and bayonets. To get into the grounds they had to scale a wall about six or seven feet high, and with the aid of the ladders they were soon all over, and advancing under cover of the huge trees towards the open rocky ground half way up the hill.

While the action was going on here at Chapultepec, a strangely horrible scene was being enacted under General Twiggs at Miscoac, the small town in which our division had been quartered during the armistice. Twenty of the deserters who were taken at Churubusco had been brought out on a plain for execution, General Twiggs commanding the troops appointed to witness the sentence carried into effect. From the plain where they were to be executed they had a view of the castle of Chapultepec about three miles distant, and could hear the sound of the firing, and see distinctly the smoke of the guns and muskets of its defenders and assailants, and here they were launched into eternity.

While the infantry advanced on the castle we hitched the horses into the battery and stood waiting to pursue the enemy, who we were confident would not make a long resistance, as the bombardment of the previous day had done great execution on the building. The firing from the castle soon commenced on our assaulting party, who at first suffered severely, but after about two hours' hard fighting they scaled the steep ascent and drove the enemy from the ramparts. General Bravo and several hundred of the Mexican soldiers were taken prisoners in the castle. The remainder of the garrison escaped by the opposite side of the castle from which our troops entered, and ran in confusion along the highway to the city. Just as we commenced to follow in pursuit, a shower of grape from the castle killed two horses and wounded several others, while almost miraculously their riders did not receive the slightest injury. The shot came from a gun at an angle of the castle, which continued to fire for some time after our men had gained the ramparts, and until our men had shot down the most of those who were working it. This delayed our battery several minutes until we cut the harness and hauled the horses to one side of the road. Near the place where this accident occurred the enemy had cut a trench across the road, which delayed us some time until it was filled up. While a party of infantry were at work filling up the trench, two citizens of the class called army followers rode over to where three Mexican soldiers were endeavouring to conceal themselves behind some bushes about a quarter of a mile off the road. The

Mexicans, who were probably wounded and unable to fly with the rest of the garrison, got upon their knees in the attitude of supplication, when these inhuman scoundrels deliberately shot them down by firing repeated shots of their revolvers. A loud murmur of disapprobation at this atrociously savage act burst from the soldiers on the road who observed it, and a ball from an infantry soldier's musket whistled past their ears as they approached the road. On their return they received a shower of curses and epithets, showing the detestation in which their infamous conduct was held.

The ditch being filled up we continued the pursuit of the flying enemy, and as we went at a fast gallop we had soon left the infantry far behind, and found ourselves entirely unsupported. A large body of the enemy's cavalry were now perceived advancing on us from the city; we immediately unlimbered and began to fire shell and round shot among them with the utmost rapidity, when they made a precipitate retreat. Several riderless horses scouring wildly over the fields on our left, which none of them stayed to catch, and which were valuable prizes to some of our infantry afterwards, showed us that our firing had made an impression, and explained the reason of their sudden change of purpose. If these lancers had charged us boldly, they could have cut us to pieces and taken possession of our battery with ease, as we had no support within a mile of us. Our company only numbered at that time about sixty men, armed with sabres, which none of them knew how to use, and which would have been a poor defence against their lances. A body of cavalry and infantry arriving soon after, we continued our march until we arrived at the suburbs of the city. Here our battery and a regiment of infantry were posted to defend a road leading to Toluco, on which a large body of the enemy's cavalry had been observed moving off in the morning. Colonel Duncan's battery and a regiment of infantry were now engaged in driving the enemy from the San Cosmo gate, half a mile nearer the city. Here the enemy had a breastwork of earth built across the road, behind which were two nine-pounders. There was also a mortar on the flat roof of a house on the left of the gate, several shells from which dropped into our position, killing and wounding a number of the infantry stationed with us to defend the entrance to the city from Toluco. This was also carried after two or three hours' fighting, leaving us in complete possession of that entrance to the city.

Generals Worth and Quitman had commenced their attack on the opposite side of the city early in the morning, and after driving the enemy from several of their outworks in succession, had succeeded after a severe fight in carrying the citadel by assault. The latter was the enemy's stronghold, where they had a strong battery of heavy guns, and after it was taken the Mexican troops retired in disorder from the city by the Penon and Guadaloupe gates, having utterly abandoned all idea of further resistance. Their large army of 18,000 men was now completely scattered and disorganized, and this by a force not exceeding one-third of their number, acting as assailants, and having to drive them from strong fortifications. Santa Anna, according to his usual custom, retired with a strong body of cavalry before our troops had gained possession of the citadel. He has not entered the capital since, and I question if all his cunning will ever be sufficient to reinstate him in the good opinions of any large or influential class of his countrymen again. Some desultory fighting took place on the following day, the 14th, between our troops and parties of patriots, principally criminals who had been released from their cells and sta ioned in the steeples of churches for the purpose. These were soon quelled, and before night the city was perfectly quiet, and considered quite securely in our possession. General Scott entered the city on the 14th, the day after the battle of Chapultepec and the storming of the citadel. By his excellent arrangements in quartering his troops in the suburbs for a few days, he succeeded in securing order, and preserving his men from those excesses which might have been apprehended from the description of troops under his command.

CHAPTER XXIV.

Ravages of War—Entry into San Cosmo—Character of the population—Markets—The cemetery.

WE had now reached the halls of the Montezumas, and still the honourable peace, with the sole design of conquering which America protested she had taken up arms, seemed to elude our grasp. The legislative body had retired to Queretaro, vowing war to the knife, and it was said that a considerable portion of the routed army had collected there also. In the meantime they were fortifying Queretaro, and preparing for another struggle; and, according to the current opinion, the war, so far from being ended, was only just commencing. But just at present the patriots might debate, and the troops might fortify at their leisure, our force was small enough to garrison the capital without marching on new conquests. These victories, gained with ease, if one takes into account the number of the enemy, and the advantages of their position, had not been altogether without cost. In the short space of six weeks, our force had decreased from ten thousand effective men with which we left Puebla, to little more than six thousand on entering the city of Mexico. In the various actions fought in the vicinity of the city during that time, we had lost in killed and wounded upwards of two thousand, and the deaths from disease and the large number of sick reduced our total effective strength to little more than six thousand. In our short campaign of about a year and a half, General Scott's expedition alone, it is said, cost the lives of at least ten thousand men; the proportion of those who died of sickness being as four to one of those killed or who died in consequence of wounds received in action. I saw a statement in an American paper estimating the loss of life incurred by the States during the whole war with Mexico at thirty thousand. Five thousand of these were said to have died on the field and of wounds received, and the remainder of the diseases incidental to the campaign.

Nearly all the houses in the suburbs of the city outside of the San Cosmo gate, had been deserted by their inhabitants, many of them evidently very hurriedly, as they still contained quantities of furniture, books, pictures, and other valuable articles. A number of wealthy people had resided in that quarter, the only suburb containing similar residences in the city. From a feeling of curiosity I entered one of these houses with several soldiers belonging to our battery on the morning after the city was taken. It had belonged to a General of the Mexican army, whose family had just quitted it when they saw the Mexican flag pulled down from the castle of Chapultepec. A number of oil paintings, chiefly on religious subjects, and a large collection of books in the Spanish language in rich bindings, among which I recognised Don Quixote, with illustrations, lay scattered in confusion on the tables and floors, with the litter of all the drawers in the apartment. Among other articles we observed a number of children's dresses, and a variety of toys and dolls. I could scarce help thinking what an event in those children's lives who were old enough to retain the impression, the arrival of *los Americanos*, the fightings in the vicinity, and their hurried flight from home would seem, when they grew old. It will form a theme for them to recur to during the remainder of their lives. A number of soldiers, most of whom seemed actuated by curiosity more than love of acquisition, strolled through the different apartments. Occasionally a soldier would select a few articles, intending to carry them off, but on reflecting on the trouble he would have in taking care of them, they were again pitched down on the floor. A number of the chairs and tables, and a large mirror, had been broken in sheer wantonness by some of our men. I saw one fellow, after examining admiringly a very handsome cabinet of finely-polished wood, exquisitely veneered and inlaid with mother-of-pearl and ivory, seize a leg of a broken chair and deliberately smash it to pieces, exclaiming at the same time, "D—n you, if I can't have you nobody else shall."

For a few days after the entrance of our troops into Mexico, the shops were all closed, with the exception of one here and there, and the prevailing aspect of the place was that of a deserted city. But in less than a week things had assumed their usual appearance, the shops being all open, and the streets busily thronged with population. The officers and soldiers of our army also thronged the principal thoroughfares, gratifying their curiosity by an inspection of the celebrated architectural features of the splendid city. For several weeks after our entrance, a number of the houses continued to display the flag of some foreign nation from their roofs or windows, as a signal of their neutrality and a claim for protection. Among these, the English, the French, and the Spanish, predominated; but the flags of almost every European nation were to be seen flying from some of the buildings. From all that I observed or learned, however, those houses which displayed none were respected equally with those which did. There were a few, and only a few, isolated attempts at plundering by small parties of ruffians, some of whom are always ready to seize the opportunity offered by these occasions. But these parties were equally discouraged, many of their number being shot by the inhabitants, who defended their property bravely, when they found the scoundrels trying to force into their premises; showing that even Mexicans will fight, when they have something worth fighting for. In fact for several nights after our victory, the number of dead bodies of soldiers found on the streets, was a proof that midnight robbery and plunder was about as difficult, and fully more dangerous, than in many cities of the States. To put a stop to these proceedings, strong patrols were sent through the streets at night, to apprehend soldiers found out of their quarters, and for the preservation of good order, and the security of life and property. These measures tended to assure the inhabitants of General Scott's good intentions; and in a very short time the most complete confidence was restored, and the inhabitants and soldiers mingled everywhere on mutual good terms. That a number of individual cases of ruffianism did occur during the campaign it would be absurd to deny. I believe scoundrelism exists to a large extent in the best constituted armies; but considering the description of troops of which our army was composed, and the loose state of discipline prevalent, I think the crimes and outrages committed by our army were comparatively few. I would even go further, and say that I think the army at large deserve credit for the general tenor of their conduct towards the inhabitants throughout the whole of the campaign. A considerable portion of this result may be justly ascribed to the conciliatory system adopted and uniformly acted upon by General Scott.

After remaining at the gate of San Cosmo for a few days, our battery moved into the city, where we found tolerable quarters in a large Meson. On entering the city, General

Scott demanded from the Mexican authorities, the sum of 200,000 dollars, as compensation for the hardships suffered by the troops in taking the city, and as the price of the protection extended by the American army to all descriptions of property. One half of this sum was to be expended for the benefit of the sick soldiers, and those doing duty were to be furnished with a new blanket and two pairs of boots each with the other half. The Mexican *Ayuntamiento* (town council) cheerfully complied with this moderate demand, very glad apparently to escape so easily. We had now leisure to take a walk occasionally through this strange city, which so intimately blends the extremes of splendour and squalor, dirt and grandeur. Of some of the more prominent features in it I will attempt to give an idea, though perfectly aware how utterly inadequate all description of mine is to convey anything like a correct impression of the city as a whole.

The city of Mexico, which was commenced in 1524, is built on piles. The streets are sufficiently wide, and run nearly north and south, east and west, intersecting each other at right angles. They are all well paved, and have side walks of flat stones, which are worn so smooth as to be quite slippery, and in some places rather dangerous to the incautious pedestrian. In looking along any of the streets in Mexico, the fronts of several churches or other religious buildings are prominent objects from almost any point of view. The quaint, old-fashioned, and mixed style of architecture peculiar to these buildings, which are usually highly ornamented with carving and sculpture, and painted with the most brilliant colours, which the purity of the atmosphere preserves unimpaired for a long time (charcoal being the only fuel consumed in Mexico), gives a highly picturesque appearance to the streets, such as I have never seen in any other city. The public squares are spacious, and surrounded by buildings of hewn stone, and of very good architecture. The private buildings being constructed either of porous amygdaloid, or of porphyry, have an air of solidity, and even of grandeur. They are of three and four stories high, with flat terrace roofs, and many of them are ornamented with iron balconies. The houses of Mexico are all square, with open courts. The corridors or piazzas of these courts are ornamented with large porcelain vases, in which are planted the most beautiful and rare flowers and evergreens that money can procure. A magnifico who owned one of these houses had retired with his family to a country residence, when our troops were attacking the city; and, as was customary at that time, one of our Generals entered into possession of it. The owner had left the principal part of his furniture in the house, which appeared to give him no concern; but he came frequently to look at his flowers, and finally sent a servant to live there for the purpose of attending to them. He said they had cost him 2,000 dollars, and he would not part with them for double that sum. Many of those courts have fountains in the centre, which, with the shade of the high buildings surrounding, and the flowers and evergreens ranged along the balustrades, or projecting from the railings of the piazza, give a refreshing coolness to their seclusion. The entrances to these houses lead through magnificent archways in the centre of the buildings, generally from ten to fifteen feet high, and surmounted by carved and projecting pediments. These are closed at night by large folding gates, three or four inches thick, and studded with large bolts of iron, or covered with plates of the same metal, or of copper. A small postern, which opens inside, is used until morning, and is attended by a domestic called the *porteria*, until all the household have retired for the night. All the lower windows, and in many cases those in the second story also, are guarded by iron bars—a precaution common throughout the whole country, where a man's house is his castle in the most literal sense of the term. But these precautions are indispensable, as there are no banks or issues of paper money in Mexico; and merchants and gentlemen have consequently immense quantities of specie in their houses, amounting to hundreds of thousands of dollars in many cases. Indians may be seen in some of the business-streets, trudging along with bags of dollars on their shoulders, at all hours of the day—of course they are always in charge of a clerk or other responsible agent.

Such are the palaces of the rich : the abodes of poverty are not in the interior of the city. Reversing the usual custom of England and America, the suburbs are almost wholly occupied by the lowest portion of the community, the *ladrones* and *leperos* (the thieves and beggars), with the lower class of itinerant vendors of paltry commodities, and labourers. It is calculated that 20,000 of the inhabitants of this capital, the population of which does not exceed 150,000, have no permanent place of abode, and no ostensible means of gaining a livelihood. After passing the night, sometimes in the open air, sometimes under cover, they issue forth in the morning to prey upon the community. If they are fortunate enough to gain more than they require to maintain themselves for a day, they get drunk on pulque and mezcal, a brandy distilled from pulque, wrap themselves up in their blanket, and lie down under a church porch, or any convenient shelter that may offer.

The *ladrones* are the sharpers and higher class of pickpockets in Mexico. They go well dressed, and would scarcely be taken for thieves by their appearance, except by a person acquainted with their habits. They are very dexterous in levying contributions upon the public; and some of their ingenious stratagems, having that object in view, would do no discredit to the genius of a London or Parisian adept. The *leperos* are the *canaille* of rascaldom; they combine the professions of thief and beggar; they want the inventive genius of the ladrones, fly at lower game, and have a dirty and suspicious appearance, that would put an observant person on his guard. It is said that they are occasionally employed by the rich and jealous to put a successful rival out of the way, or to revenge some insult, after the manner of Spain and Italy. When our troops first entered the city, a great number of our men fell by the knives of these miscreants, being stabbed by them when strolling intoxicated through the suburbs and low quarters of the city at night. In fact, so numerous were these street assassinations for several nights, that General Scott issued an order adverting to the fact, and cautioning soldiers against leaving their quarters, unless in small parties and well armed. But a more effectual check was put to this evil by the men themselves, a number of whom, irritated by these cowardly assassinations, resolved on applying the *lex talionis*, and sacrificing a few of those fiends to the manes of their slaughtered comrades. Armed with bowie-knives and revolvers, several of them sallied forth late at night, and counterfeiting the actions of drunkenness, they killed a number of those whom they suspected of designs of that nature. This was a harsh remedy; but desperate diseases require desperate remedies. Certain it is that this mode of treatment operated an effectual cure, as the *leperos* grew very shy of approaching drunken soldiers afterwards, or even of being out in the streets at a late hour. After this there were few cases of soldiers being stabbed in the streets; but during the eight months our army occupied the city, it was an invariable practice of the soldier in walking the streets alone late at night, to draw his weapon, sabre, bayonet, or pistol, and in suspicious places to prefer the middle of the road.

A very disgusting feature in the street scenery of Mexico while we lay there, was the number of drunken Indians and Mexicans of low caste, both male and female, who roamed the streets in a state of beastly intoxication. They were often to be seen lying across the footwalks of the most public streets and thoroughfares, especially in the vicinity of the market, dead drunk, and often in a state of almost complete nudity. The police seemed to take no notice of them, and they were allowed to wallow there like hogs until sufficiently recovered to get up and stagger off.

The letter-writers, *Evangelistas*, whose occupation consists of writing letters, memorials, petitions, &c., for those who have not acquired the art and mystery of writing, are a numerous and notable class in Mexico. Thirty or forty of them were constantly to be found ranged along the edge of the parapet, in a street adjoining the market, seated on stools, and with small tables in front of them placed on the carriage-road. Their stock in trade consists of a basket containing a few sheets of paper, pens, and ink-horns. They write a very plain and distinct hand, but they write slow, and ornament their writing by a profusion of flourishes, as all Mexican clerks do. A sheet of paper containing a specimen of their handwriting is usually exhibited on the table where they sit. To judge from their appearance, they did not appear to be a very thriving craft. But as my comrade Bill Nutt remarked, while commenting on their poverty-stricken appearance, "An armed republic is not the place for the encouragement of men of letters."

In front of all the churches, in all of which mass is celebrated daily, there were always congregated a multitude of beggars, exposing deformities and frightful ulcers, and chanting with endless monotony their "*caridad por l'amor de Dieu*" (charity for the love of God). Many of them were cripples who had lost their limbs in the civil wars and revolutions, of such frequent recurrence lately in Mexico. Their number had also been augmented by the late battles with our troops. I have frequently seen them hold up the stump of an amputated arm, or leg, when an American officer or soldier was passing, and repeat the names of the engagements in which they had lost them, as "Cerro Gordo," "Chapultepec," &c., adding a few imprecations on Santa Anna, an ingenious ruse, which often extracted a few clacos from their generous victors. Soldiers disabled while serving in the army are specially permitted by the Government to beg, as a compensation for the wounds they have received in the service of the republic. Certainly a most economical mode of quartering pensioners on the public, and a practical illustration of the voluntary system, remarkable in a nation so far behind in the doctrines of our modern political economists.

The market is a spacious square near the Plaza, with a tall column in the centre, on which stands a statue of Santa Anna. Fruits and vegetables are the staple commodities of which the supply is most abundant. The stalls are formed in lines facing each other, leaving ample space between the rows for purchasers. They are decked with a variety of beautiful flowers, which are always in great demand for the adornment of shrines, or to grace a festival or a funeral. From nine to eleven o'clock in the forenoon the buzz and bustle of the place are at their height, at which time it presents a very animated appearance, being thronged with Mexicans of every class and colour, from the pure Spanish haughty-looking senora, down to the poor, shrinking, bare footed, elfin-looking and half-naked Indian girls, with their baskets of fruits or vegetables. English potatoes are sold here at about twopence a pound. They are of very good quality, but from their dearness in comparison with other commodities, the yield is probably very small. Cabbages, turnips, and other vegetables of the English garden, are plentiful and moderately cheap. Of fruits, I saw abundance of apples, peaches, pears, and other fruits of temperate climates, with almost every variety of tropical fruits. The quantities of capsicums, and peppers of every shape, size, and colour, which one sees in a market in Mexico, seem to a European most ludicrously disproportionate to the rest of the commodities. Huge baskets of them meet the eye everywhere, or they are piled up in heaps on a mat, or piece of coarse cloth on the ground. These peppers, which they. call chili, are, when dried and ground, the cayenne pepper used in England. All classes of the inhabitants use them to almost every article of food, and every tienda or grocery is furnished with an unfailing supply of this indispensable condiment, dried, squeezed flat, and packed in boxes like raisins.

The pulquerias, shops where pulque is sold, are very numerous in the city of Mexico. They are all very gaudily painted in brilliant water colours, or fresco, from the top to the bottom of the walls inside, with representations of landscapes, animals, battles, &c., the subject of the painting being illustrative of the title of the pulqueria. These paintings, though of a rather exaggerated description, are generally executed with considerable artistic skill and taste. The pulquerias are furnished with a row of large open tubs, kept scrupulously clean, containing the pulque, which arrives from the country fresh every morning, and is generally disposed of and the shop closed before evening. These shops are the constant resort of a number of leperos, Indians, and greasers the latter term generally applied by the American army to the male portion of the lower class of Mexicans, is of rather obscure derivation. A genius of our company, "Ned Lonergan," gave the following definition:—"Greaser," quoth Ned, "is plainly a corruption of kreeser, and the term has originated from their custom of using the knife, a knife for stabbing being called a kreese in the East Indies." However, a plain matter of fact being suggested, that the term probably owed its origin to a greasy appearance they had from the habitual disuse of soap, Ned's ingenious definition was considered demolished. These greasers, and a sprinkling of leperos, and half-clad Indians, male and female, congregate in and around the pulqueria perpetually; now quarrelling and fighting, now hugging and kissing each other, and occasionally joining in some popular song in praise of their favourite liquor. The burden of one of these songs runs thus, "Who does not love pulque, the divine liquor which the angels drink in heaven?"

In the village of Miscoac, about four or five miles from Mexico, where the division to which I belonged was stationed during the truce after the battles of Contreras and Churubusco, there were several plantations of the maguey; and I have frequently seen their mode of treating the plant for the extraction of its juice. When the plant is on the point of flowering, which occurs from its fifth to its tenth year, according to soil and situation, they cut out the central part or heart, which should bear the flowers, and scoop out a portion of the interior pith, leaving a round cavity or reservoir, capable of containing from one to two gallons according to the size and capacity of the plant. The entrance to the cavity, which is about five or six inches in diameter, is carefully covered with a flat stone to prevent the evaporation of the juice, and to hinder the cattle, who are very fond of it, from drinking it. Plants will yield from a gallon to a gallon and a half a-day for a period of four or five months, when the juice of the plant being exhausted it withers and dies. The following is the mode of collecting the juice. The man who collects it carries a pig-skin on his back, one end of which is attached to his right shoulder; the other end, containing the mouth of the skin, he carries over his left shoulder, holding it with his left hand. In his right hand he has a hollow gourd about two inches in diameter at the thick end, and tapering to a point; it is about eighteen inches long and perforated at each end. Thus equipped he goes along the rows of the maguey (or agaves), and removing the stone from the cavity, he inserts the thick end of the gourd, and applying his mouth to the hole at the small end he rapidly fills it by suction; then putting his thumb on the hole to exclude the air, he withdraws the gourd full of the liquor, and transfers its contents to the pig-skin. It is generally collected in the morning and evening only, though it is sometimes also collected at noon. When taken from the plant it is sweet, and in taste and appearance somewhat resembles sugar and water. It is then poured into barrels or tubs, when it soon undergoes the fermenting process, which converts it into pulque. After it has fermented about twenty-four hours it has a pleasant sweet subacid taste, and is called pulque fresco (fresh pulque); when a day older it is called pulque fuerte (thoroughly fermented pulque); it has then a slightly putrid smell, and tastes very acidulous; most seem to prefer it in the latter stage. It is nearly as intoxicating as English ale, and in Mexico is sold for about sixpence a quart; but in the country it is a great deal cheaper. The pulquerias in Mexico are all kept by men, and their owners are invariably fat.

As they are the only fat class, and indeed with the exception of a few priests, the only fat individuals I saw in Mexico, it would seem to possess the property of fattening in no small degree. It is reckoned a wholesome beverage by Europeans as well as Mexicans, and our surgeons generally recommended its use to our men as a cure for diarrhœa and bowel complaint. They distil a strong intoxicating spirituous liquor from pulque, which they call Mexcal; it has a sort of smoky taste, very much resembling Irish poteen.

The grand cathedral is situated at one end of the Grand Plaza, the spacious square affording full display to the architectural beauties of a very large and finely-proportioned building, the front of which has a very imposing effect when viewed from the extreme end of the square. On a near view, however, the carving in front of the building exhibits a considerable degree of the gingerbread style of architecture. But it is in the interior that one sees most to admire. The magnificence and splendour of the grand altar, and the numerous shrines that adorn the walls of the vast pile, astonish equally by the profusion, the richness, and the variety of their decorations. The interior of the dome is very well painted with scriptural subjects, and as they receive a good light, and the colours are brilliant, the paintings show with admirable effect from the floor of the cathedral. There are a number of good paintings in the building, though I believe none of any extraordinary merit; rich and gaudy ornaments, and gilding, being evidently more appreciated than the works of the celebrated masters. A picture occupying the left side of the grand altar, as we advanced by the principal entrance, attracted the attention of our party. It was a representation of purgatory, and a number of priests, bishops, and dignitaries of the Church in full canonicals, and with mitre, crozier, and other insignia of their office, appeared in the foreground, as the principal figures, tossing in agony amidst the flames. These wretched-looking beings, who one would think ough: to have been stripped of their gowns if worthy of such severe discipline, seemed vainly imploring the assistance of the angels and cherubs, who hovered round for the purpose of rescuing those sufficiently purified. Several of these angels were engaged in ascending to heaven with a wretched-looking lepero, or ragged beggar, while those who remained seemed unanimously of opinion that the churchmen were not yet entitled to their offices. " Well, Findlay, what would your countryman John Knox say if he could rise from his grave and see all the splendour of this building ?" asked Nutt, of a Scotchman belonging to our party, as we were quitting the cathedral. "Hoot man! he would just say it was ane of the richest diamonds on the whore o' Babylon's petticoat," was the somewhat characteristic reply of honest Findlay.

The Alameda is a large square about a mile and a half in circumference, thickly planted with magnificent umbrageous trees, and intersected with spacious walks bordered with flowering shrubs and adorned with fountains and jets d'eau. Being a most delicious shady retreat, and within a short distance of the most central part of the city, it is much resorted to in warm weather by all classes. There is a fine shady avenue for equestrians all round it, while in the, interior walks, rich and splendidly dressed dons and donnas rub shoulders with the blanketed lepero. Exclusivism at least is a vice that has no footing in Mexico, and the extreme ends of society jostle each other without that air of defiant surprise which their casual encounter seems to elicit in some more highly enlightened countries.

The burial ground of Santa Maria deserves notice. It is situated on the outskirts of the town, and is enclosed with a thick wall about fifteen feet high and ten thick. In the inside of this wall, from the bottom to the top, there are recesses in regular order, into which the coffins are inserted, a plate containing the epitaph being placed over the end of each coffin, and cemented into the wall. There is a piazza round the inside of the wall, and a number of the coffins have shrines in front of the epitaph plates, which are lit up on festival nights, when the burial ground is a favourite promenade of the relatives and friends of the deceased interred there. The area of the burying ground, which contains about ten or twelve acres, is laid off in gravel walks bordered with flowers and shrubbery, and in it are a number of very handsome marble tombs. The grounds are very tastefully kept, and altogether the place has more the aspect of cheerfulness, than the gloom which usually accompanies the sight of a graveyard. Among the ornamental shrubs were some of the most luxuriant specimens of broom in full flower, that I ever beheld. Several of these shrubs were about twelve feet high, and being completely covered with their golden blossoms, they had a most glorious appearance. It was the first broom I had seen in Mexico, and it seemed like an old friend, its appearance irresistibly carrying me back to the broomy knowes of my native land. The burial ground is the property of the church, and as the sums charged for the privilege of interring in it are enormously high, of course none but the rich inter in it. The lower classes bury in other places and without coffins. They are carried to the grave on a rude sort of litter, the corpses of children and women being profusely decked with roses and other flowers.

CHAPTER XXV.

CONCLUSION.

As the Mexican Government showed no signs of wishing to terminate the war, refusing to correspond with the American commissioners, although a large party in Mexico were avowedly in favour of peace, we had still the prospect of a few more engagements. The Mexican war party were encouraged by the dissensions among our officers, a cabal of whom had managed to get General Scott superseded in the command by General Butler—a change very unpalatable to the troops, who idolized their veteran commander, so uniformly successful, and whose triumph over the weak machinations of his contemptible adversaries is now matter of history. The desertions of our soldiers to the Mexican army, which were still numerous, in spite of the fearful example of the execution of those taken at Churubusco, also served to inspire that party with hope.

As the majority of these deserters were Irish, the cause commonly assigned by the officers for their desertion, was, that as they were Roman Catholics they imagined they were fighting against their religion in fighting the Mexicans. There was a portion of truth in that view of the subject, but it came very short of the whole truth. I have good reason to believe, in fact in some individual cases I know, that harsh and unjust treatment by their officers operated far more strongly than any other consideration to produce the deplo· rable result. The various degrading modes of punishment, often inflicted by young, headstrong, and inconsiderate officers, in their zeal for the discipline of the service, for the most trivial offences, were exceedingly galling to the fiery, untameable spirit of the sons of the Green Isle. And I have not the slightest doubt that those barbarous modes of punishment in common adoption, and the want of sympathy generally existing between the officers and their men, were the exciting causes of the majority of these cases of desertion so lamentably frequent.

One of the modes of punishment practised while in the city, consisted in placing the culprit standing on a barrel in the open street, exposed to the heat of the sun all day, and the derisive admiration of the street passengers. Of course a sentry was in attendance to shoot or run him through with a bayónet if he attempted to escape from his uncomfortable position. Another mode consisted in placing the victim on a high wooden horse, and I knew of one man losing his life, in consequence of being compelled to sit for a series of days and nights in that position; one night while asleep, he fell from the back of his inanimate steed, which was about eight feet high, on the hard pavement, and was so severely injured that he died shortly afterwards in consequence.

But the favourite punishment was that called the buck and gag; which is administered after the following manner. The culprit being seated on the ground, his feet are drawn up to his hams, and his wrists tied firmly in front of his legs; a long stick or broom handle is then inserted between his legs and arms, going over his arms and under his bent knees, a gag is then placed in his mouth and tied firmly behind his head. In this helpless condition, unable to move hand, foot, or tongue, he is left for a series of hours, or even days, according to the humour of his tormentor. This revolting and disgusting punishment, which is often inflicted at the mere whim of an officer, has long been, and, I am sorry to say, still continues a favourite mode of punishment in the American army.

But the expectations of the Mexican war party were soon damped by the vigour with which the United States seemed resolved to prosecute the war to an honourable issue. Large reinforcements arrived in January and February, making up our total strength to at least 12,000 effective men. And the whole army being kept at diligent drill, by the end of March we had by far the most efficient army that had been in the field since the commencement of the war. This wise policy of the States tended greatly to facilitate the treaty which General Scott and Mr. Trist had begun to negotiate with the Mexican Government, who at length seemed willing to come to terms.

About the middle of April, it was currently reported, much to our satisfaction, that the basis of a treaty had been agreed upon between the Mexican Government and Mr. Trist, which had been despatched to Washington for the action of the Legislature. The war was now considered over, all agreeing that the States were tired of the contest, and would withdraw from it as soon as they could without a palpable sacrifice of the national honour. Still, as the result was by no means certain, our commander continued to maintain the efficiency of the troops by rigid discipline and a wholesome system of drill.

It was about the beginning of May when the news of the French Revolution reached Mexico, creating a vast deal of excitement and speculation among all classes of the army; indeed, to judge from the triumphant expression of countenance worn by the more enthusiastic of the worshippers of democratic government, they seemed to believe that the millennium of republicanism had arrived at last, the refulgency of their glorious stars having at last penetrated and dispelled the noxious fogs of European despotism. Perhaps if these too sanguine worshippers of the goddess of liberty could have foreseen the events of the last few years—*par exemple*, the spectacle of the Pope forced on his unwilling subjects, and propped in the fisherman's chair by French bayonets—it might have moderated their enthusiasm.

The news of the ratification of the treaty of peace arrived about the middle of May, an event infinitely more interesting to us all, than the downfall of European dynasties. The war was now at an end, and the intelligence seemed to diffuse general satisfaction; splendid fireworks were exhibited in the Plaza, in celebration of the event; and the inhabitants generally seemed delighted at the prospect of peace. The only class who seemed to feel it a misfortune, was the numerous train of gamblers, sharpers, and other camp followers, who, like ill-omened birds of prey, hung round our army; and who seemed by their lugubrious countenances to have received a grievous blow and discouragement by this sudden end to their accursed occupations.

The division to which I belonged, left the city of Mexico on our homeward route, on the 29th of May; but owing to the scarcity of shipping at Vera Cruz, our battery had to stay a month at Jalapa, until a sufficient number of vessels should have arrived from the States. This delay was a serious misfortune, as it detained us until the period of yellow fever had commenced in New Orleans, and which we would otherwise have anticipated. Our company, with its battery and a hundred horses belonging to it, embarked in a large steamer at Vera Cruz, on the 15th of July; the cabin fitted up with stalls, contained our horses, the men occupied the upper deck, and after a fair voyage of four days we arrived at New Orleans, where we turned in our horses to the quartermaster to be sold.

We remained in New Orleans a few days, and on the 23rd of July embarked in a brig called the Patrick Henry, for New York. We left all our sick, consisting of five or six men, who were ill with diarrhœa, in hospital at New Orleans, and there were nine men absent without leave; these had evidently taken the earliest opportunity of bidding good bye to Uncle Sam's service on landing in the States. We were towed down the river by a steamer on the 24th, and on the 25th, the wind being fair, we made sail. Before we had been a day out, two of our men fell sick, complaining of pain in the head, and in a few hours after, we had about a dozen on the sick list, and the symptoms of the disease, vomiting and delirium, confirmed our worst fears; we had the virulent and deadly tropical plague, the dreaded yellow fever, on board. The surgeon, whose name I have forgotten, was most diligent and untiring in his efforts to arrest the progress of the fatal malady, and relieve the sufferings of the sick; by his own directions he was wakened every two hours during the night, that he might observe the state of his patients and administer medicine; but in spite of his exertions, the fatal disease claimed a number of victims, and before we reached New York, sixteen of our number had been consigned to the deep. At one period of the voyage more than two thirds of those on board were on the doctor's list, and our prospects were gloomy in the extreme; more especially as the season was that in which calms are prevalent in the gulf; and to be becalmed for days, perhaps weeks, in our floating pest-house, every one felt would be the destruction of one-half or two-thirds of those on board. As a climax to our misfortunes, the medicine which our surgeon had been using, and on which he depended for the successful treatment of the disease, was nearly exhausted, and many began to consider themselves only spared from the Mexican bullets to die a more horrible death. In the midst of these gloomy anticipations, we had the good fortune to meet a large vessel bound to Charleston; having signalled her, as she was going under easy sail, she lay to till we sent a boat with our surgeon over to her, when, fortunately, the captain was able to supply him with a quantity of the medicine he required. To add to our good fortune, a fine breeze sprang up in the evening, which lasted until we reached New York, on the morning of the 12th of August, when we dropped anchor opposite Staten Island.

Soon after our arrival a surgeon came on board, and ordered all our sick to be taken ashore to the hospital at Staten Island. The vessel was to remain at quarantine until thoroughly cleansed and fumigated; but the remainder of the soldiers were to be landed at Governor's Island as soon as possible. Accordingly, our sick, amounting to between thirty and forty, were sent ashore, a number of them having to be carried up from the hold, and handed down the side of the vessel into the boat. The disease communicated to several of the hospital attendants, a few of whom died of it. A number of the inhabitants also caught the dangerous infection; and for a month after cases of yellow fever were of frequent occurrence on that side of Staten Island; in fact, though a favourite resort of summer parties from New York, steamers ceased to ply to and from it for some time, on account of the prevailing disease, the public being warned by the papers from visiting it.

The remainder of our company were put on board a small

sloop, and carried up to Governor's Island, where we landed about seven o'clock in the evening. I thought it a curious coincidence that I was landing in Governor's Island again on the evening of the 12th of August, having landed there on the 12th of August three years before. To complete the coincidence, it was at the same hour, and exactly the same sort of a lovely evening. We were lodged in some empty rooms in the castle for that night, and the next day went into tents out on the field. These tents had no wooden bottoms or flooring, as they certainly ought to have had, where they could have been so easily procured. Many of the men were weak from the effects of fever; and several who fell ill and died at that time were evidently victims to this disregard of the health of the soldier.

About sixty of the company, who had enlisted for the duration of the war in Mexico, were discharged a few weeks after our arrival. The remainder of our company, after we had been about a month on Governor's Island, our sick having nearly all joined us from Staten Island, were sent to Baltimore. There I passed the remainder of my enlistment, being discharged on the 12th of August, 1850. As the remaining two years which I passed in the service present only the usual barren and monotonous features of a soldier's life in garrison, I have resolved on concluding the narrative with my return from Mexico.

And now, tired reader, in conclusion, allow me to say a few words deprecatory of your severe criticism. The foregoing rather sketchy and imperfect narrative was written, without the help of notes, some years after the events which it describes occurred. Trusting to memory for details and statistics, I am aware that a few slight unintentional mistakes might be detected in the course of the narrative.

However, satisfied of truthfulness of intent, I feel that I have throughout endeavoured to "Nothing extenuate, nor set down aught in malice." I am also confident that should any of my old fellow-comrades ever read this narrative, while acknowledging the general accuracy of its descriptions, they will heartily subscribe to most of the opinions expressed in it.

THE END.

ELEGANTLY ILLUSTRATED EDITION

OF

COOPER'S NOVELS.

EMBELLISHED WITH FIVE HUNDRED ORIGINAL DRAWINGS

By F. O. C. DARLEY.

This beautiful Edition of COOPER'S WORKS was commenced February 1st, 1859, and will be completed in THIRTY-TWO MONTHS from that date, a volume containing a novel complete, being published on the first of each month. The volumes are uniform in size and binding, and each contains TWO ENGRAVINGS ON STEEL, and TWELVE SKETCHES ON WOOD, designed by DARLEY, expressly for this edition, and engraved by the FIRST ARTISTS OF THE COUNTRY.

THE SERIES EMBRACES:

THE PIONEERS,	LIONEL LINCOLN,	JACK TIER,
RED ROVER,	THE SEA LIONS,	THE RED SKINS,
LAST OF THE MOHICANS,	THE WATER WITCH,	THE TWO ADMIRALS,
THE SPY,	HOMEWARD BOUND,	THE HEIDENMAUER,
WYANDOTTE,	THE MONIKINS,	MERCEDES OF CASTILE,
THE BRAVO,	HOME AS FOUND,	OAK OPENINGS,
THE PILOT,	SATANSTOE,	AFLOAT AND ASHORE,
WEPT OF WISH-TON-WISH,	WING AND WING,	MILES WALLINGFORD,
THE HEADSMAN,	THE CHAINBEARER,	THE CRATER,
THE PRAIRIE,	THE PATHFINDER,	THE WAYS OF THE HOUR,
	PRECAUTION, THE DEERSLAYER.	

The first Twelve Volumes are issued in the above order; the remainder will follow the same arrangement as nearly as possible. As a

NATIONAL ENTERPRISE

the publication of this edition exceeds, both in magnitude and importance, any thing of the kind before undertaken in this country. COOPER has been justly styled

... **"THE GREAT AMERICAN NOVELIST,"**

and the Publishers believe they have not mistaken the tastes of his countrymen in offering them this complete and elegant edition of his Works.

Publishing by subscription, at $1 50 per volume, for which they will be sent, post-paid, to any address in the United States, under 3,000 miles. The work can be obtained from local agents (generally the principal Booksellers) in all the large cities.

BOOKSELLERS and others desiring an Agency where none has been established, can ascertain terms, &c., by addressing the Publishers.

W. A. TOWNSEND & Co., Publishers,
No. 46 WALKER STREET, N Y.

COOPER'S WORKS.

DARLEY'S ILLUSTRATED EDITION.

OPINIONS OF THE PRESS.

The Boston Traveller.

We are at last to have a perfect edition of Cooper's noble works, one which his multitudinous admirers will not be ashamed to place alongside of the best edition of Scott. The publication has been commenced by Messrs. W. A. Townsend & Co., of New York, well known for liberality and enterprise, and who can be depended upon to redeem their pledges to the reading world. This edition will consist of thirty-two volumes, each volume to contain a work complete, and will embrace all the author's novels, from the "The Pioneers" to "The Ways of the Hour." One volume will be published on the first day of every month, until the edition shall have been completed, commencing February 1st, 1859. Nothing has been left undone to render the edition as perfect as art, enterprise, and liberal expenditure can render it. The typography is of the most elegant description. The paper is of the very first class of that manufacture, strong, clean, and smooth as the palm of a lady's hand. The binding is at once durable and beautiful. The size is the crown octavo, universally allowed to be the best both for convenience and preservation. The illustrations, which will be five hundred in number, will all be designed by that consummate genius, F. O. C. Darley, who will be thoroughly at home on the pages of Cooper. Sixty-four of the illustrations will be on steel, engraved by the Smilies, Alfred Jones, Delnoce, Burt, Girsch Phillibrown, Andrews, Pease and Schoff. Those on wood will be the work of leading artists, among whom are Edmonds, Whitney, the Orrs, Bobbett, and Anthony. Thus much for the externals of the volumes. In other respects they will be found equally worthy of the attention of the public. Each volume will contain the last corrections of the author, and will on that account alone present an unrivalled claim to superiority over any other edition. The publication opens with "The Pioneers," one of the best of the author's works, as it was one of the earliest of them. It is a true picture of American life as it was nearly seventy years ago, and as it is now on the remote western frontiers of the republic. The origin of Templeton, and the manner of life there, are things familiar to thousands of Americans. Perhaps there is no one of Cooper's works that is, on the whole, so agreeable as the "Pioneers." The scene is far removed from city life, most of the characters are by no means remarkable, and the incidents are not often "strong," yet the author has made of his ordinary materials one of the most attractive tales in the language, and which has been translated into almost every language that has readers. He takes us through the seasons as they were in the olden times, opening with winter, the characteristics of which in our climate were never more forcibly drawn than they are in this most readable of novels; while those of summer and spring are in their turn described, and the charms of autumn are briefly introduced. "The Pioneers" is the first of those of Cooper's works that have been specifically denominated the "Leather Stocking Novels," and which have been not less popular than his admirable sea stories. Natty Bumppo here first appears, not in the order of his life, but in the order of the author's creation. Perhaps Cooper's fame depends as much upon this one character as upon most of his other creations combined. He has made the most of him, and now it will be seen that Darley, laboring on this shadowy yet real being in the realms of romance, has given him a new title to general admiration. We venture to predict that this edition of Cooper will be eminently successful, that it will find its way into the hands of every person of taste, and that no library, public or private, can afford to be without it.

The Boston Advertiser.

We have been highly gratified with the examination of specimen pages of a new edition of Cooper's Novels and Tales, to be published in New York by Messrs. W. A. Townsend & Co., with illustrations from steel plates, from drawings made expressly for the work by Mr. F. O. C. Darley. Mr. Darley is excelled by no artist in the delicacy and elegance of his delineation of figures. His illustrations of Cooper's works have been, as we understand, a "labor of love" with him for a long period. He thoroughly appreciates the author, and is able to give expression to the true spirit of his works. If we are not mistaken, Cooper is destined to be still more popular with succeeding generations than he was with his cotemporaries; and this is saying a great deal. He is thoroughly American, and original; he gave permanent place in literature to the traditions and usages of a people who have now almost wholly disappeared from the continent formerly all their own. His "Deerslayer" and "Last of the Mohicans," cannot possibly be imitated with success by any future writer. They must always remain the great specimens of their class of tales. Cooper's sea stories are scarcely less remarkable. But it is superfluous to speak in praise of the value or interest of these works. We have only now to do with the new edition, which promises to be a fitting dress for the author's text, with the appropriate ornaments of illustration. We predict for the work a large and permanent sale.

The Providence Journal.

We are glad at last to call attention to an American edition of Cooper's novels, which promises to be an honor to both publisher and author. It will contain the latest revisions, will be printed in good type on smooth and handsome paper, bound in richly ornamented covers, and illustrated by Darley with drawings on wood, and steel vignettes, executed in the highest style of art. The volume before us, the first of the series, is a beautiful book, and reflects great credit upon the publishers.

If Messrs. Townsend & Co. carry out their design as they advertise to do, this edition of Cooper's novels will certainly be a magnificent enterprise, and a worthy monument to the fame of the illustrious author.

The Boston Evening Express.

Messrs. W. A. Townsend & Co., of New York, have commenced the publication of a new and beautiful edition of this series of works, one volume to be issued on the first of each month until the whole set of thirty-two novels shall be presented to the public in a style of elegance, neatness and value which they deserve, but have never attained.

"The Pioneers," one of the earliest and most popular of the series, has been selected by the publishers for their initial number, and it now lies upon our table. Its letter-press, typography and binding are worthy of all praise; while its illustrations from steel plates—one representing the killing of the deer, in the first chapter, and the other Leather Stocking reading the inscription on the tomb-stone of the Sagamore, in the last chapter—from drawings made expressly for the work by F. O. C. Darley, are very artistic and excellent in their execution.

If "The Pioneers" may be considered a sample of the entire series, we may say unhesitatingly, that the work upon which the enterprising publishers have entered, will be an honor to the trade.

OPINIONS OF THE PRESS.

The Utica (N. Y.) Herald.

We clap our hands and are glad at the inception of this first really worthy edition of Cooper's novels. With a full appreciation of Walter Scott, and the *par nobile fratrum* of living British novelists,—with a knowledge not limited of contemporary fiction, and some acquaintance with Fielding, Smollett and Sterne, were we to have the privilege of perusing the works of but one novelist, we should, as an American, select above all others, those of J. Fenimore Cooper. Estimating, too, the effects of fiction on the mind, its tendency to give color to the imagination, topics to the fancy and to reflection, and fuel to ambition and the affections, we know that love for nature, an enlightened patriotism, kindly regard for humanity, pride in the beauty of our scenery, and sympathy with our early history, spring from every page of the Leather Stocking and Revolutionary Tales.

Take "The Pioneers," for example. Its scene is laid in Otsego county, in our own State. It is descriptive of the early settlers in that region. Leather Stocking, a connecting link between Europeans and Indians, is one of the finest creations in all fiction, deserving to rank with Robinson Crusoe, or the best of Scott's heroes. The spirit and circumstances of the early settlers can be better gathered from this work than from tomes of history. No New Yorker should read any novel before he has perused not only "The Pioneers," but the rest of the Leather Stocking series.

The present edition is issued in beautiful style. The type is large, clear and open, the paper beautiful, and the binding tasteful and solid. Besides several small wood engravings, the present volume has two fine steel engravings from drawings by Darley; one the death of the deer, the other, Natty at the grave of the Mohegan. The former is a capital scene of forest and hunting life; the latter still and solemn and beautiful. They are worth studying as works of art, and are strong allurements to every beholder to peruse the story they so well illustrate.

All of Cooper's novels are to be issued in this handsome style, and if we could have our wish, would supplant nine-tenths of the current works of fiction.

"The Press," Philadelphia.

In this new and beautiful edition we have two engravings on steel, executed with delicacy and yet with force, from drawings by Darley, and a dozen beautiful and characteristic head-pieces, executed on wood, after designs by the same artist, who really seems to have taken to illustrating Cooper, as a labor of love, so congenially has he translated the author's idea into that expression which an able artist sometimes happily seizes, which Darley never misses. This new edition of Cooper will probably have as large a sale as any series of volumes ever published in this country. It is emphatically one of the most splendid collections ever issued—equalled only by the embellished Abbotsford edition of Scott's Novels, which is too bulky in size and delicate in adornment for daily use. On the contrary, *this* Cooper is equally adapted for the Parlor and the Library.

The Boston Transcript.

AN AMERICAN LITERARY ENTERPRISE.—Such is emphatically the new edition of Cooper's novels. The initial volume, containing "The Pioneers," has just appeared. It is printed from the most neat and distinct type, on white, substantial paper, and bound in a handsome and appropriate style. A good library edition of Cooper has long been a desideratum. W. A. Townsend & Co. have chosen a seasonable moment for supplying this national want. There is a comparative lack of good new fiction, and readers gladly resort to old favorite and standard reading in this department. The time which has elapsed since Cooper's death, has made his fame and works more precious to his countrymen. The success of the Household Waverley, proves that the most familiar of popular authors was universally welcome in a new and attractive shape. Libraries are forming throughout the country, and to each of these a handsome edition of Cooper is indispensable. Every intelligent and patriotic American desires to own one, for the appreciation of native productions has vastly increased within the few past years. For these and many other reasons, we call the publication of this edition *seasonable*.

And now, a word or two as to its peculiar merits. We have spoken of the mechanical execution; we must refer to the correct text, and to the full introductions—to the convenient arrangement—each novel being complete in one crown octavo—as superior to anything before realized. The price—a dollar and a half per volume, is very moderate. It is proposed to issue the series in successive volumes, beginning on the first of February, and continuing on the first of each month until the set is complete. Thus thirty-two volumes will include all the tales and romances, with the author's latest revisions.

In addition to these claims, this new and beautiful edition of Cooper, has received its crowning distinction from the vigorous, skillful, and, we must add, *sympathetic* pencil of F. O. C. Darley. His drawings are universally admired for their expression, correctness and beauty; but in these illustrations of Cooper, he seems to have found his most congenial sphere. No designs executed in this country can compare with them for masterly finish and effect. His genius is akin to Cooper's in a certain facile energy; he catches the very spirit of the novelist's scenes and characters. In each volume there are two steel plates and twelve designs on wood: the drawings are full of spirit—the groups eminently dramatic; they are finished up in the most refined style of execution—elaborately conceived and executed in line and etching. In a word, taking in view the joint triumphs of author and artist, and the liberal taste of the publisher, we consider this edition of Cooper a memorable and precious example of native genius and enterprise, and a landmark in the progress of American literature and patriotic feeling.

The Boston Journal.

Although Cooper is pre-eminently a national novelist, we have no library edition of his works comprising his latest revisions and handsomely printed. The one now commenced is in every respect desirable. It is printed on tinted paper, with new type, each work complete in one volume, and is bound in a substantial style, suitable for a library. Its peculiar excellence, however, lies in its superb illustrations by Darley, an artist who is fitted for his task not less by his long study and delicate appreciation of the author than by his acknowledged skill in his art. So entirely has he made the creations of the novelist's fancy his own, that they stand out with the same bold, vivid individuality in the sketch of the artist as on the page of the author. Every detail is given with fidelity, so that nothing detracts from the pleasure of a harmonious whole. Each work contains two fine engravings on steel and twelve on wood.

The Northampton (Mass.) Gazette and Courier.

It is truly a magnificent undertaking, and is to be carried out in a generous and liberal manner. Each volume is beautifully illustrated with two steel engravings, designed by F. O. C. Darley, and numerous smaller wood-cuts by the same master hand. When the leading American artist brings his genius to the task of illustrating the works of America's greatest writer of fiction, the result will be something of more than ordinary merit. The enterprise is truly American, and commends itself to the reading public in general, and will be hailed with special delight by all admirers of Cooper. The first volume, "The Pioneers," just issued, is beautifully printed on thick, heavy paper, and it is a mystery how a volume of such elegance can be furnished at the low price of $1 50.

The N. Y. Evening Post.

The execution of the volume is in all respects worthy of the genius of the author whose work it perpetuates, and cannot fail to renew the interest that has for so long a time made the name of Cooper one of the most prominent in American literature.

artist, but are as original in conception as is the tale whose incidents they delineate The illustration of this series of novels has long been a favorite idea with Darley, and we can discover, not only in the two sketches of Leather Stocking, which grace the present volume, but in several others that have been shown to us, the love of the subject which the artist has brought to his labor. Henceforth the reputation of Darley will be associated with his illustrations of Cooper, and no edition will be considered complete without them.

The Buffalo Commercial Advertiser.

Messrs. TOWNSEND & Co. have engaged in the enterprise of publishing an edition of the complete works of the great American novelist, in a style of elegance in typography and binding befitting the high merits of the series. The American public owe a heavy debt of gratitude to Mr. Cooper, who was the first novelist to win for this country an enduring fame in works of fiction. Nearly all his works are purely American in character, and American in the true sense, the various personages introduced being truthful portraits of some phase of American character. His descriptions of American scenery, too, are among the most charming in our recollection. Add to this that the plot of all his tales is explicit, consequent, and clear, and his style as a writer eminently pleasant, and we have sufficient reason for ranking Mr. Cooper as the first of American novelists.

The Boston Evening Gazette.

The typographical execution and general appearance of "The Pioneers" are most creditable to Messrs. TOWNSEND & Co. Paper, print, binding, illustrations, are alike excellent. When completed, no handsomer volumes will grace the shelves of a library. It seems almost needless at this late day to urge the importance of possessing the works of Fenimore Cooper. His fictions have as yet been equalled by no American author. They possess a charm for both old and young; are unexceptionable in their tone; have a vividness of description no other romancist has approached, and are truly American in all their characteristics. But what use to praise a man who created a Leather Stocking and a Naramattah? What avails laudation of the author of "The Spy" and of "The Wept of the Wish-ton-Wish?" His stories should be familiar in every household, and to such as may not own them, we would cordially and honestly commend the edition to which we allude.

The Portland (Me.) Argus.

The style and finish of the work are such as to make it a fitting testimonial to the genius of the most fascinating of all our native writers, and it should receive the support and approval of the American public.

The New York Tribune.

In this first installment of TOWNSEND's new edition of the novels of Cooper we have a promise that the productions of the great American writer of fiction will be presented to the public in a form worthy of the author and his reputation. The edition will be comprised in thirty-two volumes, to be issued on the first day of each month, containing the latest corrections and revisions of the author, and illustrated by original designs from the pencil of Darley, and engraved in a style of superior accuracy and beauty. The volume now issued amply sustains the representations of the publishers. It has rarely, if ever, been surpassed by any production of the press in this country, in exact and finished workmanship, and in elegance of embellishment. Mr. Darley's designs have caught the genuine spirit of the novelist, and reproduce old Leather Stocking in different scenes with the fresh naturalness of the original page. The issue of this tempting edition can hardly fail to induce a host of readers to renew the pleasure with which they first made the acquaintance of this noble illustration of the genius of Fenimore Cooper.

The Home Journal. (GEO. P. MORRIS and N. P. WILLIS.)

The initial volume of this American series of novels is just published. It would be a work of supererogation to attempt an analysis of this volume. Every one is familiar with its contents. It has been read and re-read in all parts of the land; but, until the appearance of this present volume, there has been no edition of Cooper's Novels worthy, in all particulars, of his name and fame. It is the mechanical execution of the book, therefore, of which we would now speak. It is printed from clear and distinct type, and bound in a most substantial and handsome manner. Each novel will be complete in one crown octavo volume, and the price—a dollar and a half—is moderate. The edition will contain all the tales and romances of Cooper, and will be comprised in thirty-two volumes, to be issued on the first day of each month till the work is completed. An attractive feature of this edition will be the skillful and admirable designs of Darley, embodying the very spirit of the novelist's scenes and characters. Each volume will contain two steel engravings and twelve wood-cuts. The steel plates will be executed in the style and finish peculiar to bank-note engraving, and are, indeed, executed by the best note-engravers in this country. They are a combination of line and etching, and are elaborately and charmingly executed.

The Rochester Union and Advertiser

A GREAT AMERICAN ENTERPRISE—SPLENDID EDITION OF COOPER'S NOVELS.—It fell to an American publishing house to bring out the first really beautiful illustrated edition of Scott's Novels, and however much we felt bound and pleased to commend an enterprise so creditable, we felt that our own great novelist, Cooper, speaking for his country, deserved a like remembrance. Not that we admired the man, but his genius stands unquestioned at home and abroad. His works have done as much to perpetuate the memory of revolutionary heroism, pioneer enterprise, and naval gallantry in our people, as all the history ever written. Cooper had his faults, and they were not few, but all who have read his charming stories of fiction will be ready to forget the peculiarities of the writer if they cannot forgive his errors. The tales of Leather Stocking, the noble hero of five of his novels, the story of "The Wept of Wish-ton-Wish," are vivid pictures of pioneer life, when civilization was contending against the savage possessors of this continent. "The Spy" and "Lionel Lincoln" are tales of the Revolution, which cannot be read too much. The "Pilot," "Red Rover," and "Water Witch" are charming sea tales, and illustrate the gallantry of our early seamen. We say that we felt that our great novelist should not be forgotten. We are happy to see it announced that his works have not been forgotten, and that an edition of these novels will soon begin to appear from an American press that will excel any thing of the kind ever issued in this or any other country.

The Troy Daily Times.

We have before alluded to Townsend & Co.'s republication of the works of J. Fenimore Cooper. No American author was ever more versatile or successful. He was well called a writer "who had the sea as his empire and the forest as his home." Of his long list of books, there are none that have ceased to be popular, and several rank with the most generally circulated literature of the country. With these may be reckoned "The Red Rover," one of the finest sea tales ever written, just issued in admirable form for permanent preservation, and illustrated with two magnificent engravings, from drawings by Darley. For sale in Troy, West Troy, Lansingburgh, and Cohoes, by W. B. Jones, agent.

Concord (N. H.) Democrat.

COOPER'S NOVELS—A SPLENDID EDITION.—W. A. Townsend & Co., New York, book publishers, are engaged in an enterprise which should meet with the enthusiastic approval of the American public. They are issuing a new and splendid edition of the works of J. Fenimore Cooper—an edition which should be found in every well-assorted library. No handsomer or more *luxurious* volumes than those of this edition of Cooper's Novels the most epicurean book taste could desire. The works of Cooper have become classic; and have contributed more than the productions of any other single author, to give American literature a distinct and proud personality among the literatures of the world. We read Cooper's Novels, years ago, but find it such a luxury to peruse them in this edition, that we mean to go over them again. Such will be the experience of many, we trust.

The Baltimore Patriot.

As we expected, this best edition of the greatest of American novelists has proven a complete success. It is gratifying to notice the promptness with which the admirers of the distinguished novelist have responded to the prospectus of the publishers, and placed beyond a doubt the regular and perfect issue of an edition of his immortal works that shall be an honor to his memory, and a credit to American taste and American art. Considered as a national enterprise, it merits this success, and, as we have said, we are glad to chronicle it. Messrs. W. A. Townsend & Co. have spared no outlay or labor to make the work, as it is, the most elegant and satisfactory ever issued from the American press.

The Philadelphia Daily News.

This is a great enterprise. The publishers have already invested an almost fabulous sum in the present series. The five hundred illustrations alone, all designed by Darley, and including sixty-four engravings on steel, would involve a handsome outlay. But there will be no risk. The American people possess sufficient taste, liberality, and patriotism to render it worth while to present them a model edition of their favorite representative novelist. We will not offend the intelligence of our readers by attempting any analysis of novels whose characteristics are so universally known wherever the English language is read or spoken, as those of Cooper. Suffice it to say that they are now being "dressed" in admirable style.

The New York Leader.

We made the inevitable remark, in reviewing the first number of this admirable series, that it could only be a work of supererogation to attempt criticism upon the novels of Fenimore Cooper, at this late day. The issue of the second number of the series—"The Red Rover"—recalls the observation, and necessitates its repetition. It is well known to all writers, and to most readers of fiction, that the "Red Rover" was the great original and type of a class of works which have since so well filled the shelves of booksellers, and the attention of readers: *i. e.*, the nautical tale, with character painting as a component. Few novelists who enjoy opportunity for the study of character ever know enough about a ship to distinguish the spanker-boom from the cat-head, or to know that "splicing the main brace" is any thing more than a nautical evolution; and the result is a series of tales which may embarrass landsmen, but can only provoke a smile upon the faces of salt-water sailors. Cooper was sailor as well as student—had seen blue water and smelt powder; and the "Red Rover" was the best result. We need only add that this second volume of Messrs. Townsend & Co.'s series is quite up to the mark of the former in paper, type, and binding; and equally excellent, though less profuse, in the inimitable illustrations by Darley.

The Buffalo Courier.

Too much cannot be said in praise of the typographical execution of this edition, and of the spirited illustrations which accompany each volume. Nothing which the present advanced stage of the book-making art can command has been neglected in their publication. Beautiful as these books are, they are not too ornate nor too substantial to be the fitting mediums of acquainting the American people more fully with the writings of the great American novelist. We learn that there are about one hundred subscribers in this city. The number certainly ought to be doubled.

The Philadelphia Ledger.

W. A. Townsend & Co., publishers, New York, are issuing an illustrated edition of Cooper's Novels, with drawings in steel and wood by Darley. The volumes issued so far are the "Pioneers" and "Red Rover," and, judging from these specimen volumes, the collection will be the most beautiful edition of these national romances which has ever come from the press. They are a credit to the publishers, and their enterprise deserves the highest success. Each volume is printed on superfine cream-tinted and calendered paper from the most perfectly-formed type, in a large crown octavo page, elegantly bound in embossed cloth, with bevelled edges. In elegance and artistic finish they are not to be surpassed.

The Rome (N. Y.) Sentinel.

Messrs. W. A. Townsend & Co., of New York, have commenced the issue of their new and splendid illustrated edition of Cooper's works, which was announced some time since. The first of the series, as it now appears, is the "Pioneers," a story of Southern New York. The book, in mechanical appearance, exceeds even our expectations from the promise made by the publishers. Nothing ever issued from the press, except it be something of the parlor annual kind, can compare with this work. The paper, printing, binding, and all else are in keeping with the illustrations by Darley, which are his crowning triumph as the first American artist. In such a garb the capital tale of the "Pioneers" looks like a new story. The tales of Cooper are, many of them, of an historic kind, intended to portray American character, and they are as pure as any fiction ever written. If parents and others in charge of the young would introduce to them literature as pure as the writings of Cooper, the literary taste of the youth of our country would not become vitiated and poisoned as it now is by the stuff which is pouring daily from the press in the various forms of romance.

The Springfield (Mass.) Republican.

The second volume of Townsend & Co.'s beautiful edition of Cooper's Novels contains the "Red Rover." Of the style and value of this edition we have spoken before in sincere commendation. If any body supposes it is too highly praised, let him look at it. The edition is one of the finest specimens of the typographical art ever issued by the American press.

The Wilmington (Del.) Gazette.

The present volume contains the "Red Rover," the second of Cooper's great sea stories in the order of production, it having been written in 1827, but unequivocally the greatest of them all. We are glad to see that this elegant edition of the greatest of American novelists is a grand success. From all parts of the country it has been hailed with delight and admiration, the promise of the publishers that it "shall excel in elegance, artistic beauty, and mechanical perfection any publication heretofore issued in this country," thus far being vindicated to the letter. The volumes are published monthly, and should find a place in every American library.

The Hartford Courant.

This edition, from the elegance of its binding, the clearness of its typography, the fineness of its paper, and the beauty of its embellishments, is far superior to any of the previous editions of this famous novelist. In fact no American fiction writer has ever before been honored by so splendid a dress.

"The Red Rover" first appeared in 1827, being the second of Cooper's sea stories. It created a great sensation in the reading world, particularly in England, where it was repeatedly dramatized. The older of our readers will remember the interest attracted by Cooper's tales—scarcely surpassed by Sir Walter Scott's—and "The Red Rover" is one of the best. In its new dress it cannot fail to be pleasurably received by the numerous subscribers to the edition. The illustrations—drawn expressly for this edition by Darley—are in his well-known, inimitable style; a style that cannot be surpassed by any living artist.

The Boston Herald.

THE RED ROVER.—This is the second volume of the finest edition of Cooper's Novels that has ever yet been given to the public, and the admirers of our unapproachable American should not fail to improve the present opportunity to possess Cooper in this elegant form.

The Home Journal. (MORRIS & WILLIS.)

"The Red Rover" is the last issue of the new edition, published by Townsend & Co., of America's greatest novelist. The engravings excel even the ones that illustrated the first of the series—"The Pioneers." No such excellent illustrations have appeared in any work ever published in this country. They are truly admirable, both in design and execution. In its typographical appearance, the book is charming; the contrast it presents to the same work, as published thirty years ago, is certainly most wonderful.

The New York Evening Post. (WILLIAM CULLEN BRYANT, Editor.)

In the appearance of this remarkable sea-story, which has probably never been surpassed, if equalled, we have additional evidence that neither the illustrator nor the publishers have relaxed in their efforts to make this edition worthy of the subjects they delineate. It affords us great gratification to be enabled to state that the publishers have not been mistaken in their judgment of the want of a proper edition of Cooper's novels, and that the large expenditure which has been made for illustrations and typographical execution is likely to prove highly remunerative.

The St. Louis Republican.

THE RED ROVER.—This novel is part of the series of Cooper's novels which has already been mentioned in our columns. This edition is beautifully illustrated by engravings from drawings by F. O. C. Darley, and in the excellence displayed in its paper, print, and binding, is most creditable to the book manufacturing art in our country; the admirers of Cooper's fictions will be pleased with this opportunity of possessing them in so elegant a form.

The Commercial Bulletin, Boston.

THE PIONEERS.—There are numerous editions of Cooper's works, and the sale of every edition is large, thus proving how popular his writings are; but no first class edition of his works, complete, and embracing all of his novels in uniform shape, with illustrations has been attempted until now. Some of his novels have been selected for the higher typographical honors, but even those lacked illustrations. Messrs. Townsend & Co. have commenced supplying the want that has been felt, and in "The Pioneers" have given us the first volume of an edition of the best American novels in a style quite worthy of their intrinsic merits, their great popularity, and the estimate in which they are held throughout the whole reading world. Nothing more beautiful has ever been published by an American house. Every thing used in getting up the volume is perfect in its kind—paper, type, binding, engravings, and so forth—and the combination of all these good things is a splendid volume, of which any publishing house might be proud, and which is worthy to be placed among the finest collections of books in this or any other country. That the publishers do not mean to spare any cost on this edition, and that it will be illustrated in a style worthy of the author, are facts established by their having engaged the services of so admirable an artist as Darley, than whom no man is more familiar with Cooper's writings. His drawings have been engraved by many of the leading artists of the age, and are all that could be asked by the most fastidious taste, or demanded by the most ardent admirer of the first American novelist.

The Providence (R. I.) Press.

THE COOPER NOVELS.—Messrs. Townsend & Co., of New York, are doing for our great American novelist, what Messrs. Black, of Edinburgh, did for "The Wizard of the North"—giving him a publisher's lease of immortality, in sumptuousness of edition. The "Abbottsford Waverley" is not a whit more elegant than the new edition of Cooper's works, now issuing from Townsend's press, in crown-octavo volumes. Five hundred designs by Darley will illustrate the edition, and of these sixty will be engraved on steel by Smillie, the best engraver of this country.

The Utica (N. Y.) Observer.

It is our pleasure to draw attention to even a nobler monument to the fame of Cooper than the one which is to be raised at Cooperstown. It is a monument which will make him known to the thousands who can never view the contemplated shaft over Cooper's grave, and which will help to perpetuate his name long after the marble shall have crumbled, and been prostrated by the forces of the seasons.

It is a great National Publishing and Artistic Enterprise to which we allude. It is in the hands of W. A. Townsend & Co., 46 Walker st., New York. That enterprising firm have already commenced the issue of "A splendid illustrated Edition of Cooper's Novels, issued in a style of unsurpassed elegance, and beautifully illustrated by five hundred Original Drawings, by Felix O C. Darley, executed on steel and wood in the costliest style, by the most eminent engravers in the country." We do not put too much emphasis on this, when we say that it is one of the most deserving artistic and publishing enterprises of the day. As Cooper stands at the head of our national novel writers, so does Darley, that great master of design, stand at the head of his profession. And thus we are to have the works of the greatest American novelist illustrated by the greatest American designer.

The publishers, Messrs. Townsend & Co., in announcing their intentions, some time ago, did not promise more than they intend to fulfill. This we can say, because the first two novels of the series—which will number thirty-two volumes, one of which is to be issued every month—are before us.—They are "The Pioneers," and the "Red Rover." The handsome type, the superfine, cream-tinted and calendered paper, the large crown-octavo page, the elegant binding with embossed cloth and bevelled edges, the designs on wood, and, above all, the vignettes on steel, executed with bank-note finish, fall not one whit behind what Townsend & Co. gave the reading world reason to expect.

The Bangor (Me.) Daily Times.

A SPLENDID ILLUSTRATED EDITION OF COOPER'S NOVELS.—The lovers of beautiful books, and the admirers of the great American novelist, will hail with pleasure the splendid national edition which Messrs. Townsend & Co., of New York, have commenced issuing from their press. What Messrs. Ticknor & Fields have just accomplished for the Waverley, in their beautiful household edition, the New York publishers will far excel in the presentation of Cooper, whose genius will be honored with a style of dress and a beauty of illustration never equalled or attempted for a work of similar extent in this country, and which will reflect the highest credit upon American bookcraft.

The New York Daily Times.

Messrs. W. A. Townsend & Co. have performed a most acceptable service to American literature, by the publication of their new edition of Cooper's novels, of which three volumes, "The Pioneers," "Red Rover," and the "Last of the Mohicans,". have already been issued. The style in which these classical romances are published is the very highest that has been attained in American book-making. The designs of Darley, of which there are two in each volume, engraved in line on steel, and the wood vignettes, are among the finest specimens of illustrative art. The "Death of Scipio," one of the illustrations of the "Red Rover," ranks among the most successful efforts of the artist's pencil. The original of the picture was in the exhibition of the National Academy, last year, where it excited great admiration.

The Rochester (N. Y.) Democrat.

THE LAST OF THE MOHICANS.—This is the third of the sumptuous edition of Cooper's novels, illustrated by Darley, the eminent designer. The genius of the American novelist has here portrayed the Indian character, as it was found to exist among the tribes who inhabited New York and the Canadas previous to the Revolution. The English and the French alternately engaged the fierce aborigines as their allies, and fearful massacres of white men, by the treacherous savages, was the natural consequence. One of the scenes depicted by the masterly pen of Cooper, is the massacre at the surrender of Fort William Henry to the French. Another, is a battle between two Indian tribes—the Delawares and Hurons. A love story, with adventures and hair-breadth escapes, captivity and rescue, tragedy and humor, all lend interest to a historical novel, in which the red men, who are now so nearly extinct in this part of the country take a conspicuous part. When they are no more seen, these novels will present the character of the "Lost Tribes" in a life-like and masterly manner to future generations; and the writings of Cooper will never die.

The Mobile (Ala.) Advertiser.

There is no question that J. Fenimore Cooper held the very front rank as a writer of fiction; his popularity in this respect has had no parallel in this country. He originated a distinct class of fiction, national in its character, and patriotic in its aims and teachings. Notwithstanding the fertility of his pen, and the rapid production of his novels, he managed to preserve a remarkable freshness of style, and so to keep up the interest of the story, that the reader's attention never flags, nor his taste becomes cloyed.

We regard this enterprise as in some sort one of a national character. The first of American designers illustrating the works of the first of American novelists, treating altogether of American subjects and scenes, would certainly seem to entitle the completed work to the special consideration of American readers.

The Concord (N. H.) Patriot.

By a singular coincidence, two very decided recognitions of Cooper's genius transpired on the first instant. Townsend & Co. issued the third volume of their magnificent, new, illustrated edition of his novels, which chanced to be "The last of the Mohicans," and the United States Navy Department decided to name the new war steamship now building at Portsmouth navy-yard, the "Mohican." This action of the department has proved conclusively that the "Last of the Mohicans" was not the *last* "Mohican," and is also a proud display of the lasting hold Cooper has upon the national heart. . . . . The illustrations in this volume are, if possible, better executed than those in the two previously issued. We could not suggest an improvement to this edition. It is entirely satisfactory, and we can but advise those who desire to possess Cooper's novels—and who does not ?—not to let slip this opportunity to get the best edition which will ever be offered to them.

The Boston Recorder.

The first volume of the series we have now before us, and it is in a style to meet the reasonable wishes of the author's greatest admirers. The paper is excellent, the type good, and the form and binding every way satisfactory. We seldom look upon a fairer page, or take in hand a more tasteful volume.

Of the particular work before us, the "Pioneers," we shall enter into no minute criticism. It is confessedly one of the most interesting of all the author's numerous and characteristic tales. Not to have read it, argues an oversight of a book with which every well-read American should be acquainted. The reading public are under great obligations to Messrs. Townsend & Co. for this unequalled edition of an author whose name is an honor to the nation, and whose fame is in all civilized lands, and of whom the Edinburgh Review has said:

"The empire of the sea has been conceded to him by acclamation; and in the lonely desert or untrodden prairie, among the savage Indians, or the scarcely less savage settlers, all equally acknowledge his dominion.

"Within this circle none dare move but he."

The New Haven Palladium.

The specimens shown us of the work are enough to captivate any body. The binding is elegant, and yet heavy and durable; the paper is manufactured expressly for this purpose, and is richly tinted and calendered: the size is appropriate—a large crown octavo, and the page is most beautifully printed. The illustrations, by the first of American artists, are truly creditable to him, and worthy of the work which they embellish. Whether in the design or the execution they can hardly be surpassed. It is stated that the engravings alone cost $20,000.

Cooper's novels deserve such an elegant dress better than any other American fiction, because they alone are truly American in every sense. When Bryant said of him, "The creations of his genius shall survive through centuries to come," and Webster said, "While the love of country continues, his memory will exist in the hearts of the people," they but render a just tribute to his remarkable creative powers, and to the spirit of nationality that inspires all his writings.

The New York Commercial Times.

AN AMERICAN BOOK.—The "Pioneers" of Cooper, illustrated by Darley, has just been issued by Messrs. W. A. Townsend & Co., as the first of a series of the works of the great novelist, whose bold conceptions of the woods and woodsmen of America have found a worthy illustrator in the artist by whose graceful and spirited pencil each of the volumes of the series is to be adorned. This edition, which is dedicated by the publishers to the "American People," will compare favorably, in all the mechanical departments of type, paper, and binding, with any work of the kind hitherto issued on either side of the Atlantic. But the distinguishing feature of the book before us is the conscientious rendering by Darley of two of the most striking descriptive scenes in the story. The conception of Leather-stocking as he calmly reloads his rifle, in the opening scene with Judge Temple, and the grim sarcastic expression which the artist has infused into the hard old features of that stark *coureur des bois*, are beyond all praise, the whole figure teeming with *character*, which extends even to his rifle, and down to its very butt. Another design is an illustration of the closing scene—Old Leatherstocking visiting the graves of the "Major," and the "Mohegan," and is a very touching embodiment of a touching incident, full of pathos and expression. These designs are admirably engraved, the one by Girsch, and the other by Wrightson. The volume is one of which the publishers may justly be proud; for seldom has there been issued in popular form, a more elegant edition of a truly American book.

The Newark (N. J.) Advertiser.

THE PIONEERS.—The issue of the splendid edition of Cooper's Works which is now commenced by the publication of "The Pioneers," is an undertaking of no little magnitude and importance. It was an era in American authorship when Cooper issued a work, and the standing order of $5,000, made by Bentley of London for the English copyright was considered a matter of national pride. But those days are gone by. Cooper is not now the only (with Irving) American author with a European reputation. We have our works reprinted by hundreds, till we are no longer proud to have them stolen. May we soon be so grieved as to be willing to have an international copyright! Newer writings may have temporally hidden the works of the great American novelist, but none in Europe can compete in popularity with him. And now we are glad to see that a new *édition de luxe* is to honor the writer, and inspire a new enthusiasm into our own people. The style in which this edition is issued is worthy of the man and his rank among our foremost native writers, Darley, the best of our native draughtsmen, a man fully imbued with the picturesqueness and nationality of the country, whose keen eye notes the type of the red man, the sky, and foliage of the American prairie, the shape of the lithe antelope, the heavy bear, who feels the spirit of the scenes described, in whose drawings you will find no anachronisms. Darley contributes two illustrations to each of the thirty-two volumes which compose this set. We have seen some dozen or more of these spirited sketches, and can safely say that no more exquisite works of art have ever illustrated any work issued in this country, if in Europe. Nor is illustration all. The edition is faultless in type, printing, paper, and binding. Particularly we note the *cloth* binding of this edition as one of the neatest and most durable of its class. We have thus made especial mention of this enterprise on account of its magnitude, its artistic superiority, and its national importance, and we trust that it will be properly encouraged.

The Gazette and Democrat, Reading, Pa.

The paper, printing, pictorial embellishment, and binding of these volumes are so superior as to call forth the most unqualified praise of the press, both in this country and in England; and, indeed, it may be safely said that no American books were ever issued which excel them in tasteful design and elegance of execution. They form an edition of Cooper's Writings eminently worthy of their distinguished author; and, indeed, the only one fit to grace the library. The new volumes contain "The Last of the Mohicans" and "The Spy," the illustrations to which are really splendid. The vignette to the latter, representing the escape of Harvey Birch, is a perfect gem. "The Spy" contains two of the best characters ever drawn by Cooper—Harvey Birch, the Spy, and the grave but gallant gentleman, Mr. Harper, who eventually appears as Washington himself. Prefixed to this edition is the author's introduction, giving a history of the writing of the book, and the real incident which suggested it.

Cincinnati Daily Gazette.

COOPER'S NOVELS, ILLUSTRATED.—Messrs. Townsend & Co.'s new edition of Cooper's Novels, with illustrations by the inimitable Darley, will prove a lasting benefit to the public, and we trust also to the publishers.

Of the thirty-two volumes which will complete the series, three have already appeared—viz.: "The Pioneers," "The Red Rover," and "The Last of the Mohicans." They contain the author's final revisions, two steel engravings each, which, though executed with marvellous finish, still retain all the spirit of the designer, beside a large number of tasteful vignettes. The typography is truly elegant, the paper soft-tinted, smooth, and clear, the binding neat, strong, and appropriate. Altogether the edition promises to do honor to a writer who, with all his faults, deserves the name of the American Walter Scott.

The price of the volumes is exceedingly reasonable, being but $1.50. Robert Clarke & Co. are the Cincinnati agents for the sale of the series.

The National Intelligencer, Washington, D. C.

COOPER'S NOVELS.—We have before us several volumes of the above novels, and, on looking over them, have been so delighted that we cannot withstand the temptation to congratulate the public upon this latest magnificent issue from the New York press.

The publishers have indeed done justice to the ever-fresh and ever-welcome creations of J. Fenimore Cooper, our national author, the Walter Scott of America. He needs no encomium from us. The eagerness with which each generation of readers seizes upon his glowing and truthful portraitures proves the firm hold he has upon the public heart and fancy; but if by chance there is any one who has not followed the author in his graphic description of the varied adventures of those who "go down to the sea in ships," or who is not familiar with his luimitable scenes of the forest and prairie, of the customs and every-day life of the red man, who is so surely passing away, and will soon live only in Cooper's magic pages, this intellectual omission should be remedied at once by obtaining this beautiful set of novels, and, our word for it, he will not repent his bargain. To add to the charm of these works (if such be deemed possible), the services of Darley have been brought into requisition, a host in himself; and these illustrations are worthy of his fame as the first designer in our country, and not inferior, in the estimation of high English authority, to Retsch himself. Many of our readers, we doubt not, have seen the evidences of his wonderful artistic conception and faithful expression in that remarkable book "Margaret," also in his etchings of "Rip Van Winkle," while Hood's "Bridge of Sighs" has also been exquisitely interpreted by his delicate and vivid pencil.

Messrs. Townsend & Co. have brought out these books in a substantial form and beautiful finish, which may successfully compete with English and French editions *de luxe*, and of which they may well be proud. Their intention is to publish a volume monthly, each to contain a novel complete. Those which have already reached us are printed from perfectly-formed type, in crown octavo, on beautiful cream-tinted paper manufactured expressly for this edition, solidly and elegantly bound in cloth, stamped with designs new and appropriate to the subject-matter.

The Vox Populi, Lowell, Mass.

There is a grateful flow of satisfaction in sitting down to notice a work that we know will warrant all we could desire to say in its favor. Of Cooper's Novels there is nothing to be said. Like Bunker Hill, and Lexington and Concord, "there they stand." They are a fixture in the hearts of the people and the literature of the world. It is the captivating *style* of the work that strikes us forcibly and favorably. This is to be an entirely new edition, published exclusively by subscription, at $1.50 a volume. One volume will be published every month, each containing a novel complete, a convenience to subscribers, to whom the payment will thus be made light and easy. They are to be illustrated with designs on wood, and vignette drawings on steel, in *line* and *etching*, by F. O. C. Darley.

"The States," Washington, D. C.

SPLENDID ILLUSTRATED EDITION OF COOPER'S NOVELS.—It is a desideratum to witness the perfection to which the publishers have attained in the display of this work, and it may compare most favorably with the productions of the English press. The paper is unusually fine and heavy, type distinct and good size, and binding such as will prove an heir-loom for several generations, as it appears adapted "not for a day, but for all time."

The price is low—$1.50 per volume—considering the beauty of the work, illustrated as the thirty-two volumes will be, each with two large designs, the work comprising, in all, 500 original drawings by Darley, who stands at the head of his profession. No library should be viewed as complete not comprising Cooper's works, if the proprietor designs having one on general literature, as Cooper is identified in his works with both modern and ancient countries. No edition that we have yet seen reflects so much credit on publishers; and we hope this is but the commencement of a new era in solid, substantial binding—made to last.

The Newburgh (N. Y.) Daily News.

COOPER'S WORKS.—It was no light advantage to the cause of American literature that at its very outset it was lifted far beyond the level of mediocrity, in the department of historical fiction, by the genius of Cooper. And this advantage has not been confined even to the circle of letters, wide and genial as its influence is—but the impress of the great novelist's creations has stamped itself upon our nationality, and made it instinct with the fresh and vivid beauty of the soil. What Shakspeare was to the older civilization of England—and Scott to the Mountain homes of Scotland—what Beranger is to the *bourgeoise* of France, that Cooper is to America. We would not be understood by this to place the American author on a par with Shakspeare; but that in taking up and giving immortal shape and life to the genius of the times as they *were*, and not as they may be, and for rendering us affectionately familiar with the scenic grandeurs of our land as they will be forever, Cooper must occupy a foremost rank in our literature while its language endures. He does, it is true, color somewhat too highly his Indian heroes; though it must be remembered that we are not familiar with the Indian character as he was; but his descriptions of American scenery are true to the life. Who, for instance, can read his Spy, and not feel deeper interest in our Revolutionary war, as well as a better appreciation of the scenery of our own river.

We have all read Cooper, and hardly need any eulogy to quicken our admiration of his genius—the zest with which each generation peruses his volumes needs no suggestions from the critic. But we have been led into these remarks by the publication of an edition of his works illustrated by Darley. This is indeed a happy combination—the masterly touches of Darley's weird-like, yet truthful pencil, will give new developments of beauty to the creations of the novelist. No writer opens a wider or nobler field to the artist's pencil; and few, if any, have found a more truthful delineator. . . . . We are indebted for this felicitous union of artistic and literary excellence to Townsend & Co., publishers, of New York, who are bringing out a beautiful edition in handsome volumes on the best paper, and with the clearest type. The designs are engraved on steel in line and etching—bringing out the beauty of the original. The binding is worthy of the work, and the whole will make this the finest and most complete edition of the great novelist yet published. The price is only $1.50 per volume—one of which is issued every month, containing a complete novel.

The Toledo (Ohio) Herald.

MOHICANS.—It is nearly a quarter of a century since James Fenimore Cooper wrote his story entitled "The Last of the Mohicans," and we venture to say that no work of the kind ever published has met with more popular favor amongst the truly intelligent portion of the community than this. Yet, considering the long lapse of time since the first editions of the work were issued, and the improvements and inventions which have been made in printing, engraving, binding, and book-making generally, it is quite time that some patriotic and enterprising American publisher should give us, for our libraries, an edition of Cooper's Novels, gotten up in all the elegance of our day. And it is with great pleasure that we notice the volumes just published by W. A. Townsend & Co., of New York. We congratulate that firm upon their success in introducing an edition of Cooper's works which compares, in typography and finish, with the substance and beauty of the text.

The Utica (N. Y.) Observer.

THE SPY.—This is one of the earliest and best of those pre-eminent American historical romances, which have gained a celebrity scarcely inferior to those of Sir Walter Scott. The scene of the story is the neutral ground in the south-eastern section of this state, in Westchester county, where neither the Americans nor British held complete sovereignty. The hero of the story is one of those *sui generis* characters who are content to submit to all sorts, and the worst misconception of motive and design, for the sake of advancing to the best of their abilities some cherished cause. "The Spy" was, in reality, a patriot, as the sequel proved. He was employed by Washington, but often appeared to be an adherent of the British—his purpose being to affect Tory principles in order the better and more surely to advance the object of the leader of the American armies. When, after the war, Congress put into the hands of a prominent statesman funds to amply reward the self-sacrificing services of the Spy, the noble-hearted patriot refused to accept it, on the ground that he owed the country the services he gave her, and she was too poor to grant him the pecuniary recompense offered. This was a real incident, and the novelist has woven around it a tale of enchanting interest, written in the most elevated style, furnishing at once an entertaining story of the Revolution and a literary model. The delineation of character is forcible and truthful. .... American youth will find in these stories of the past history of their country sources of true and unalloyed enjoyment, far bet er and more wholesome than the meretricious, superficial, dissipating fictions so prolific at the present day, and which cost their writers so little real thought and earnest labor. The family library which contains these volumes will possess a real treasure.

The Philadelphia Bulletin.

A SPLENDID WORK.—It was quite time that the illustrious novelist, Cooper, should receive the honor of a splendid edition, and we are pleased to see that W. A. Townsend & Co., of New York, are issuing a truly magnificent one, which adds to all the attractions of exquisite type, paper, and binding, those of *five hundred original designs* by Darley, executed on steel and wood, in the costliest style, by the most eminent engravers in the country. The publishers have, in fact, begun this series with the determination of issuing an edition which shall excel in elegance any collection of works ever before given in this country. There have been more expensive and showy single volumes published here, but no series of volumes equal to these.

This series is doubly interesting from the fact that it is illustrated by Darley. Retsch was not more appropriately the artist of Goethe than is Darley that of our great American novelist. This has long been understood and anticipated, since all of Darley's works point in this direction. The London *Athenæum*, in calling on Darley to illustrate Cooper, once said: "We shall then enter upon a new region of art, as dramatic, picturesque, and vivid as any artist lover has had the pleasure of first attempting."

We have before us the "Spy," "Pioneers," "Mohican," and "Red Rover," and, turning over their beautiful, tinted pages, we feel that the work is truly the most appropriate monument of genius. The introductory illustrations and the vignettes are in the very spirit and life of the incidents; nothing could correspond more perfectly to the impressions formed of all the varied, motley, strange company who pass through the deeply-stirring scenes of truly American life. There are to be thirty-two volumes in all, containing the latest corrections of the author, and, in fact, rendered as perfect as possible in every respect, whether literary, mechanical, or artistic.

The Century, New York.

The new illustrated edition by Townsend & Co. of the Novels of Cooper is receiving the attention to which its merits fully entitle it. It appears simultaneously with a new English illustrated reprint of the Waverley Novels, to which the series bears a parallel name and fame. The American publishers were already in possession of a set of stereotype plates of the works of Cooper, which they have laid aside to give place to this more elegant edition. In typographical excellence it leaves nothing to be desired. The engagement of Mr. Darley as its illustrator has added greatly to its value. The variety of subject, rural, Indian, military, naval life, gives the best opportunities to his pencil, which has acquired a distinguished reputation in all these departments. The wood-cut vignettes are also very happy in design. A volume of this publication appears monthly, at a very reasonable price.

The New York Day Book.

JAMES FENIMORE COOPER.—No American writer has achieved so world-wide a popularity as he whose name stands at the head of this article; none has been at once so much admired at home and so generally read abroad. Indeed, his reputation is even greater in Europe than in America. His works have been republished again and again, in half a dozen of the capitals of the civilized world, have been translated into half a dozen languages, and great Parisian critics have not hesitated to rank Cooper along side of Walter Scott. Many causes combined to procure for him this enviable fame. Of course the greatest was his genius, but peculiarities of his character assisted in making this greatness. His genius and his character were both essentially American: he chose for his themes the deck of the American frigate, the life of the American sailor, or the paths of the American forest, and the strife between the American Indian and the American pioneer. The very names of the novels indicate the intense nationality of his mind. And this nationality not only, as it should have done, endears him to those with whom he shared it, and not only was a claim, gladly recognized, upon the consideration of his countrymen, but won for him the appreciation of others. .... Messrs. W. A. Townsend & Co., of New York, are engaged in the publication of a complete edition of Cooper's works, which is designed to be in every way worthy of the great American novelist. The spirit in which it has been begun is a worthy tribute to his literary excellence. .... Three are already before us, "The Pioneers," "The Red Rover," and "The Last of the Mohicans.' They are gotten up in the most admirable style of the publisher's art. The paper, binding, printing, are all of the first class; the size is convenient, and the whole appearance of the book elegant. .... No previous edition of Cooper's works is at all comparable with this of which we speak.

The Knickerbocker Magazine.

W. A. Townsend & Co.'s edition of Cooper's Novels is attracting the attention, and securing the wide popularity which we predicted for it some months since, while the great enterprise was as yet almost in embryo; but the materials to be employed and the superb original illustrations, indicated with sufficient plainness what the public had good reason to expect. Nor will public expectation in any degree be disappointed. The pioneer of the series was "The Pioneers," which has been succeeded by "The Red Rover," and "Last of the Mohicans." It would be idle, at this late day, to speak of the *character* of these or other kindred works, which have made Cooper's name and literary fame known not only "wherever the English language is read and spoken," but as well where many *other* languages are read and spoken. Hence, it remains only to be stated, that in the conception and execution of the engravings by Darley, who has the rare faculty of entering into the very spirit of his author; in the firm and beautiful paper, made expressly for this edition; in the clear and elegant typographical execution; and in that rich and tasteful binding of the volume, there is nothing left to desire, save the ability to purchase them; and this, fortunately, the publishers place within the easy reach of all good book-buyers.

The New York Tribune.

THE SPY.—The unrivalled illustrations of this edition by Mr. Darley, give each successive volume a new interest as it issues from the press. The artist has caught the very spirit of the author in his characteristic designs, which are reproduced with excellent effect by the skill of the engraver. In every respect, this beautiful library edition deserves to be in the hands of the admirers of Fenimore Cooper.

The Independent, New York.

COOPER'S NOVELS.—Messrs. W. A. Townsend & Co., of this city, are publishing a beautiful edition of Cooper's novels, large duodecimo, printed in fair type upon substantial paper, and illustrated with steel and wood engravings by the first artists. "Red Rover," the first of the series, is illustrated in a spirited manner, by Darley, whose skill is not surpassed by any European artist. The works of Fenimore Cooper are as fresh to-day as when first they fired our youthful imagination with the stirring scenes of border life, and the braveries and perils of the sea. The American novelist still remains without a peer in that department of fiction which his genius so brilliantly illustrated; and he will be read—always, we hope, with that moderation which should control our reading of fiction—so long as American literature shall have a name. This attractive edition will greatly enlarge the circle of Cooper's readers and admirers.

The Pittsburgh Gazette.

THE SPY.—This is the fourth volume of the uniform edition of Cooper's Works now in course of publication by Townsend & Co., of New York. We have before referred to the enterprising spirit manifested in getting out this superb edition, and take occasion again to recommend it. In the beauty of its typography it is unequalled, while the illustrations are of the first order, and the binding most substantial, rendering it the handsomest library edition of any work ever issued in the United States.

"The Spy" was one of the most popular of Cooper's novels, at the time of its issue, and deservedly retains its popularity. It is a thrilling romance, worthy of the enlarged fame of the author. We hope to see this edition attain a wide popularity.

The Daily Advertiser, Detroit.

"THE SPY."—Messrs. Townsend & Co., of New York, who are issuing Cooper's novels in a style far superior to any with which they have ever before been clothed, have just published the fourth volume of their admirable series. It is "The Spy," one of the best of the charming works which made their author famous. Like the volumes which preceded it, it is clearly and elegantly printed on beautiful paper, and its illustrations are by that prince of artists, F. O. C. Darley. The publishers attempted a great enterprise in publishing the productions of the great American novelist in this superb style, and we are glad to learn that it is likely to prove successful. The subscriptions to this series are largely and constantly increasing, and promise to them a circulation which they richly deserve.

The Daily Enquirer, Cincinnati.

We have received from Robert Clarke & Co., No. 55 West Fourth-street, Cooper's "Spy," from the press of W. A. Townsend & Co., New York, with illustrations by Darley. What more could we add in the way of praise? The first of American novelists, and the first of American designers. The letter-press of the book is beautifully clear and perspicuous, and the tale itself was the most popular novel of the day in which it was issued, and its interest is as fresh now as ever.

"The Press," Philadelphia.

W. A. Townsend & Co., of New York, have published another volume (the fourth) of their magnificent edition of the novels and romances of Fenimore Cooper, with first-class engravings, on steel and wood, from original drawings by Darley, whom we are proud to claim as a Philadelphian. Even the London *Athenæum*, always so difficult with American books, smiles grimly upon this superb edition of Cooper, and admits that in paper, binding, printing, and illustration, every thing has been done to make it worthy of the most liberal patronage. The new volume contains "The Spy," which was the first of Cooper's American novels. The illustrations are beautiful. The vignette (on steel) representing the escape of Harvey Birch, is a perfect gem. "The Spy" contains two of the best characters ever drawn by Cooper—Harvey Birch, the Spy, and the grave but gallant gentleman, Mr. Harper, who eventually appears as Washington himself. Prefixed to this edition is the author's introduction, giving a history of the writing of the book, and the real incident which suggested it.

The New Orleans Daily Picayune.

We are indebted to J. C. Morgan & Co., Booksellers, Exchange Place, next the Post Office, for three volumes of the new edition of Cooper's works, published by W. A. Townsend & Co., New York, and illustrated by Darley.

"The volumes are the "Pioneers," the "Red Rover," and the "Last of the Mohicans." The illustrations from Darley's drawings are very beautiful indeed, whilst the binding, printing, types, paper, and general style of the edition are exceedingly handsome.

DARLEY'S
COOPER VIGNETTES.

ARTISTS' PROOFS.

The superior beauty and excellence with which Mr. DARLEY's Designs for the NEW ILLUSTRATED EDITION OF COOPER'S NOVELS, have been reproduced upon the steel, have led the undersigned, at the request of numerous artists and amateurs, to cause a limited number of Proofs on India before Letter, to be taken from each plate, with a view of issuing them in a series of Folios, with the proper descriptive letter-press.

The remarkable spirit and power evinced in all the designs from the pencil of Mr. Darley, have signally and eminently characterized those illustrating the scenes and characters of Cooper's novels. The artist's long familiarity with the pages of our great novelist, and a hearty love and appreciation of his genius, have resulted in the production of a series of drawings, which, for dramatic, picturesque, and vivid interest, have perhaps no superiors in modern art. These drawings have been engraved with a faithfulness and care worthy their reputation, by the acknowledged first artists in the country, exclusively in *Line* and *Etching*, and with a scrupulous regard to the requirements of first-class art. In their nationality, and their great superiority over ordinary book illustrations, they especially commend themselves to all connoisseurs of the Fine Arts.

The Proofs will be issued in eight folios, each folio containing eight proofs, and each proof accompanied with a page of letter-press descriptive of the picture, embellished with a design on wood by Mr. Darley. The proofs are printed with the utmost care, on India, and backed on the finest French Plate Paper. Each folio will be in a cover of highly ornamental design, printed in tint.

FOLIOS ONE AND TWO are now ready, and the remaining Six will follow at intervals of two or three months.

PRICE TO SUBSCRIBERS—THREE DOLLARS PER FOLIO.

As the proofs are limited to a small number (only 500 impressions from each plate, after which the plates are lettered, so that no more can be taken), no subscription will be received except for the full set.

W. A. TOWNSEND & CO.,
No. 46 WALKER STREET, NEW YORK.

www.ingramcontent.com/pod-product-compliance
Lightning Source LLC
Chambersburg PA
CBHW022025240426
43667CB00042B/1179